Teacher Inquiries
in Literacy Teaching-Learning

Learning to Collaborate
in Elementary Urban Classrooms

Teacher Inquiries in Literacy Teaching-Learning

Learning to Collaborate in Elementary Urban Classrooms

Edited by

Christine C. Pappas
University of Illinois–Chicago

Liliana Barro Zecker
DePaul University

2001

LAWRENCE ERLBAUM ASSOCIATES, PUBLISHERS
Mahwah, New Jersey   London

Lawrence Erlbaum Associates, Inc., Publishers
10 Industrial Avenue
Mahwah, NJ 07430

Cover design by Kathryn Houghtaling Lacey

Library of Congress Cataloging-in-Publication Data

Teacher inquiries in literacy teaching-learning : learning to collaborate in elementary urban classroms / edited
by Christine C. Pappas, Liliana Barro Zecker.
    p. cm.
    Includes bibliographical references and index.
    ISBN 0-8058-2400-6 (alk. paper)
    1. Language arts (Elementary)—Illinois—Chicago. 2.
Education, Urban—Illinois—Chicago. 3. College-school
cooperation—Illinois—Chicago.   I. Pappas, Christine, C.
II. Zecker, Liliana Barro.
    LB1576.T365 2001
    372.6'09773'11 —dc21   00-025451
                                       CIP

Printed in the United States of America
10 9 8 7 6 5 4 3 2 1

Contents

Preface

This book consists of the stories of 13 urban elementary teacher–researchers' year-long inquiries around literacy topics. As part of a collaborative school–university project, these teachers—all of whom taught in two Chicago elementary schools during the year of their studies—attempted to transform their teaching practices to meet the needs of students who came from diverse ethnic and linguistic backgrounds. These teachers' inquiry efforts, as their chapters show, resulted in developing more collaborative styles of teaching.

Collaborative classroom interactions occur when teachers move away from teaching-as-transmission approaches to ones in which they share power and authority with their students. They happen when teachers view their urban students not as at risk, but instead as at promise. This was an underlying tenet that all teachers believed, despite the commonplace deficit view of urban children held by many urban personnel and by society at large. Each teacher posed and grappled with difficult questions in his or her inquiry: How do I hear the voices of my students and at the same time have them hear my voice as a mediator of the culture at large? How do I include my students' local and culturally varied knowledge in literacy-learning transactions and also create ways for integrating my expertise? People argue for teachers taking on the role of guides or facilitators, but what does that really mean in my everyday teaching practices? Thus, it is one thing to want to enact literacy routines so as to both appreciate and value students as knowers and to encourage and appreciate students' meanings; it is another to actually pull it off. There are both ups and downs in such a process. Consequently, these teacher researchers have been candid in discussing the critical points of their inquiries in their chapters, for they think too many of the accounts of teacher researchers sound too rosy.

The everyday interactions between teachers and students are realized by the social talk in the classroom. Thus, in our project we analyzed classroom discourse to study and document the teacher researchers' efforts to make changes in the locus of power in literacy teaching and learning. Their chapters, therefore, are filled with classroom discourse examples to illustrate their points. They show the struggles and successes involved in moving away from teacher controlled *IRE patterns of talk*—that is, teacher *I*nitiating, child *R*esponding, and teacher *E*valuating—to developing alternative, collaborative discourse. They explain how they found ways to encourage their students' questions, ideas, and comments, and how they discovered strategies to respond to these student meanings.

The chapters represent teacher inquiries conducted in various elementary grade levels from kindergarten to the eighth grade. Three occurred in bilingual classrooms and one in a special education classroom. The inquiries cover a range of literacy topics: reading aloud, language richness, writing, literature discussion groups, drama, pretend reading, and so forth. The first and last chapters, written by the editors, provide the background and theoretical underpinnings of the project. They also attempt to pull together the major themes of all of the teacher researchers' chapters and they discuss the political implications of these urban teachers' efforts to change literacy teaching and learning in their urban classrooms.

We acknowledge the support of grants from Spencer Foundation and the Center for Urban Educational Research and Development at the University of Illinois at Chicago for the research reported in this book, as well its companion book on the project also published by Lawrence Erlbaum Associates and edited by Pappas and Zecker (2001), *Transforming Literacy Curriculum Genres: Working with Teacher Researchers in Urban Classrooms*. The data presented, the statements made, and views expressed in both books are solely the responsibility of the authors.

Chapter 1

Introduction: Creating Collaborative Relations of Power in Literacy Teaching-Learning

Christine C. Pappas
University of Illinois at Chicago

Liliana Barro Zecker
DePaul University

This book features the stories of 13 urban, elementary, teacher– researchers' year-long classroom inquiries into various literacy topics. They made these inquiries as part of a school–university collaborative project. All of these teachers taught at 2 Chicago public schools during this year of study. Each made efforts to transform his or her literacy curricula to better meet the needs of students who came from diverse ethnic and linguistic backgrounds. As this introductory chapter and the teachers' chapters vividly show, this change involved these teachers taking on more collaborative styles of teaching.

The teachers' inquiries took place during the 1994–1995 school year, and were subsequently written up to be publicly shared in this book. Of course, after the 1994–1995 school year, these teachers were teaching new students, and some of them were teaching at different schools and dealing with new inquiries. Some allude to these new circumstances in their chapters.

This chapter provides the background and theoretical grounding for this book. It is organized into three sections: The first describes briefly how the school–university project evolved and how it was later structured

1

while the teachers conducted and wrote up their inquiries. It also describes the two schools in which the teacher researchers worked. The second section covers the conceptual background that informs the studies, including the role that classroom discourse played in the project. It also outlines the major methodological features of the teacher research in the collaborative school–university project. The third section provides a summary of important ideas in the chapter. An Appendix at the end of the chapter contains a key for classroom-discourse transcriptions, so you can understand the examples to be found in all of the chapters.

BACKGROUND OF THE COLLABORATIVE SCHOOL–UNIVERSITY PROJECT

The 1989 Illinois Chicago School Reform Act resulted in many changes in the Chicago Public Schools. For example, it mandated governance changes. A major feature was the formation of a local school council (LSC) at each school, charged with primary responsibility for setting the school's educational policy. An integral aspect of this reform initiative was the 5-year School Improvement Plan, which was developed by the principal at each school in consultation with teachers, the LSC, and the community. This plan mapped out the school's strategies for improving student achievement and for reaching other goals set out in the reform legislation.

The 13 teachers in this book taught in 2 elementary schools whose School Improvement Plans included the use of a whole-language curriculum and related approaches. Various faculty at the University of Illinois at Chicago (UIC) became involved in some of these schools' activities, already having an ongoing formal connection between UIC and the schools (as well as several other Chicago schools). Chris Pappas, who had just joined the UIC faculty, worked with teachers at the two schools that had specifically requested help with implementing whole-language ideas. After this inservice was completed, some individual teachers from each school contacted her to take up her invitation to work collaboratively in a more long-term basis as they attempted to change literacy teaching and learning in their classrooms.

From 1990 to 1993, a small group of teachers at each school met regularly (usually weekly) with Chris to discuss their inquiries about their efforts to enact more collaborative styles of teaching literacy. Chris also periodically observed in the classrooms, audiotaped interactions in various literacy activities or routines, and kept fieldnotes that she shared with the teachers to foster ongoing investigation and discussion. Finally, external research support from Spencer Research Foundation and the Center for Urban Educational Research and Development, UIC, made it possible to extend and document this school–university collaborative-action research in a more systematic way so that its findings could be shared with a larger audience through this book (and its companion volume *Transforming Literacy Cur-*

riculum Genres: Working With Teacher Researchers in Urban Classrooms, Pappas & Zecker, 2000) and other papers and articles.

After receiving this external funding, other university researchers joined Chris in the project. Liliana Barro Zecker worked with the teacher researchers in the bilingual classrooms, and also provided expertise for the project as a whole. Other university researchers, who were graduate students at UIC (Diane Escobar, Shannon Hart, Linda Montes, Jane Liao, Caitlyn Nichols, Dian Ruben, and Hank Tabak), also became collaborators. They were the team members who worked closely with teacher researchers and are specifically identified at the beginning of each teacher's chapter.

About the Two Schools

Both Chicago public schools serve lowsocioeconomic students, almost all of whom qualify for federally assisted meals. The support for the project from principals at both schools—Fausto Lopez at Joseph Jungman Elementary School and Peggy Iska, principal at Hans Christian Andersen Elementary School until 1995, and Suzanne Dunaway, the current principal —was invaluable over the years.

Jungman has mostly a Mexican and Mexican–American student population. In the past few years, a small number of African-American and other non-Latino students have also attended. It is very close to the UIC in the Pilsen area of the city. The community surrounding the school consists of mostly Spanish-speaking families and businesses. The school has a prekindergarten through sixth-grade program. Six teacher researchers taught at this school while they conducted their inquiries, three of them taught in trailers (since removed), next to the main school on the edges of the parking lot.

Hans Christian Andersen (now renamed Hans Christian Andersen Academy) offers a prekindergarten through eighth-grade program. The community surrounding the school is diverse, and is showing early signs of gentrification. Seven teacher researchers did their inquiries in this school. The school is located further from the university than is Jungman and has a more diverse student population. The majority of the students are from families originally from Mexico, Puerto Rico, and other Latin American countries. There is a also substantial number of African-American students, as well as a small minority of Anglo students (many of Polish or eastern European descent).

CONCEPTUAL UNDERPINNINGS

Emphasis on Teacher Research

An important feature of the project from the beginning was its emphasis on *teacher research*—the pursuit and the examination of teachers' own questions, concerns, and issues about their teaching practices and their students' learning of literacy. It was thus quite different both from approaches taken by many typical professional development programs and from mainstream educational research studies.

Most traditional educational research dichotomizes theory and practice. More specifically, the typical view has the theoretical background for all and any educational innovation being produced by researchers from the university. Such a process assumes the following: (1) There are general solutions to practical problems; (2) Such solutions can be developed outside of particular, practical classroom situations (that is, in universities or research laboratories, etc.); and (3) These solutions can then be translated into the teachers' actions in the classroom through various training, publications, or administrative directives (Altrichter, Posch, & Somekh, 1993). Clearly, this is an "outside–in" conception that sees knowledge for teaching being generated at the university and then disseminated for use in schools (Cochran-Smith & Lytle, 1993). What has been missing in this arrangement has been the teachers' voices. Indeed, as Gitlin (1990) argued, traditional educational research rarely involves question posing from teachers and therefore "strengthens the assumptions that practitioners do not produce knowledge, that their personal knowledge is not useful" (p. 444).

Teacher research is defined as systematic, intentional inquiry by teachers (Cochran-Smith & Lytle, 1993). It is *systematic* because there are ordered ways in which teachers can gather and document information and experiences about teaching and learning in written and other forms. Ordered ways are used to recollect, rethink, and analyze classroom events. Although insights can always be gained through more spontaneous teaching–learning activities, teacher research is an *intentional,* planned enterprise. It is *inquiry* because it involves reflection by teachers to make sense of their own experiences, questions, and problems that emerge and emanate from classroom events. There is a "REsearching" here (Berthoff, 1987)—looking and looking again at what happens in the classroom. Teacher research consists of taking on a learning stance toward classroom or school life (Pappas, Kiefer, & Levstik, 1999).

Thus, in contrast to the "outside–in" conception, teacher research is "inside to outside" because it calls attention both to teachers as knowers and to the complex ways that knowledge and teaching are interrelated and embedded in the contexts of daily classroom life (Cochran-Smith & Lytle, 1993). Teacher research promotes a new, distinctive way of knowledge of teaching because it privileges teachers as those with the authority to know about teaching. Consequently, the teacher research reported in this book (and in many other books and publishing outlets) provides useful knowledge for teachers themselves, and it has also generated knowledge for the larger educational community by contributing to the general knowledge base for teaching.

Features of Teacher Research in Our Collaborative School–University Project

As already noted, the teacher research reported here was conducted in collaboration with university partners. It is important, then, to describe this particular relationship because the arrangements in school–university collaborative research projects can vary (Pappas, 1997). Here are some of the important features of our project during 2 years in which the teachers conducted their inquiries and then wrote them for this book.

Teachers Identified Their Own Inquiries.   This is probably most important facet of the project. At the beginning of the year (1994–1995 school year), teachers decided what they wanted to investigate, and when during their school day would be the most likely time for these inquiries to occur. Each of the teachers had questions, areas of concern, and impressions of difficulty and tension they wanted to pursue, but defining the particulars of their research took time. In the beginning, however, most of these research topics were quite nebulous. In the first month or so they became more clarified. This is not to say that everything was then set, for one of major characteristic of teacher research (like much of the other qualitative, interpretative research approaches to which teacher research is related and part of) is that its focus frequently changes as teachers rethink and modify their roles in teaching as a result of what occurs during inquiry. What was notable is that teachers gradually became clearer on their first directions or steps during their studies.

Teachers Kept Research Journals.   The teachers kept notes on the teaching–learning experiences in their classrooms related to their inquiry. Details were sometimes shared at weekly meetings. The teachers reviewed their journals when they prepared for their end-of-year interviews with university researchers about what stood out for them during their year of inquiry. They also used journals in writing their chapters for this book and for other texts coauthored with university researchers.

Teachers Reviewed Ongoing Fieldnotes.   A two-member team of university researchers worked with each of the teacher researchers throughout his or her inquiry. One member took fieldnotes, and the other operated the video camera to capture the classroom interactions (and classroom discourse) during the part of the day in which the teacher was conducting his or her study. These fieldnotes were given to the teacher a few days later. Chris Pappas, the director of the project, spent time in all of the teachers' classrooms at both schools. She also provided short versions of fieldnotes that she called *Summary/Queries*. Over the years, teachers used both kinds of fieldnotes extensively. During the first year they helped teachers think about emerging issues in their inquiries; during subsequent years they aided teachers' further reflections of their previous work as they analyzed and wrote about their findings.

Teachers Viewed and Analyzed Videotapes and Transcriptions.

At weekly meetings, one or two teachers shared edited versions of video classroom footage. Here, teachers gained feedback about the status of their inquiries from the other teacher–researcher colleagues and from university–researcher partners. Showing and talking about particular features of their teaching that were working well gave the teachers feelings of accomplishment and demonstrated strategies that others might try (even though the other teachers might not be doing a similar inquiry). On the other hand, airing difficulties or vulnerabilities in inquiries afforded opportunities to obtain new ideas or directions to consider.

In later years of the project, teachers used videotape transcriptions provided by the university–researcher partners to further examine and identify critical points of their inquiries. These transcriptions also documented and illustrated the findings presented in the teachers' chapters in this book.

Teachers Conversed and Conferenced With Other Research Project Members.

Throughout the years of the project, teachers had many conversations with university researchers in addition to the weekly videotaped meetings. These conversations were frequently audiotaped. (During the 1994–1995 year of inquiry, sometimes relevant comments from these conversations were included as additions to fieldnotes.) Teachers also engaged in a long end-of-the-year interview with university researchers where, often reviewing their journals and fieldnotes in advance, they talked about what stood out for them—the critical points they saw in their inquiries. Subsequently, university researchers provided an outline of the points the teachers covered in this interview. University researchers also gave them any transcriptions the teachers felt they needed for their own analysis in writing their chapters.

Finally, there were many conversations about various drafts of the chapters in this book, as well as discussions over coauthored chapters in the companion volume that accompanies this one (see reference at end of this chapter) and other conference papers and journal articles written by project members.

"New Literacy" and Struggles to Share Power and Authority in Collaboration With Students

Beginning in 1989, the teacher researchers began work together with Chris to develop the "whole-language" programs specified in their School

Improvement Plans. To implement this change required designing alternative, more student-centered approaches to teaching literacy. Such approaches challenge traditional transmission-oriented curricula, a model that Freire (1972) criticized as the "banking concept of education." A major concept in the transmission-oriented approach to teaching and learning is that the function of teachers is merely to make deposits of knowledge into learners' heads, thought of as empty vessels. This traditional approach to education treats students as having no theories, prior ideas, or knowledge about topics. Thus, teaching based on this model frequently results in unchallenging rote learning for students. This is especially the case for nonmainstream children of low-income families of various ethnic or linguistic groups who populate urban schools (Bartolome, 1994; Cummins, 1994; Moll & Gonzalez, 1994).

It is hard work to develop alternative curriculum and teaching practices that recognize learners as active and constructive. Some of the teacher researchers in this book had many years of experience using a teaching-as-transmission approach and felt that they had much to overcome; the newer teachers found the alternative approach difficult to conceive of, because they had never observed or directly tried it personally.

Very early in the collaboration among Chris and these teachers, a persistent theme emerged in the teachers' efforts to change their teaching. Questions of when and how to share authority and power with their students became a major focus in their inquiries. To believe that students are active meaning makers required these teachers to develop different forms and structures of social interaction in teacher–student and student–student classroom literacy routines. The process of reconceptualizing the teaching–learning relationship in terms of social transaction rather than in terms of transmission entails creating new roles as teachers (Wells & Chang-Wells, 1992). That is, it involves teachers trying to figure out how to fashion instructional interactions so they can share their expertise, but at the same time can still foster children's construction of their own knowledge and expertise. Although the teacher researchers in the project asked different questions and addressed different facets or aspects of literacy teaching and learning, all of the chapters in this book share this common thread.

Creating "New Literacy" Approaches

The assumption that students (all humans) construct their own knowledge in various social contexts (including classrooms) is known as a *socioconstructivist perspective on literacy*. It represents a fundamental shift from the idea that meaning resides within texts, to a sense of literacy as active transformation of texts. Meaning is seen as being created through an interaction of readers, writers, and texts in particular social contexts. Written texts are seen to be constructed and used to serve social goals; reading and writing are thus social and cultural acts.

The implications of this perspective for teaching are immense. It means that reading and writing and the curriculum in general must be more connected to the real lives of students. Making reading and writing more personally meaningful, and making the processes of literacy more powerful for students is what Willinsky (1990) called the *New Literacy*. Central in this transformation is changing the power relationships in literacy activities in the classroom, for both teachers and students. In Willinsky's words:

> The New Literacy speaks directly to teachers reasserting control over the work that goes on in the class, even as it attempts to hand a greater part of the locus of meaning over to the student. It represents a taking hold of the curriculum by the teacher at a fundamental level by challenging the meaning of literacy in the classroom as well as the nature of a teacher's work with the students. (p. 19)

New Literacy, then, calls for teachers to have more autonomy over what happens in their classrooms, and to reevaluate the everyday instructional patterns of interactions they have with their students. To reiterate, basic issues of power and authority are at the root of the changes generated by a New Literacy approach.

The teaching–learning relationship being sought is not one based on transmission by teachers and reception by students, but is rather, one that is based on collaborative interaction. This approach counters individualistic conceptions of learning by emphasizing that learning activities take place not within individuals, but in transactions between them (Wells, 1994b; Wells & Chang-Wells, 1992). Thus, it reflects a sociocultural theory based on Vygotsky's (1962, 1978) view of learning, which has been extended by others (e.g., Gutierrez, Rymes, & Larson, 1995; Moll, 1990; Newman, Griffin, & Cole, 1989; Wells 1994a, 1994b, 1998; Wertsch, 1985, 1989, 1991). From such a perspective, the teaching–learning relationship represents the coconstruction of meaning and knowledge in which the teacher shares his or her expertise to guide and assist learners. As Kreisberg (1992) expressed this idea, the emphasis here is on power *with*, not power *over*.

Using Classroom Discourse to Document the Critical Points in Inquiries

The regular routines and interactions between teachers and students are enacted through the social use of language. Because so many of the processes of teaching and learning are realized in language (Cazden, 1988; Edwards & Mercer, 1987; Green & Dixon, 1994; Lemke, 1985), in our project we used classroom discourse analysis to study and document teachers' efforts to innovate changes in the locus of power.

Many classroom discourse studies (Cazden 1988; Edwards & Mercer, 1987; Young, 1992) indicate that typical classroom talk in everyday instructional activities is usually quite different from the talk in most other settings. First, this talk is usually dominated by teacher questions, typically ones called *pseudoquestions*—for which the teacher already knows the answers (Dillon, 1994; Ramirez, 1988; Young, 1992). Second, these teacher questions are frequently embedded in a particular type of structure called the *initiate–respond–evaluate (IRE) sequence* that is controlled by the teacher. In this IRE pattern, the teacher *initiates* an interaction, the student *responds* to this initiation or question posed by the teacher, and finally the teacher *evaluates* what the student has said before calling on the next student, and on and on. This IRE structure is the essence of traditional transmission-oriented education.

All children have unique personal characteristics. In schools where students come from a variety of cultural and linguistic backgrounds, they also bring their own complex "ways with words" to classroom interactions (Heath, 1983). The traditional IRE talk structure, with its strict teacher-dominated, turn-taking format, does not provide many opportunities for negotiation or consideration of these children's styles of interaction.

What is central in our project, then, is how the urban teacher researchers tried alternatives to these IRE patterns to realize New Literacy ideas. By giving their students more control of their own literacy learning, they attempted to transform and develop literacy activities so that *both* teacher and student voices are privileged in collaborative interactions.

This does not mean that teachers remain silent as they provide space for students to present their own ideas and knowledge. Teachers' questions and comments—their expertise—are still to be heard, but serve different functions in literacy instructional interactions.

As already noted, this effort on the part of the teachers—and students, many of whom are used to traditional transmission-oriented classrooms—has not been easy. Thus, along with the successes, you will hear in these teachers' stories their difficulties as they worked to enact New Literacy ideas. It should also be noted that their endeavors represent more than taking on new teaching–learning approaches; frequently the impetus for their inquiries had deep personal and autobiographical roots. Just as they encouraged their students to take risks in learning, they also took risks and experimented—with the support of the other members of the project team—to try out new and different ways to teach. The teachers here have commented that too many of the accounts of teacher researchers sound too rosy, so they tried to be candid about both the ups and downs in their attempts to change teaching and learning in their urban classrooms.

CONCLUSION AND OVERVIEW OF THE BOOK

Conclusion

The teachers' inquiries presented in this book cover a range of literacy top-ics: reading aloud, language richness, writing, literature discussion groups, drama, pretend reading, and so forth. You might want to hop around to read different chapters, based on your own interest in grade lev-els or topics. However, it is critical that you always remember to connect this chapter with any particular chapter you are reading. We decided not to include overlapping information in the teachers' chapters on back-ground theory, or on data about the project and the two schools, but to confine it to this introductory chapter, which informs all of the others. Finally, it is important to keep in mind that the appendix to this chapter provides the transcription key to decipher classroom discourse examples found throughout the book.

Overview of the Book

The teachers' inquiries are organized by grade level, starting with kinder-garten and progressing up through eighth grade. Three are accounts of studies done in bilingual classrooms. In addition, issues of bilingual educa-tion and learning English as a second language (ESL) are incorporated throughout the book.

The teacher researchers come from diverse ethnic and linguistic back-grounds, have differing educational and other professional experiences, and had varying degrees of teaching experience at the time of the inquiries they conducted. Information about the background of individual teachers is provided within their own chapters, of course, but is also included in Edi-tors' Comments sections preceding each chapter, and in the teachers' bio-graphical sketches that follow their chapters. The Editors' Comments also offer ideas to look for and think about as you read the teachers' stories.

The last chapter of the book, again written by the two editors, summa-rizes and further examines important ideas and findings found in the teachers' chapters. It also considers the political implications of teach-ers creating collaborative relations of power in teaching literacy to urban students.

ABOUT THE AUTHORS

Christine C. Pappas is a professor in the College of Education at the Uni-versity of Illinois at Chicago where she teaches courses on language, class-room discourse, and literacy. Her current interests involve the research and teaching–learning of genre and teacher inquiry.

Liliana Barro Zecker collaborated with all of the teacher- and university researchers in this project as a postdoctoral fellow at the University of Illinois at Chicago, focusing especially on the bilingual classroom inquiries. She is currently an assistant professor in the School of Education at DePaul University where she continues to explore with her students, pre- and inservice teachers, young children's development and learning of language and literacy.

APPENDIX: CONVENTIONS OF TRANSCRIPTION FOR CLASSROOM DISCOURSE EXAMPLES

Unit:	Usually corresponds to an independent clause with all dependent clauses related to it (complex clause or T-unit). Sometimes includes another independent clause if there is no drop of tone and is added without any pausing. Units here are punctuated as sentences.
Turn:	Includes all of a speaker's utterances or units.
Key for Speakers:	First name is listed for teacher researcher. C, C1, C2, and so forth are noted for individual children (with "m" or "f" to refer to the gender of a child): C is used if a child's voice cannot be identified; Cs followed by a number are used to identify particular children in particular sections of the transcript (so that C1 or C2, etc., is not necessarily the same child throughout the whole transcript). Cs (or SCs) represents many or some children speaking simultaneously.
——	False starts or abandoned language replaced by new language structures.
...	Small or short pause within unit.
... ...	Longer pause within unit.
....	Breaking off of a speaker's turn due to the next speaker's turn.
< >	Uncertain words.
(...)	One word that is inaudible or impossible to transcribe.
(... ...)	Longer stretches of language that are inaudible and impossible to transcribe.
Italic	Emphasis.
# #	Overlapping language spoken by two or more speakers at a time.
CAPS	Actual reading of a book.
{ }	Teacher's miscue or modification of a text read.
[ ]	Identifies what is being referred to or gestured and other nonverbal contextual information.
....	Part of a transcript has been omitted.

REFERENCES

Altrichter, H., Posch, O., & Somekh, B. (1993). *Teachers investigate their work: An introduction to the methods of action research.* London: Falmer Press.

Bartolome, L. I. (1994). Beyond the methods fetish: Toward a humanizing pedagogy. *Harvard Educational Review, 64,* 173–194.

Berthoff, A. E. (1987). The teacher as REsearcher. In D. Goswami & P. R. Stillman (Eds.), *Reclaiming the classroom: Teacher research as an agency for change* (pp. 28–39). Portsmouth, NH: Boynton Cook.

Cazden, C. B. (1988). *Classroom discourse: The language of teaching and learning.* Portsmouth, NH: Heinemann.

Cochran-Smith, M., & Lytle, S. L. (1993). *Inside/outside: Teacher research and knowledge.* New York: Teachers College Press.

Cummins, J. (1994). From coercive to collaborative relations of power in the teaching of literacy. In B. M. Ferdman, R.-M. Weber, & A. G. Ramierz (Eds.), *Literacy across languages and cultures* (pp. 295–331). Albany: State University of New York Press.

Dillon, J. T. (1994). *Using discussion in the classroom.* Buckingham, England: Open University Press.

Edwards, A. D., & Mercer, N. (1987). *Common knowledge: The development of understanding in the classroom.* London: Routledge & Kegan Paul.

Freire, P. (1972). *Cultural action for freedom.* Hammondsworth, England: Penguin.

Gitlin, A. D. (1990). Educative research, voice and school change. *Harvard Educational Review, 60,* 443–466.

Green, J. L., & Dixon, C. N. (1994). Talking into being: Discursive and social practices in classrooms. *Linguistics and Education, 5,* 231–239.

Gutierrez, K., Rymes, B., & Larson, J. (1995). Script, counterscript, and underlife in the classroom: James brown versus *Brown v. Board of Education. Harvard Educational Review, 65,* 445–471.

Heath, S. B. (1983). *Ways with words.* Cambridge, England: Cambridge University Press.

Kreisburg, S. (1992). *Transforming power: Domination, empowerment, and education.* Albany: State University of New York Press.

Lemke, J. L. (1985). *Using language in the classroom.* Victoria, Australia: Deakin University Press.

Moll, L. C. (Ed.). (1990). *Vygotsky and education: Instructional implications and applications of sociohistorical psychology.* Cambridge, England: Cambridge University Press.

Moll, L. C., & Gonzalez, N. (1994). Lessons from research with language-minority children. *JRB: A Journal of Literacy, 26,* 439–456.

Newman, D. P., Griffin, P., & Cole, M. (1989). *The construction zone: Working for cognitive change in school.* Cambridge, England: Cambridge University Press.

Pappas, C. C. (1997). Making 'collaboration' problematic in collaborative school-university research: Studying with urban teacher researchers to transform literacy curriculum genres. In J. Flood, S. B. Heath, & D. Lapp (Eds.), *A handbook of research on teaching literacy through the communicative and visual arts* (pp. 215–231). New York: Macmillan.

Pappas, C. C., Kiefer, B. Z., & Levstik, B. S. (1999). *An integrated language perspective in the elementary school: An action approach.* New York: Longman.

Pappas, C. C., & Zecker, L. B. (2000). *Transforming literacy curriculum genres: Working with teacher researchers in urban classrooms.* Mahwah, NJ: Lawrence Erlbaum Associates.

Ramirez, A. (1988). Analyzing speech acts. In J. Green & J. O. Harker (Eds.), *Multiple perspective analyses of classroom discourse* (pp. 135–163). Norwood, NJ: Ablex.

Vygotsky, L. S. (1962). *Thought and language.* Cambridge, MA: MIT Press.

Vygotsky, L. S. (1978). *Mind in society: The development of higher psychological processes.* Cambridge, England: Cambridge University Press.

Wells, G. (1994a). The complimentary contributions of Halliday and Vygotsky to a "language-based theory of learning." *Linguistics and Education, 6,* 41–90.

Wells, G. (1994b). *Changing schools from within: Creating communities of inquiry.* Portsmouth, NH: Heinemann.

Wells, G. (1998). Some questions about direct instruction: Why? To whom? How? And When? *Language Arts, 76,* 27–35.

Wells, G., & Chang-Wells, G. L. (1992). *Constructing knowledge together: Classrooms as centers of inquiry and literacy.* Portsmouth, NH: Heinemann.

Wertsch, J. V. (1985). *Vygotsky and the social formation of mind.* Cambridge, England: Cambridge University Press.

Wertsch, J. V. (1989). A sociocultural approach to mind. In W. Damon (Ed.), *Child development today and tomorrow* (pp. 14–33). San Franscisco: Jossey-Bass.

Wertsch, J. V. (1991). *Voices of the mind: A sociocultural approach to mediated action.* Cambridge, MA: Harvard University Press.

Willinsky, J. (1990). *The New Literacy: Redefining reading and writing in the schools.* New York: Routledge & Kegan Paul.

Young, R. (1992). *Critical theory and classroom talk.* Clevedon, England: Multilingual Matters.

Chapter 2

Exploring Language Richness in a Bilingual Kindergarten Classroom

Sonia White Soltero
Andersen Elementary School

EDITORS' COMMENTS

Sonia was amazed at the "language richness" of her Spanish-speaking kindergartners. Her goal was to discover the sources of these funds of knowledge possessed by her students. In doing so, she challenged the deficit theory that is frequently applied to the abilities, experiences, and intellectual resources of the children she teaches.

Sonia illustrates in varied curricular routines how she and her students created "conversations," in which students' ideas and wordings were used to build new knowledge about a range of topics they crafted together. Along with these successful negotiations with her student informants, she describes the rough times when classroom talk went off course. Thus, lots of reflection on her questioning, and other interactional strategies to foster critical thinking, can be found throughout.

The introduction chapter of this book provides the theoretical and methodological background for the larger collaborative school–university action-research project and this chapter about Sonia's inquiry on language richness.

University researchers, Liliana Barro Zecker and Caitlyn Nichols, collaborated with Sonia in her inquiry.

BACKGROUND OF THE INQUIRY:
QUESTIONING DEFICIT THEORIES

The questions I sought to answer in my inquiry all had to do with the notion of "language richness." What or who are the sources of this language sophistication? How does this relate to my mostly Mexican-immigrant kindergartners' abilities to process complex ideas and thoughts? And, how do I, their teacher, incorporate these findings into how and what I teach? This led me to inquire about the children's funds of knowledge and to collaborate with them to explore their sources of information. This collaboration and sharing of power indirectly led the children to become independent and self-respectful participants in their own learning.

My interest in this inquiry originated with my own concerns about the traditional and often-heard "deficit theories," which refer to the assumption that some children are inferior to others due to genetic, cultural, or experiential differences; that is, due to a deficit. According to Nieto (1992):

> [Deficit] theories that hypothesize that some people are deficient in intelligence and/or achievement either because *genetic inferiority* (because of their racial background) or because of *cultural deprivation* (because of their cultural background and/or because they have been deprived of cultural experiences and activities deemed by the majority to be indispensable for growth and development). (p. 306)

As a teacher, I strongly believe that these types of explanations as to why certain groups of children fail educationally are dangerous and misleading. In a sense, these theories places all the blame on the children's homes, their families, their economic status, and their ethnic groups. Even supposing that social, cultural, or economic factors may put some children at a disadvantage, they still have the learning potential of any other group of children. It is important to note that race, ethnicity, social class, and language do not cause school failure. Rather, as Nieto pointed out, when students' culture, language, and class are perceived by the schools as inadequate and negative, the schools' failure with this group of children is more easily explained.

A good example of this is the way in which the trips of immigrant or working class families to visit their original states or countries are seen. Such trips are usually not viewed by the mainstream school system as an enriching activities, rather they are viewed as detrimental to the students because they miss conventional instructional time in the classroom. What children learn on these trips is usually ignored by the school, in spite of the obvious learning benefits the trips may offer. On the other hand, similar trips taken by more mainstream families are considered as valuable and enriching.

When teachers accept deficit theories, their expectations can be too low or too high. In the first case, students do not have access to challenging instruction. That is, the educational environment and curriculum are reduced to a remedial, back-to-basics orientation. In the second case, teachers' expectations may be too far from the students' actual learning potential or their *zone of proximal development* (ZPD) (Vygotsky, 1978). Vygotsky coined this term and proposed that all children have an *actual developmental level,* which is the potential for learning that exists within a particular domain, if under the guidance of adults or more capable peers (Moll, 1990). So, when the teachers' instruction and content are too high from this ZPD, development does not take place.

Personal Roots of My Interest in Language

My interest in the relationship between variations of language levels and academic performance among poor immigrant children began when I was teaching in a trilingual school in the outskirts of an Indian reservation in Tucson, Arizona. It grew when I began to teach at Andersen. This interest in language also made me reflect on my own learning as a child. I am the youngest of four children and was born in Buenos Aires, Argentina. I also lived in Uruguay, Brazil, Costa Rica, and the United States, with my parents, and was lucky enough to visit them twice in Cameroon, Africa, when they resided there for 3 years. In Argentina, I attended a bilingual British boarding school, where I must say, I had a great time (not what people usually say about boarding schools!). Although I entered this school knowing little English, I experienced firsthand what it is like to be in a nurturing learning environment where people also speak your native tongue as you learn a second language. I remember the anxiety I felt at first because I perceived learning English as such a colossal task. Interestingly, I never had given much thought to this until I became involved in bilingual education and began to see the struggles of linguistic minority students.

Before I moved to Chicago, I was a graduate student at the University of Arizona. I was lucky to work with Dr. Luis Moll on his Funds of Knowledge research project. Under his guidance, I conducted visits to my students' homes, then developed curriculum based on the information we gathered. The principal aim of this project was to develop curriculum that not only was relevant to our students, but that also tapped into their existing repertoires of knowledge from home: In essence the goal was to bridge the home, the school, and the community. Thus, my experiences in this project have also influenced my inquiry. This was my first experience as a teacher researcher. In my 1994–1995 inquiry I developed even more skills.

HOW MY INQUIRY EVOLVED

The students in my classroom during my 1994–1995 year of inquiry were all Latina or Latino, 95% were Mexican and 5% were Puerto Rican. Their parents were born outside the U.S. mainland (four in Puerto Rico, one in

Colombia, and the rest in Mexico). Half of the children were born in Chicago and the other half were born outside the United States. Each seemed to have a limited extended family—mostly uncles and aunts, with grandparents still living in Mexico or Puerto Rico. Many of these young children were frequently cared for either by one of the parents or by older siblings. Some of these older siblings might have had attended several years of bilingual education and ESL instruction or both, so they may have been stronger in either English or Spanish. I also found that approximately one third of the parents did not read or write (because many asked me to read or help them fill out forms for them).

The Role of Songs in Identifying and Clarifying My Inquiry

As part of my literacy curriculum, I have always used children's songs because I like the pattern language, the rhythm, and the predictable language of the lyrics. The children and I just simply enjoy the stories told in many children's songs. I write the words to the songs on large, lined tagboard, color code certain words, and draw small pictures next to particular words so that the children have some visual clues. The songs consist mainly of fairly lengthy humorous stories about animals, objects, and events. Many of them have familiar food or household objects as the characters, and the events mostly take place within the home. Because the materials were gathered from different parts of Latin America as well as Spain, there are some vocabulary variations (comparable to English vocabulary variations from England, New Zealand, South Africa, etc.). These songs usually led to lengthy discussions about the topic and related subjects.

In using these songs and poems, I began to see, even at the beginning, that students in Chicago seemed to have a very clear understanding of the content of the material and a high level of enthusiasm whenever I introduced them. Although the children had not heard many of the words before, they appeared to use context clues from the story to decipher the meaning of new words. For instance, when I introduced a new song, we sang it several times together and then I would ask for a volunteer to read and sing (with approximations) the song by using the chart or the book on which the song was written. Students would often substitute an unknown word such as *sobretodo,* a word used for coat in Argentina, but definitely not used in Mexico or Puerto Rico, with a known word such as *abrigo* or *chamarra,* both words meaning coat.

These experiences made me start rethinking about young children's language development and the sources of their language richness. What intrigued me the most was the level of language expertise these children had, regardless of the parents' economic status or educational attainment. The children's language sophistication was demonstrated many times, especially when I would ask them to explain something or reword a statement for clarification that they might have said. I was amazed at the level of their command of Spanish at that age. They were not only capable of giving me several synonyms for a particular word, but they were also able to explain concepts or opinions in several different forms.

EARLY STRUGGLES IN MY INQUIRY

Very often, children come to school with a set of preconceived ideas about the school culture. That is, they have specific expectations about how school is supposed to work, their roles as students, and the role of the adults as teachers. Even among kindergarten children one can find quite a strong set of beliefs about schooling. This may be due, in part, to older siblings' accounts of their own educational experiences or adults in the home who influence young children's notions of what school is all about. Adults in the home may believe that certain behavior from their children is appropriate at home, and certain, different behavior from them is expected in their interactions with teachers. At schools, most often they expect a traditional view of education—children sit passively listening and learning while the teacher "teaches." In this scenario, children have little to contribute, because it is assumed that they don't know much (at least they don't know much that is of any importance) and teachers educate and instruct, because it is assumed that they know almost everything.

Challenging Students' Views of Schooling

During the first month or two of my inquiry, I struggled in changing my students' views about what they thought school ought to or could be like. Many of the students who later became eager "informants" and "ethnographers" were at first very puzzled, and even a bit nervous, about the way I conducted class discussions, which I later began to call "conversations." It is important to note here that our discussions were not mere conversations, they had structure and specific purposes. I encouraged them not only to share their experiences, but also to explore and become more cognizant about how they acquired new knowledge outside the classroom.

In the beginning, in our conversations and during journal writing, I inquired about the children's personal lives, in particular about their parents and their own countries or states of origin. This caused anxiety and alarm for some parents, who rushed to school nervously wanting to know why was I asking so many personal questions about their families. This was a very valid and immediate concern for them. I realized that I had not communicated my intent or my curricular objectives to them. This is an important point because, as teachers, we sometimes overlook informing families about what is happening in school. I discovered that most of my children's parents didn't quite know what their roles could be in their children's educational process at school. My objective was more than their setting a time and place for homework and making sure the children completed it, but to attempt to bridge the home and the school. This approach requires more involvement from the families in helping their children to explore, analyze, and formulate ideas at home by helping them tap into their prior knowledge. I believe this results in higher self-respect for the families and the students because it affirms that their homes, traditions, and culture are valued by the schools.

After the initial shock of being in such a different schooling situation the children and the parents became quite comfortable with the collaborative mode of teaching and learning I was attempting, and were eager to participate in our quest for knowledge!

Questioning My Interactional Style

Although the purpose or goal of my inquiry was clear—namely, to find out about the sources of my students' language richness and to try to use this information to create curriculum that would further their language and new knowledge—the ways in which I tried to go about investigating my inquiry questions were very problematic for me. I had many false starts! During the first 2 months of my study I frequently changed my approaches to gather data. One of the negative side effects I experienced at first was, that while trying to collect children's language, I seemed to be creating contrived teaching practices in the way I elicited responses from the children. Eager to collect all this great language sophistication, my teaching style began to change, and I became, for a short time, a very teacher-directed type of teacher. As a result, during this period, children's responses where short and lacking in the type of higher level thinking and use of rich language that I was looking for, and that I had earlier observed.

Interrogating Lidia

Example 1 illustrates this point well. In the weeks prior to this conversation we had been talking about traveling and maps. On this particular day, children brought pictures of a trip (any trip) they had taken. In order to accommodate the data-gathering process, I set the activity in a round-robin manner wherein the students were supposed to take turns talking about their pictures and trips. Here, Lidia is showing her pictures of her summer trip to Washington.

Example 1

Lidia: Alla había muchas frutas y a mi lo que más me gusto fueron los cherries.

Sonia:	¿Cómo llegaron a Washington?
Lidia:	En avión.
Sonia:	¿Cómo volvieron?
Lidia:	En avión.
Sonia:	¿Cuándo fueron? ¿En qué temporada?
Lidia:	Cuando hacía calor.
Sonia:	¿Qué temporada es cuando hace calor?
Lidia:	[No response.]
Sonia:	¿Es invierno? ¿Qué estación es?
....	[Finally someone says "verano" ("summer") and Lidia continues talking about her trip.]

Translation

Lidia:	There were many fruits over there and the ones I liked the most were the cherries.
Sonia:	How did you get to Washington?
Lidia:	In an airplane.
Sonia:	How did you come back?
Lidia:	In an airplane.
Sonia:	When did you go? During which season?
Lidia:	When it was hot.
Sonia:	What season is it when it is hot?
Lidia:	[No response.]
Sonia:	Is it winter? What season is it?
....	[Finally someone says "verano" ("summer") and Lidia continues talking about her trip.]
	{Fieldnotes 10/26/94}

In this interaction, I initiated all the leads and my questions were of a lower level reasoning kind. The responses I elicited from Lidia were dull and uninteresting ones, I believe, due to my temporary lapse into a traditional mode of questioning, or better put, interrogation. In this instance I should have followed up on Lidia's first comments about fruit and cherries. This might have led her into a conversation about migrant workers and fruit picking, which I later found was the family's reason for going to Washington. Unfortunately, after Lidia, I approached each child's contribution in exactly the same way.

These types of exchanges made me reflect more and more on the importance and relevance of dialogues that foster higher level reasoning from students in the classroom. Too often, students are just bombarded, either with information or with questions about that information. Instead, the role of the teacher should be to guide students to explore and find knowledge on their own, and also to allow them to make connections to their experiences and prior knowledge. In this way, students can become truly engaged and interested and that is when they truly learn. The following example illustrates how this latter kind of thinking took place among my students when I guided the conversation areas that children were not only highly interested in, but of which they had some previous knowledge.

A Better Conversation: Students' Questioning Boundaries and Wetbacks

Example 2 was part of an ongoing unit, "Travel and Our World." Initially the other kindergarten teachers and I had planned this thematic unit to superficially cover aspects related to travel, including geography. It was not my initial intention to do a more in-depth study on Mexico, but the children's enthusiasm when we initially discussed the country led me to this curricular direction. Here, half of my class (the other half was at the computer lab) was sitting around a table facing a board with a map of North America.

Example 2

1	Sonia:	Aquí dice México. Esto es Estados Unidos, esto es México. [pointing to them on the map]
2	Esteban:	Pero de todos modos México no es——no es chiquito, cuando ellos robaron——la tierra, todavía es grande, México.
3	Sonia:	México era grande antes. ¿Y quién le robó la tierra?
4	Esteban:	Los de aquí.
5	Sonia:	Ooooh. ¿Y quién te contó?
6	Esteban:	Mi papá.
7	Sonia:	Tu papá. ¿Y tú sabes qué parte era de México que ya no es? [I wait but there is no response.] ¿Qué parte sería esa? Esto es México. [pointing on the map] ¿Cuál era la parte que era de México antes?
8	Esteban:	Esto——era——era——era de aquí pa' allá. [pointing towards the map]
9	Sonia:	¿Para abajo?
10	Esteban:	(... ...).

11	C1:	Aquel no era, Maestra.
12	Sonia:	Pero Estados Unidos está acá arriba. Esos son otros países. [pointing to countries south of México in the map]
13	Cf:	Aquel, Maestra, aquel.
14.	Sonia:	Yo creo que acá arriba, acá, esta era la parte que tu papá te contó que era de México....
15	Esteban:	A lo mej——a lo mejor——es——este es un lugar famoso porque también hay un——un país que es famoso por——porque ahí los mexicanos no——no pueden pasar a través de——de la línea (...).
16	Sonia:	¿No pueden pasar?
17	Esteban:	No.
18	Sonia:	¿A dónde?
19	Esteban:	La——la línea es de Est——es parte de Estados Unidos.
20	Sonia:	¿Acá en la——en la——en el límite? ¿Justo acá, en esta línea?
21	Esteban:	Uhum.
22	Sonia:	¿No los dejan pasar?
23	Esteban:	Ya <mi tío> lo atraparon el año pasado.
24	Sonia:	¿Quién sabía eso?
25	Esteban:	Mi papi me lo contó y también....
26	Sonia:	¿Qué te dijo? [I wait but there is no response.] ¿Quién sabia de eso que——uy, vamos a esperar a Vicente y Mariela porque están jugando. El papá de Esteban le contó a él que hay partes acá, en el límite con México y Estados Unidos, que no dejan entrar a los mexicanos. ¿Por qué sería eso? ¿Por qué no los dejan entrar?
27	Cm1:	Porque no....
28	Sonia:	¿Por qué será?
29	Cm1:	Porque....
30	Mariela:	Ell——ellos no son de este país.
31	Sonia:	¿Porque los mexicanos son de México y no son de Estados Unidos?
32	Cf1:	#Maestra....#
33	Sonia:	#Pero ustedes están acá, y uestedes son de México.... #
34	Cf1:	#Maestra ... maestra ... mi papá vino a los Estados Unidos.#
35	Cm:	#A mí si me dejan entrar, y soy de Chicago.#
36	Sonia:	Porque naciste en Chicago. ¿Y por eso te dejan entrar? Hmmm. ¿Quién mas nació en Chicago? ¿Quién nació en México?
37	Cs:	[Raise hands and talk all at once.]

38	C:	#Yo nací en Chicago.#
39	C:	#Yo nací acá.#
40	C:	#Yo igual.#
....		[I name some of the ones born in Chicago and some of the ones born in Mexico. Then I question some of them who have not volunteered information. Some do not know and I tell them to ask their mothers. Then I pose another question.]
41	Sonia:	¿Y sus mamá y papá, dónde nacieron?
42	Cf:	En México, mi mam——mamá y mi papá nacieron en México.
43	Esteban:	Mi tio es mojado.
44	Sonia:	¿En *Mojado*? [Because they were talking about being born *in* Mexico and reluctant to believe the children would know the word "mojado" (wetback) in Spanish, I initially responded to the child's comment as if "mojado" were the name of a place in Mexico.]
45	Cs:	[laughter]
46	Cf1:	Caminando … se fue caminando porque un amigo de mi mamá lo dijo.
47	Sonia:	¿Qué?
48	Cf1:	Que … e … e … e——que mojado quiere decir que se vienen caminando, de allá.
49	Sonia:	Hmmmm, y se vinieron caminando. ¿Y por qué le dicen mojado? [I wait but there is no response.] ¿Porque se mojó?
50	Cs:	No.
51	Esteban:	Pero mi papá dice que——se vino, yo creo.…
....		[I ask Cs not to touch the microphone, to sit down in their chairs and call some names, especially as Esteban wants to keep talking.]
52	Esteban:	Yo creo que——yo creo que——yo creo que se vino en un taxi de México.
53	Sonia:	¿En un taxi de México? [with emphasis as "Can this be?"]
54	Esteban:	A lo mejor.
55	Sonia:	¿En un taxi de México? Aquí está Chicago, acá arriba, tuvieron que cruzar tooooodo esto para ir a México. [pointing on the map] ¿Se habrá ido en un taxi?
56	Cs:	(… …).
57	Esteban:	(…) en lugar de en un taxi, a lo mejor se fue en un avión.
58	Sonia:	Hmmmm. Okay, estamos hablando——Esteban nos contó que alguien le habiía dicho que a la gente que se cruza caminando le dicen mojado. ¿Alguien sabe por qué? [I wait but there is no response.] ¿Qué quiere decir mojado?

59	Cm:	Que están mojados.
60	Sonia:	Que se mojó. Porque muchas personas que viven en México, cruzan por un río y se mojan. Pero le dicen mojados, pero no es una cosa muy linda que le dicen. Cuando le dicen mojado no es——no es algo lindo, es algo que no....
61	Cf:	Que no lo deben repetir.
62	Sonia:	Es un insulto. ¿Saben lo que es un insulto?
63	Cm1:	¡Maestra!
64	Sonia:	¿Qué es un insulto?
65	Cm1:	¡Maestra!
66	Sonia:	Cuando yo le digo a alguien "Eres un tonto," eso es un insulto.
67	Cs:	[laughter]
68	Sonia:	Si alguien te dice, "Eres un mojado." ¿Eso qué es?
69	Cs:	Un insulto.
70	Cf:	Es una grosería.
71	Sonia:	Es una grosería, uhum. Okay, aquí tenemos el globo, el globo terráqueo se llama.

Translation

1	Sonia:	Here it says Mexico. This is the United States, this is Mexico. [pointing to them on the map]
2	Esteban:	But yet Mexico is not——is not small, when they stole——the land, it is still big, Mexico.
3	Sonia:	Mexico was big before. And who stole the land?
4	Esteban:	Those from here.
5	Sonia:	Ooooh. And who told you?
6	Esteban:	My dad.
7	Sonia:	Your dad. And do you know what part was Mexico's and it is not any more? [I wait but there is no response.] What part would that be? This is Mexico. [pointing on the map] Which was the part that was Mexico's before?
8	Esteban:	This was——was——was from here to there [pointing towards the map].
9	Sonia:	Going down?
10	Esteban:	(... ...).
11	C1:	That one was not, Teacher.
12	Sonia:	But the United States is up here. These are other countries. [pointing to countries south of Mexico in the map]
13	Cf:	That one Teacher, that one.

14	Sonia:	I believe that up here, here, this is the part that your dad told you was Mexico's....
15	Esteban:	Maybe——maybe th——this is a famous place because there is also a——a country that is famous bec——because, there, the Mexicans cannot——cannot go in through——through the line(...).
16	Sonia:	They cannot go in?
17	Esteban:	No.
18	Sonia:	Where?
19	Esteban:	The——the line is of U——is part of the United States.
20	Sonia:	Here in the——in the——in the border? Right here, on this border?
21	Esteban:	Uhum.
22	Sonia:	They don't let them in?
23	Esteban:	And <my uncle> was caught last year.
24	Sonia:	Who knew that?
25	Esteban:	My daddy told me and also....
26	Sonia:	What did he tell you? [I wait but there is no response.] Who knew about that——ooops, let's wait for Vicente and Mariela because they are playing. Esteban's dad told him that there are parts here, in the border with Mexico and the United States, that they do not let the Mexicans in. Why would that be? Why don't they let them in?
27	Cm1:	Because they don't....
28	Sonia:	Why would that be?
29	Cm1:	Because....
30	Mariela:	The——they are not from this country.
31	Sonia:	Because the Mexicans are from Mexico and they are not from the United States?
32	Cf1:	#Teacher....#
33	Sonia:	#But you are here, and you are from Mexico....#
34	Cf1:	#Teacher ... teacher ... my dad came to the United States.#
35	Cm:	#They let me in, and I am from Chicago.#
36	Sonia:	Because you were born in Chicago? And because of that they let you in? Hmmmm. Who else was born in Chicago? Who was born in Mexico?
37	Cs:	[Raise hands and talk all at once.]
38	C:	#I was born in Chicago.#
39	C:	#I was born here.#

40	C:	#Me too.#
....		[I name some of the ones born in Chicago and some of the ones born in Mexico. Then I ask some of them who have not volunteered information. Some do not know and I tell them to ask their mothers. Then I pose another question.]
41	Sonia:	And your mom and dad, where were they born?
42	Cf:	In Mexico, my mo——mom and my dad were born in Mexico.
43	Esteban:	My uncle is wetback.
44	Sonia:	In *Wetback*? [Since they were talking about being born in Mexico and reluctant to believe that the children would know the word mojado (wetback) in Spanish, I initially responded to the child's comment as if mojado were the name of a place in Mexico.]
45	Cs:	[laughter]
46	Cf1:	Walking … went walking because a friend of my mom's said that.
47	Sonia:	What?
48	Cf1:	Tha-a-a——that wetback means that they come walking, from there.
49	Sonia:	Hmmmmm, and they came walking. And why do they call him wetback? [I wait but there is no response.] Because he got wet?
50	Cs:	No.
51	Esteban:	But my dad says that——he came, I believe….
....		[I ask Cs not to touch the microphone, to sit down in their chairs and call some names specifically as Esteban wants to keep talking.]
52	Esteban:	I believe that——I believe that——I believe that he came in a cab from Mexico.
53	Sonia:	In a cab from Mexico? [with emphasis as "Can this be?"]
54	Esteban:	Maybe.
55	Sonia:	In a cab from Mexico? Here is Chicago, up here. They had to cross aaaaall this to get to Mexico. [pointing on the map] Would he have gone in a cab?
56	Cs:	(... ...).
57	Esteban:	(...) instead of a cab, maybe he went on a plane.
58	Sonia:	Hmmmm. Okay, we are talking——Esteban told us that someone had told him that the people that cross by walking are called wetbacks. Does anybody know why? [I wait but there is no response.] What does wetback mean?
59	Cm:	That they are wet.

60	Sonia:	That he got wet. Because many people that live in Mexico cross through a river and get wet. But they call them wetbacks, but it is not a nice thing to say. When they call them wetback it is not, it is not something nice, it is something that is not....
61	Cf:	That should not be repeated.
62	Sonia:	It is an insult. Do you know what an insult is?
63	Cm1:	Teacher!
64	Sonia:	What is an insult?
65	Cm1:	Teacher!
66	Sonia:	When I tell someone, "You are a dummy," that is an insult.
67	Cs:	[laughter]
68	Sonia:	If someone tells you, "You are a wetback," what is that?
69	Cs:	An insult.
70	Cf:	It is a rude comment.
71	Sonia:	It is a rude comment, uhum. Okay, here we have the globe, the Earth globe it is called.

{Fieldnotes, videotape, 02/28/95}

This exchange is noticeably more involved than the previous one. Here the students were obviously eager and excited about the topic, so I quickly backed off and allowed them to guide the conversation. Although they were dictating where the conversation was heading, I provided springboards to construct new knowledge. For example, when the students discussed the term wetback toward the end of the example, they were unsure about where the term came from and whether this was a good thing to be or not. I provided an explanation concerning both, and then helped them to better understand what exactly is an insult. Although immigration and land appropriation are sensitive and controversial topics of conversation, I consciously attempted to have my students' perspective voiced. I found this approach to be important because I don't want to put forth my way of thinking in a way so as not to hear their ideas. So, the conversation is dotted with my phatic markers (i.e., ooooh's, humm's and aaah's) indicating to the students that I am listening and I would like to know more (see lines 5 & 58) (Halliday & Hasan, 1976).

I encouraged the children to continue the conversation by probing for more information, in particular, about their sources of information. For example, I had Esteban reflect on where he got the information about the Mexican land being stolen by "those [people] from here" (line 4), and I nudged him to explore his sources of information or funds of knowledge. At times I challenged further about such things as the likelihood that his father came from Mexico in a taxi (lines 52–57). I tried not to be judgmental about the topic at hand because I did not want to influence too much what the students had to say. That is, I did not want to influence their perceptions as to what, I, as the teacher, wanted to hear. Children often will tell you what they think you want to hear because they want to please you or because they want your approval.

MORE ON MY QUESTIONING TECHNIQUES

My questioning strategies were, at the beginning of the year, regarded with much skepticism by the children. The students, understandably, were not totally sure about the true intentions of my questioning. When I asked, "Why?" or "How do you know?", did I *really* want to know the answer? Was I *really* interested in what they had to say? Later, I realized that children are used to adults questioning them for other purposes than getting to an answer or explanation. For example, a parent or teacher may ask a child after she has broken something, "*Why* did you do that?" or "What do you *think* you are doing?" Even as adults we know that most of the time when we are asked, "How are you?," nobody really wants to know about our state of being. So, sometimes questions become mere statements, greetings, even accusations. Because my questions were open ended and I used many phatic markers, the students were surrounded by constant invitations to participate. After a time, they began to anticipate our conversations and my line of questioning. Many times students and I engaged in discussions that almost seemed like they were guiding themselves, or taking lives of their own. Of course, there were still many instances in which the discussions came to complete dead ends, like the one we had about different breeds of dogs.

Unsuccessful Attempts to Talk about Dogs

The interaction in Example 3 took place after a shared reading of a song that I had written down (with my own illustrations) in the form of a big book. The topic in the song discussed a fantasy world in which everything is upside down or backward. One of the pages mentions a Pekinese dog.

Example 3

1	Sonia:	Hay distintos tipos de perros. ¿Qué tipos de perros hay?
2	Cs:	(... ...) color.
3	Sonia:	Hay distintos tipos de perros: pekinés, collie, poodles. ¿Qué otro tipo? ¿Qué otro tipo de perro hay?
4	Cm1:	Uno negro.
5	Cf1:	Una perra.
6	Sonia:	Si, hay perros y perras.

Translation

1	Sonia:	There are different types of dogs. What kinds of dogs are there?
2	Cs:	(... ....) color.
3	Sonia:	There are different types of dogs: Pekinese, collie, poodle. What other type? What other types of dogs are there?
4	Cm1:	A black one.
5	Cf2:	A female dog.
6	Sonia:	There are dogs and female dogs.
		{Fieldnotes, 11/18/94}

In this instance I tried to build a conversation by extending the simple and silly verse that mentioned a Pekinese dog. My aim was to build on their prior knowledge, discuss types of dogs with which they might be familiar, and then introduce the concept of categories and classification. I quickly realized that the students didn't understand my questioning and seemed to have limited prior knowledge about breeds of dogs.

Although my unsuccessful initiations could be seen as fumbles, I tried to view them more as attempts at discussions that did not take hold, and as areas outside the zone of proximal development regarding students' interests, as well as outside of their knowledge. Because I saw myself as a learner too, I was also willing to take risks. I think that if children view teachers as learners and risk takers, students will be more open to share and be risk takers themselves. They will realize that in different ways, we are all learners and teachers.

More Successful Attempts to Talk about Airplanes

Example 4 represents a conversation that was more productive than the previous one; here, I was able to tap into the students' prior knowledge and interest. The discussion took place after a read aloud of *El Avion de Angela* (*Angela's Airplane*) by Robert Munsch (1988). Here we are exploring word meaning based on the students' own knowledge about airplanes. Nearby on a bulletin board is a poster showing the interior of a plane.

Example 4

| 1 | Sonia: | [reading from the book] YO ME LLAMO ÁNGELA Y SOLO TENGO CINCO AÑOS Y NO SE NADA DE VOLAR AVIONES. "DIOS MÍO, QUÉ LÍO!" CONTESTÓ LA VOZ. "ENTONCES ESCÚCHAME MUY BIEN ÁNGELA: AGARRA EL TIMÓN Y DA |

		VUELTA HACIA LA IZQUIERDA." [addressing the group] ¿Qué querrá decir el "timón"?
2	Ramón:	El volante.
3	Sonia:	El volante. [she points to the book] ¿Cómo sabías que el timón era el volante?
4	Cm1:	Porque … era así. [moves hands like steering, then looks at Ramón]
5	Sonia:	Ramón, ¿por qué?
6	Ramón:	Porque estaba pensando.
7	Sonia:	Aah! Ramón estaba pensando porque el escuchó lo que estaba diciendo el cuento. Le dijeron: "AGARRA EL TIMÓN." Tiene que ser el volante, no?
….		[Later on, the conversation moves on to plane crashes and what the children know about planes.]
8	Sonia:	Vamos a hablar un poquito de cuando hay accidentes de aviones.
9	Cm1:	Cuando chocan.
10	Sonia:	Cuando chocan con otro avión pero cuando se vienen abajo, ¿cómo se llama eso?
11	Cm2:	Estrellar.
12	Sonia:	Se estrellan.
….		[A few minutes, later Sonia turns to the nearby poster and uses it a basis of conversation.]
13	Sonia:	Y pueden mirar por la ventana. Y acá, acá está la parte donde….
14	Cm1:	Manejan!
15	Sonia:	Manejan … eeeh….
16	Mariela:	Esos dos son los jefes.
17	Sonia:	¿Son los jefes?
18	Mariela:	Sí.
19	Cs:	No.
20	Sonia:	Son los….
21	Cs:	Los pilotos!
22	Sonia:	Los pilotos, aha. Y sí, son como los jefes.
23	Cf1:	Mi hermano tiene aviones de——de juguete.
24	Sonia:	Si tienen aviones de juguete en casa, los pueden traer mañana. Los van … a traer mañana, para verlos.
25	Esteban:	Yo tengo un avión que es—es de la … de la Army.
26	Sonia:	De la Army! Porque hay distintos tipos de aviones….
….		[Sonia refers them back to poster and asks them what type of plane the one in the poster is.]

27 C: #(...) llevan gente.#

28 C: #Los de la army.#

29 C: #Llevan tanques.#

30 Esteban: #Llevan comida para los pobres.#

31 Sonia: ¿Cómo sabes? [asking Esteban]

32 Esteban: Porque—porque pasan en las noticias.

Translation

1 Sonia: [reading from the book] MY NAME IS ANGELA AND I AM ONLY
             FIVE YEARS OLD AND I DON'T KNOW ANYTHING ABOUT
             FLYING PLANES. "OH, MY GOD, WHAT A MESS!" ANSWERED
             THE VOICE. "THEN, LISTEN TO ME VERY CAREFULLY,
             ANGELA: TAKE THE WHEEL AND TURN LEFT." [Sonia ad-
             dresses the group] What would *timón* (wheel) mean?

2 Ramón: The wheel.

3 Sonia: The wheel [she points to the book] How did you know that the
             timón was the wheel?

4 Cm1:   Because ... it was like this [moves hands like steering, then
             looks at Ramón]

5 Sonia: Ramón, why?

6 Ramón: Because I was thinking.

7 Sonia   Aah! Ramón was thinking because he listened to what the story
             was saying. They told her: "TAKE THE *TIMÓN*." It has to be the
             wheel, right?

....   [Later on, the conversation moves on to plane crashes and what
             the children know about planes]

8 Sonia: We'll talk a little bit about when there are plane accidents.

9 Cm1:   When they bump.

10 Sonia: When they bump with another plane, but when they come down,
             what do you call that?

11 Cm2:   Crash.

12 Sonia: They crash.

....   [A few minutes later, Sonia turns to the nearby poster and uses
             it a basis of conversation]

13 Sonia: And you can look through the window, and here, here is the part
             where....

14 Cm1:   They drive.

15 Sonia: They drive ... uuuh....

16 Mariela: Those two are the bosses.

17	Sonia:	The bosses?
18	Mariela:	Yes!
19	Cs:	No.
20	Sonia:	They are the….
21	Cs:	The pilots.
22	Sonia:	Aha, the pilots. And yes, they are like the bosses.
23	Cf2:	My brother has——has toy planes.
24	Sonia	If you have toy planes at home, you can bring them tomorrow. You are going … to bring them tomorrow … to look at them.
25	Cm1:	I have a plane that is——is from the Army.
26	Sonia	From the Army? Because there are different types of planes….
….		[Sonia refers them back to poster and asks them what type of plane the one in the poster is]
27	C:	#(…) carry people.#
28	C:	#Army planes.#
29	C:	#Carry tanks.#
30	Esteban:	#Carry food for the poor.#
31	Sonia:	How do you know? [asking Esteban]
32	Esteban:	Because——because they show them on the news.
		{Fieldnotes and videotape, 02/12/95}

In the beginning of this conversation I guided Ramón (lines 2–7) to explore how he engaged in his own thought process about deciphering that timon must mean *volante*—there are two different words in Spanish for steering wheel of a plane or boat and that of a car or vehicle. I also consistently tried to engage students in demonstrating their knowledge and thinking about their sources of information by asking, "How do you know?" (line 31). I was always more interested in the process than in the product of students' answers or responses. That is, my focus was on having the students consciously think about their thinking and how they engage in meaning making, rather than on giving me the right answer. As a result I could take their approximations, such as Mariela's initiation about the "two bosses," and then the other children and I could extend them for more appropriate or for new understandings (lines 16–22).

THE RELEVANCY ISSUE IN CONVERSATIONS

In time, our conversations became longer and more involved, and with this came the dreaded management issue. Children were so eager both to contribute and to be heard that many times they would seemingly go off on tangents, that had either little relevance or no relevance at all, to the topic at hand. I again struggled with trying to accept and encourage children's initiations and at the same time trying to contain the conversations within reasonable time and topic-relevance constraints. This was a difficult task for me. Many times I felt I had to take the time to find out if indeed there was any relevance in a child initiation to our discussion. Many times the child's contribution was related, but two or three times removed from our conversation, even though in the child's mind it was valid and had relevance. Sometimes, because of the time constraints, I had to cut children off by making statements such as: "Are we discussing that now?" or "We can talk about that later?".

Also I sometimes made mistakes about relevancy. For example, a little later in the conversation found in Example 4, students continued to give ideas about the different types of planes they knew about. A student offered *alacran,* which in Spanish is a type of scorpion. My response was, "Are we talking about scorpions?" Ceci followed up with a statement that she had seen one in Mexico, where I said, "But we said that we were going to talk about Mexico later." {Fieldnotes, videotape, 02/12/95} In this case, I was too quick to cut the student off who had mentioned the alacran. I realized, after a review of the transcript, that I hadn't even attempted to find out what made the student think about a scorpion in the first place. I could have asked, "What makes you think of scorpion as we are coming up with the kinds of planes we know?" I missed a great opportunity. Later, Liliana, one of the university-researcher collaborators remarked that it was possible that alacran was the name of a fighter jet. This made a lot of sense and made me reflect more on my role as a facilitator rather than a time keeper. Keeping close to time schedules is a great part of being a teacher, so the challenge, then, is to juggle time constraints and teachable moments, such as this.

CHILDREN'S CONTRIBUTIONS AS THE FOUNDATION FOR CREATING NEW KNOWLEDGE

I set as my goal to study the rich linguistic and intellectual resources that I had informally observed in my students. Underlying my inquiry where three objectives: first, to challenge the common assumption that poor, nonmainstream, Latino, immigrant children are somehow devoid of abilities and skills, and suffer from a deficit of mainstream cultural and intellectual experiences; second, to bridge the home and the school so that the students can be engaged in meaningful interactions and learning; and third, to enrich my own teaching by better understanding my role as a facilitator, and thus explicitly applying the principles of Vygotskian theory to my educational practices.

As a teacher, my principal intent was for students to feel like they are valued contributors of the classroom knowledge. I think that I had some rocky patches in my research period, but that overall I was extremely successful in all of the three areas I list. I strongly believe that this approach of valuing children's thought processes and funds of knowledge, regardless of their economic or ethnic backgrounds, promotes the development of critical thinkers and problem solvers. Students learned strategies and could evaluate and build on others' ideas to create new knowledge and understanding. This type of teaching–learning approach, I believe, has a more profound and encompassing effect. It is different from the traditional ways where the objective is often to produce merely functionally literate individuals. In my role as facilitator of learning, rather than merely as a transmitter of knowledge, I also discovered the richness of my students' linguistic, cultural, and intellectual resources. If I worked hard to look, to dig for it, there it was—a strong foundation on which to build in my teaching practices.

ABOUT THE AUTHOR

I am the youngest of four, my parents live in Maine and I have six nephews. I was born and raised in Argentina. I have also lived in Uruguay, Brazil, and Costa Rica, and have visited Africa several times while my parents resided there. I am the product of Latin American bilingual education.

I have a bachelor's degree in elementary education, a master's in bilingual education. I have recently received a PhD in bilingual education from the University of Arizona. I have been a bilingual teacher for more than 13 years, 7 of these at a Native American reservation. During the past several years I have been teaching at Andersen in Chicago.

DEDICATION

I dedicate my chapter to my husband, Jose, and to my nephew, Logan.

REFERENCES

Halliday, M. A. K., & Hasan, R. (1976). *Cohesion in English*. White Plains, NY: Longman.

Moll, L. (Ed.). (1990) *Vygotsky and education: Instructional implications and applications of sociohistorical psychology*. Cambridge, England: Cambridge University Press.

Munsch, R. (1988). *El avion de Angela (Angela's airplane)*. Toronto, Canada: Annick Press.

Nieto, S. (1992). *Affirming diversity. The sociopolitical context of multicultural education*. White Plains, NY: Longman.

Vygotsky, (1978). *Mind in society: The development of higher psychological processes*. Cambridge, MA: Harvard University Press.

Chapter 3

Pretend Reading Is for Everybody in Kindergarten—Even the Boys!

Demetrya Collier
Andersen Elementary School

EDITORS' COMMENTS

Dee's inquiry centers around her attempts to foster and assess her kindergartners' early emergent reading. Noting that her boys were especially unmotivated or interested in literacy activities, she set up a time every day for all children to engage in the pretend reading of books of their choice. In this chapter, she lays out both her struggles and her successes in motivating children in this activity, and in her scaffolding of their efforts.

An important feature of her inquiry was the way in which students collaborated with each other to support their reading of various books. Another issue for her was how to do the ongoing assessment and subsequent response to children of diverse ability and understanding. Until this inquiry, Dee had not thought much about what is involved in these early stages of reading, so her story of what she learned about this facet of emergent literacy may provide important insights for others.

The introduction chapter of this book provides the theoretical and methodological background for the larger collaborative school–university action-research project and for this chapter about Dee's inquiry on pretend readings.

University researchers, Dian Ruben and Jane Liao, collaborated with Dee in her inquiry.

THE INQUIRY: IN THE BEGINNING

Before 1989, I had doubts and reservations concerning the whole-language approaches that were being implemented in my school. However, as I learned more about the underlying philosophy, I found that I already agreed with many of the fundamental beliefs. In general I worked during the past several years to redefine my literacy curriculum so that reading and writing are related, and are meaningful and purposeful activities in my kindergarten students' lives. I moved away from a basal orientation to a more literature-based approach. I learned how to develop thematic units that enable me to integrate the curricular areas. I became aware of the quality of children's literature that is available for use in my teaching, and I explored the ways that children respond to this literature.

Classes vary from year to year. However, I found that most have a common element. It is usually not difficult to nudge the girls into the class library center or for them to be motivated in the various literacy activities I provide. However, I often had to face reluctance and lack of motivation for these literacy experiences from many of the boys. During the year of my inquiry, my class was predominantly male (14 out of 22 students—16 Latina or Latino children, 5 African Americans, and 1 Anglo child), and many of these boys loved to run, wrestle, karate chop, and roll on the rug. These little fellows would devote most of the free-time choices or breaks to activities involving physical fun. They would readily join a literacy activity only if it offered some physical activity, for example, in dramatization or role-playing experiences. They especially avoided any reading-like behavior—that is, the actual sitting down with a book to pretend read or reenact it.

Although I did previous inquiries around writing and had a pretty good understanding of young children's beginnings of writing and how I could facilitate it, I felt that I was not fully cognizant of the various ways that my young students might develop the early emergent processes of reading. Thus, I decided that my inquiry this year should involve trying to get *all* of my students more into pretend reading—especially the reluctant, physically bound boys—and then to learn new strategies that would enable me to foster their learning to read by reading. I read aloud to my students twice a day. I became interested in what they would do with the books on their own, how they would model what I had done. In short, I wanted them to see themselves as readers and I wanted to study that process.

STRUGGLES AND SUCCESSES IN ENGAGING STUDENTS IN LITERACY ACTIVITIES

During the very first month of school, I observed how my kindergartners worked, played, and interacted with each other as they moved from center to center. I had an enthusiastic, exuberant, and talkative group of students the 1994–1995 school year. However, there were great differences in their developmental levels, interests, and experiences. Also it was difficult, at best, to get some of the students—especially the majority of the males—interested in the books in the class library or in other literacy activities I offered them.

Struggles to Keep the Boys' Attention in Literacy Activities

An early thematic unit we had was Families. As part of that unit, I read Eve Merriam's (1989) book, *Mommies at Work*. After reading the book, we began to write a list of what students' mommies did. Example 1 shows the typical difficulties I had in getting the boys into literacy-related activities.

Example 1

1	Dee:	Let's make a list of some thing our mommies do.
2	Cm:	*Five Little Pumpkins.* [This is the name of a big book made by another kindergarten teacher]
3	Dee:	We're not doing *Five Little Pumpkins* now. You can do that as soon as we make a list [reaching for a marker and standing near the butcher paper ready to write]. We'll start as soon as everyone is sitting up nice and quiet. Teresa, what does your mommy do at home?
4	Teresa:	She cleans up.
5	Dee:	Does she clean the house?
6	Teresa:	I clean the bathroom.
7	Cs:	#[hands up]#
8	Cm1:	#[stands up and walks over to me]#
9	Dee:	[addressing the Cm1] Sit. Ana, what does your mom do?
10	Ana:	Wash dishes.
11	Dee:	Larry?
12	Larry:	My mommy washes dishes.
13	Dee:	Does she work outside the home?
14	Larry:	She works on carpets.
15	Dee:	Randolph. Oh!
16	Randolph:	She listens to peoples' stories. She cleans house. I help her.
17	Dee:	[briefly stopping my writing] Randolph's mom is a counselor in the next building. She used to teach third grade here.
18	C1:	My mom works at J. J. Peppers.
19	Dee:	Do you know what she does?
20	C1:	She makes donuts.
21	Dee:	Good. Larry, we need to listen.

22	SCms:	[five boys on the back of the rug are engaged in some kind of game]
23	Dee:	Let's stop. I hear voices in the back. I don't know if you're talking about mommies to a friend, but we have rules on the rug.
24	Cm2:	[sitting in a chair (not on the rug) at the back of the rug] I clean the hallway and wash windows.
25	Dee:	Your mom has a job. Do you know where she works?
26	Cm2:	Downtown.
27	Dee:	I think it might be the Mayor's office.
28	Cms:	(... ...) Power Rangers.
29	Dee:	Are we talking about Power Rangers now?

{Fieldnotes, 10/18/94}

Now, because many of the children in my class have not attended preschool before they enter my kindergarten, it is normal that some might still be learning how to act appropriately as students in school. However, although there were some boys who participated in the making of a list of how their mothers' work activities—Larry (lines 12 & 14), Randolph (line 16), and Cm2 (lines 24 & 26)—there were many who did not. It was mostly boys who were disruptive or otherwise caused distractions. For example, a boy brought up the *Five Little Pumpkins* in line 2, a boy stood up and walked up to me in line 8, a boy (Larry) was noisy in line 21, and boys brought up Power Rogers in line 28. There were many other distractions during this lesson that were not included in the example, most of which were initiated by boys. When our ESL students came back to the classroom, it was several boys who ran over to the door to let them in. As we tried to make closure to this activity by summarizing our data on the list, it was a boy, Randolph, who I had to reprimand for crawling all over the rug.

Thus, this and many other kinds of literacy activities were interrupted by boys; mostly, I think, because they did not find them interesting at all. After my afternoon reading aloud period, I set time for students to choose their own books to read, as I roved around them to encourage them to re-enact or pretend read them. On many occasions several boys had to be told to pick out a book to read, and I had to go back to them later to persuade them to try to read their books. I tried to encourage them by telling that they could read or tell the book in their own words—that that was reading. Nevertheless, there was still a group of children—boys—who continued to be reluctant to read to me.

I tried to make sure that I read books the children liked. I began having volunteer students dramatize stories to retell them, and the boys began to participate in these part-verbal, part-physical activities. I encouraged students to bring their books from home to read. The boys brought in Batman, Power Rangers, Barney, and V. I. Trooper books. These are not examples of great literature, but these boys' interest in these books made it possible for me to create opportunities to scaffold their reading. Slowly their interest in the class library began to be aroused.

An Important Breakthrough! Angel Reads *Daddies*

Then, in November, a particular book, another one from my Families unit, really ignited the interest of many of the children, but especially the boys. *Daddies* (Greenspun, 1991) is an informational book with wonderful black-and-white photographs of fathers, from a range of ethnic and racial backgrounds, with their children. The text and photographs tell and depict everyday, family events and experiences. Thus, with this content and because the book had only six sentences with one or few words per page, children were successful in approximating the book's meanings. Students read it on their own, but more often small groups would be found supporting each other in reading it.

Then one day, Angel, for whom the book appeared to be very salient (due to a troublesome family situation), asked me if he could read the book to the whole class. After practicing reading the book on his own, he stood in front of the class, who sat on the rug as they did during my read alouds. Example 2 shows his reading. Note that I have indicated those wordings of the text found on the left- versus right-hand side pages with a slash mark, and that my few contributions are placed in double parentheses. During his reading, Angel showed the pictures to the audience and tried to point to the words (although, as you will see this was not always done in a one-to-one correspondence).

Example 2

Text	Angel's Reading
Daddies/ hold babies, [picture]/ push strollers,	DADDIES HOLD BABIES. DADDIES PUSH STROLLERS [calls a name to get the student's attention]
share feelings,/	DADDIES [turns book around so Dee can see words] ([Dee: SHARE ... I can't see the rest of it. Oh, FEELINGS. Okay.]) DADDIES SHARE FEELINGS.
read stories.	DADDIES READ STORIES [looking up to watch his audience]
Daddies have shoulders to stand on,/	DADDIES HAVE SHOULDERS TO SIT——TO STAND ON.

bellies to sit on,	DADDIES HAVE BELLIES TO SIT ON.
backs to climb on,	DADDIES (... ...).
hands to hold.	DADDIES (... ...). [Calls out a student's name]
Daddies give hugs/	DADDIES GIVE <HUGGLES>.
and kisses,	DADDIES GIVE KISSES [calls a name]
tickles and giggles,/	DADDIES (...) GIGGLES.
piggyback rides.	DADDIES HAVE—DADDIES GIVE PIGGYBACK RIDES [calls a name].
Daddies teach/	DADDIES TEACH
how to	HOW TO
swim,/ and dive,	DADDIES ... TEACH HOW TO DIVE.
ski,/ [picture]	DADDIES SKI.
catch/ and throw,	DADDIES (...) HOW TO CATCH AND THROW.
win,/ and lose.	DADDIES KNOW HOW TO WIN AND LOSE.
Daddies take us/ to parades,	DADDIES TAKE US TO PARADES [calls a name]
and home again,/[picture]	AND HOME <WORK>—AND HOME <WORK> AGAIN
on picnics, /	DADDIES TAKE US TO PICNICS.
to parties,	DADDIES TAKE US TO PARTIES [calls a name]
to the zoo. /picture	[Skips a page]
Daddies need/ hugs and	DADDIES GIVE US <HUGGLES>.
kisses,	DADDIES GIVE KISSES.
smiles,/ and tickles,	DADDIES [turns book to me for help] ([Dee: AND TICKLES.]) AND TICKLES.
Jokes,/and giggles, and	DADDIES GIVE GIGGLES.
"I love you."	I LOVE YOU.

{Fieldnotes, videotape, 11/25/94}

I was amazed at Angel's close approximations to the written text. He also modeled some of the things I do in class, telling students to pay attention and turning the book around to show the illustrations. I noticed his directionality and visual attention to print. He utilized pictorial clues in order to support his reading, adding extra "Daddies" as subjects for the verbs in the sentences of the book. (By the way, by May he was correctly reading this book from print.)

Angel's reading spurred a desire in the class to read out loud for me and others. Subsequently, I ended up providing a period of time at the end of the pretend reading time every day during which several children took turns to read to the class. Many other children—even boys—wanted to read *Daddies* and did not need to be nudged into the class library.

Andre Makes New Steps

Angel began to be a great collaborator and he was frequently found assisting others to read *Daddies* and other books. For a period of time, he ended up as the official reading buddy of Andre, who by the beginning of February, was still unwilling to read. I was very puzzled about Andre. He was quite capable in creating interesting dictations and did some writing on his own, but he was completely uninterested in reading. So, when he put his hand up to volunteer to read to the class one day, I was amazed. He had chosen the book, *When I Was Sick* (Hillman, 1989) to read, attempting first on his own and then with Angel, who came up to stand next to him to help—see Example 3.

===

Example 3

1	Andre:	WHEN I WAS SICK....
2	Dee:	(... ...) [distracted with another student]
3	Andre:	[turns the page]
4	Cs:	(... ...).
5	Dee:	[I take the book and try to close it because children are noisy, causing it to fall to the floor.] Wait a minute. We don't have a good audience. Let's just stop. #[reaches for the fallen book]#
6	Andre:	#[reaches for the fallen book]#
7	Angel:	Ms. Collier, you want me to help him?
8	Dee:	Help him? Stand here. [motioning to Angel to stand next to Andre] [to Andre] Do you need help?
9	Andre:	Uhhuh.
10	Dee:	Yeah!
11	Derrick:	He said "no."

12	Dee:	He said "yeah.' [to Angel] Okay, let's let him read first.
13	Andre:	[has the book open now reading] (... ...).
14	Donald:	WHEN I WAS SI....
15	Angel:	[takes the book and closes it to point to the words of the title on the cover, while Andre reads along] #WHEN I WAS SICK.#
16	Andre:	#WHEN I WAS SICK.# [opens the book and reads from the title page] WHEN I WAS SICK.
17	Dee:	Show the pictures.
18	Andre & Angel:	[both holding the book and reading together] WHEN I WAS SICK, I DIDN'T WANT TO EAT (...).
19	Andre:	THINNER [holding up the book to show the pictures]
....		[I stop the reading to get students to be quiet and be more attentive. After a few seconds, the two boys begin to read again.]
20	Angel:	#WHEN I....# [pointing to each word]
21	Andre:	#DIDN'T WANT TO# EAT....
22	Angel:	No!. WHEN I WAS SICK I——I DIDN'T WANT....
23	Dee:	Okay. I GOT THINNER ... AND....
24	Angel:	AND....
25	Dee:	THINNER. Okay, let's let Andre show the pictures. [taking the book, turning it for Andre]
26	Andre:	#[holds up the book for the students to see]#
27	Dee:	#And let's see if Andre can try and read some of it for us.#
		{Fieldnotes, videotape, 02/02/95}

This was a big day for Andre, and everyone knew it. Because Angel initiated helping, I let him do it when Andre agreed to his assistance. Later on I asked them if they could continue to be reading buddies, and they both agreed. Even when it was almost time to go home, Angel was found aiding him in another reading of the book (with a couple of other boys who joined in as well).

Thus, although I had lots of struggles in getting everyone engaged in the pretending reading experiences in the beginning, by the end of the year everyone was excited by the activity and learned a lot from it. All saw themselves as readers.

STRUGGLES AND SUCCESSES IN SCAFFOLDING

Some students easily modeled my reading, and I think I was successful in scaffolding reading strategies and techniques when I worked with many of the children, individually or in small groups. However, I still had many difficulties figuring out the best way to support students' attempts because of the diverse developmental range in my classroom. Below are three examples that show my attempts to assist three children—Samantha, Jimmy, and Teresa—who lie on the developmental continuum. I think I did the best job with Jimmy, an African–American child who was in the middle on that continuum. My interactions with the two girls, who were at either end of the continuum, showed the kinds of challenges and difficulties I had to deal with.

Samantha

Samantha was a creative and energetic Latina student. Both the preschool program she had attended and her mother's efforts in her education and learning had already laid a good foundation for kindergarten. In the beginning of the school year, when many of the students spent their time to playing during the free times, she was among those who frequented the class library.

Samantha was also an attentive listener during our Shared Reading Times, and she initiated questions and other comments about the books I read aloud. She was able to draw pictures about the stories that showed she understood them, to dictate her own stories, and she was beginning to write on her own. Samantha always wanted to volunteer to read to me. While reading, she showed knowledge of directionality and word to word correspondence. She was not solely using pictures to read books. In fact, she was attempting to read from print. However, when she came across a word she did know, she looked to me to give her the word. The problem I had is that I got caught up in doing just that—see Example 4. This example begins about the sixth page of the book, *I Like Me* (Carlson, 1988). The illustrations identify the "I" as a pig character.

Example 4

Text	Samantha's Reading (with my aid)	
I like to take care of me	1 Samantha:	I [looks at me]
	2 Dee:	LIKE
	3 Samantha:	LIKE TO [looks at me]
	4 Dee:	TAKE
	5 Samantha:	TAKE OF [looks at me, pointing to "care," but skips it]
	6 Dee:	CARE

	7 Samantha:	CARE OF ME.
I brush my teeth.		I BRUSH MY TEETH.
I keep clean and		I KEEP MYSELF CLEAN.
	8 Dee:	Okay. I KEEP CLEAN AND
I eat good food.	9 Samantha:	I EAT GOOD FOOD.
When I get up in the morning	10	WHEN I GOT UP IN THE MORNING,
I say, "Hi, good		I [looks at Dee]
looking!"	11 Dee:	SAY
	12 Samantha:	SAY <HUH>
	13 Dee:	HI
	14 Samantha:	HI [looks at me]
	15 Dee:	GOOD LOOKING
	16 Samantha:	GOOD LOOKING.
I like my curly tail,		I LIKE MY CURLY TAIL,
My round tummy,		ME....
	17 Dee:	MY
	18 Samantha:	MY [looks at me]
	19 Dee:	ROUND
	20 Samantha:	ROUND TUMMY,
And my tiny little feet.	21 Dee:	AND
	22 Samantha:	AND MY
	23 Dee:	TINY
	24 Samantha:	TINY
	25 Dee:	LITTLE
	26 Samantha:	LITTLE FEET.

{Fieldnotes, videotape, 02/02/95}

As you can see, most of the time I just simply gave Samantha the words she didn't know when she looked to me (lines 1–7) or seemed to hesitate at all (lines 21–26). Now, that might have been an okay thing to do if I was trying to launch a beginning reader (see what I do with Jimmy in the next example), but this was not going to help Samantha to learn new strategies.

Samantha did not want to take many risks in reading. I soon discovered that her mother might have been partially responsible for that because she wanted her to read "real" words and told me that she corrects all of Samantha's "mistakes" in reading at home. Unfortunately, I was doing the same thing at school. For example, on line 7 Samantha gave a good approximation of the text ("I keep myself clean" for the book's "I keep clean"), yet by my saying "okay" and then repeating the book language, I gave her the message that what she had read was incorrect. Also, because I jumped in so much in giving the actual words that she had no opportunities to self-correct. That happened, for instance, when Samantha correctly read, "I like my curly tail," and began the next part of the sentence of the book ("my round tummy") with "me." I quickly corrected her and gave her no chance to reconsider it on her own. I did the same thing in lines 12–14.

Thus, Samantha thinks that reading is getting all the words correct, and I didn't act in any way to show her any other way. There were so many things I could have done. I could have just have waited more to see if she could self-correct. When she looked at me, I could have said, "What do you think?" I could have suggested that when she skipped a word she didn't know she could read rest of the sentence and then go back and figure out what that word could be. In other words, although I knew at the time I wasn't scaffolding her reading the best way, it is only since I have had time to review and reflect on transcriptions that I have really come up with the best strategies I might have used with Samantha. I guess I did get better over the rest of the year, but I could never fully accomplish what I could have done.

Jimmy

Example 4 is Jimmy's reading of *The Napping House* (Wood, 1984), which was a favorite book of the children. The book is about a slumbering mouse, a snoozing cat, a dozing dog, a dreaming child, and a snoring granny on a cozy bed, all of whom are awakened by the bite of a wakeful flea. Jimmy is an African-American child who joined my class in October. His reading of this book occurred late in the year, March, but it was a big step for him in seeing himself as a reader. Until then he was motivated to look at books, and he often talked about the pictures of books with his classmates. However, he would usually choose very easy books and he made no real attempts at pretend reading them. He really liked a book version of "Old MacDonald's Farm" and he used his memory of the song to get through the book. He never tried to take what he had remembered about the song and map it to the pages to come up with text approximations. That is, this book was just used by him as a way to sing the song he knew.

Thus, before this reading of *The Napping House* book, Jimmy had never seriously taken on the role as reader. In the beginning of the example, I am reading the book to him, and then with my own and other students' help, Jimmy began to read on his own. Although others give him suggestions, he is insistent in giving his own reading of the book.

Example 5

Text		Jimmy, Myself, and Other Readers
And in that house there is a bed, a cozy bed in a napping house, where everyone is sleeping.	1 Dee:	Okay, see … #AND IN THAT HOUSE THERE IS A BED … A COZY BED IN A NAPPING HOUSE#
	2 Jimmy:	#AND IN THAT HOUSE THERE IS A BED … A COZY BED IN A NAPPY HOUSE#
	3 Dee:	WHERE EVERYONE IS….
	4 Jimmy:	SLEEPING [in a louder voice, then turns page]
And on that bed there is a granny, a snoring granny, a snoring granny on a cozy bed in a napping house, where everyone is sleeping.		IN THE NAPPY HOUSE….
	5 Dee:	Now who's on the bed? [pointing to the picture]
	6 Cm:	THE GRANDMA.
	7 Teresa:	A DOZY GRANDMA.
	8 Dee:	What kind of bed is it?
	9 Angel:	A COZY BED.
	10 Dee:	In what kind of house?
	11 Cs:	A NAPPING HOUSE.

And on that granny (...
there is a child, a ...).

dreaming child on a

snoring granny on a

cozy bed in a napping

house, where everyone

is sleeping.

12 Dee:	Where everyone is doing what? [looking directly at Angel but seems to be expecting responses from the group]
13 Cs:	SLEEPING.
14 Jimmy:	[Turning the page]
15 Dee:	What is the granny doing?
16 Guill:	SNORI....
17 Dee:	SNORING. And what kind of bed are they on?
18 Angel:	#COZY#
19 Jimmy:	#COZY#
20 Teresa:	COZY BED.
21 Dee:	What type of house?
22 Jimmy:	NAPPY HOUSE.
23 Dee:	Where everyone is....
24 Jimmy:	#SLEEPING#
25 Cs:	#SLEEPING#
26 Dee:	Okay.
27 Jimmy:	AND THE NAPPY HOUSE ... IT WAS NAPPY ... IN THE NAPPY HOUSE ... IT WAS ... EVERYBODY SLEEPY.

And on that child

there is a dog, a

28 Dee:	Okay, now who's on top of the dreaming child

dozing dog on a		now?
dreaming child on a	29 Jimmy:	(...).
snoring granny on a	30 Angel:	DOG....
cozy bed in a napping	31 Dee:	What kind of a dog?
house, where everyone		A DOZING DOG.
is sleeping.	32 Teresa:	AND THE CAT....
	33 Jimmy:	No! Hey, don't tell me.
	34 Dee:	Okay, we're not going
		to tell you.
	35 Jimmy:	IS A NAPPY——IN A NAPPY
		HOUSE ... <IF A> ... ALL THE
		PEOPLE SLEEPING IN A
		HOUSE. [putting his
		hand to his head and
		looking down as if to
		say, "I know that's not
		exactly what it says,
		but I did it."]

{Fieldnotes, videotape, 03/28/95}

In the beginning I read *with* him, but by line 4 his louder voice showed me that he was ready to read alone. However, between lines 6 and 13, he lost his role as single reader, while I asked questions about the pictures while other students participated in the reading by providing approximations. This book has repetitive language and has illustrations that support the wordings on the pages, so my questions about what was happening in the book, I thought, were good scaffolding for them. After that, Jimmy attempted to regain his role as reader, but because he spoke so quietly, Angel and Teresa took over. Later on, he made another effort to be the solo reader at lines 22 and 24, but especially in line 27, when he sort of summarized the text we had been working on. At line 33, Jimmy indicated that he wanted to do it himself as he told his classmates, "No! Hey, don't tell me." I agreed that he has the right to be the lone reader at line 34 and Jimmy continued to try to make sense of text by pretend reading it.

Later in the same reading, which is not provided in the example above, other emergent skills were present as he read the book. He seemed to look at the print more, pointing at words with his finger. He was aware that he wasn't reading the actual words of the book, but he showed me that he realized that the message of the book was coming from the print. I was good in not interrupting too much when he hesitated, so he frequently would self-correct a part on his own to come up with an approximation that was closer to the book meaning. Sometimes he would use suggestions of classmates, but throughout he kept telling them not to tell him the words.

Thus, Jimmy was on the middle of the developmental continuum, showing lots of good emergent-reader behaviors. He was paying attention to print, he knew a lot about its format in books, and he understood the book and provided a good version of the text language. He was self-correcting, and after this experience, he was quite eager to be a solo reader on his own. And I think I gave him the appropriate support to launch him into pretend reading.

Teresa

Teresa, an African-American student, was a very beginner in emergent reading. She had no preschool experience and virtually no academic support at home. Teresa was always a cheerful and effervescent child. She had an active imagination that led her to create the text from the pictures of books. However, she frequently picked books that did not support the pretend reading process at her developmental level or books that had not even been introduced to class before. I constantly had to nudge her back into the class library to choose another book, perhaps with pattern language that would more successfully support her reading.

In Example 6 she read *Imogene's Antlers* (Small, 1985), which is about a girl who wakes up to find that she has grown antlers during the night.

Example 6

Text	Teresa's Reading (with my aid)	
On Thursday, when	1 Teresa:	(… …) … I HAD THESE
Imogene woke up,		THINGS ON TOP OF MY
she found she had		HEAD.
grown antlers.	2 Dee:	Okay.

Getting dressed was difficult,	3 Teresa:	MY SHIRT GOT——MY SHIRT HAD (...) [bends down very close to the book, looking intently].

.... [There are many interruptions as several students come over to me asking questions.]

and going through a door now took some thinking.	4 Teresa:	(... ...) OUT OF THE DOOR. [turns page]

Imogene started down for breakfast ... but got hung up.		SHE SLIDE DOWN THE STAIRS.[turns page] SHE HUNG ON THE THING.
	5 Dee:	Okay, this is the light fixture [pointing to the picture]
"OH!!" Imogene's mother fainted away.	6 Teresa:	IT WAS [looking intently at the left-hand page while pointing to words on the right-hand page]
	7 Dee:	[pointing to the words on the right-hand side page] IMOGENE'S MOTHER FAINTED AWAY.
The doctor poked, and prodded, and scratched his chin. He could find nothing wrong.	8 Teresa:	[turns page] AND THE DOCTOR CAME.
	9 Dee:	Okay.

.... [Teresa reads the next page and then they are disturbed by other children. Teresa continues to read, but realizing that she had skipped a page, she goes back to it.]

Her brother, Norman,	10 Teresa:	THE BROTHER WAS
consulted the encyclo-		THINKING—THE BROTHER WAS
pedia, and then		READING A BOOK. HE HAD
announced that		TO DO HIS HOMEWORK.
Imogene had turned		
into a rare form of	11 Dee:	Oh, okay. That's a good
miniature elk!		interpretation of that.
Imogene's mother		What's happening
fainted again and was		here? [pointing to the
carried upstairs to bed.		next page]
	12 Teresa:	THE MOTHER FELL OUT.
	13 Dee:	Okay, she fainted again.
Imogene went into the	14 Teresa:	[turns the page and
kitchen. Lucy, the		points to the middle of
kitchen maid, had her		the right-hand side page]
sit by the oven to dry		THE MOM....
some towels. "Lovely	15 Dee:	Okay, over here [pointing
antlers," said Lucy.		to the left-hand side
		page] Start at this
		page, from left to right.
	16 Teresa:	THE MOMMY PUT TOWELS ON
		THE THING. IT WAS WET. SHE
		PUT IT ON.

{Fieldnotes, videotape 02/02/95}

Teresa rarely used finger pointing when she read. Yet she tried it this time when I modeled it on line 7, although I did not expect that there would be word-to-word correspondence in her reading. Because she began to point to words, I was able to notice that she did not understand that readers need to consider the left-hand side page before attending to the right, and I was able to show her that particular feature of book reading. So, I think I did a good job on supporting some important understandings about directionality and other aspects of print in books.

However, I don't think I used great strategies in scaffolding her construction of the content or meanings of the book. I did okay at some places. For example, in line 6, when Teresa appeared to start a sentence that wouldn't match the text ("It was ...") and hesitated so long, I read the text ("Imogene's mother fainted away"). That seemed to get her going again, and she provided a great approximation about the doctor in line 8, which I was able then to affirm. In many other places I think I could have intervened differently and more effectively. Because she was paying so much attention to the pictures, I might have helped her produce a better story from them. For example, instead of my saying just "okay" when she called the antlers "the things" in line 1, I could have pointed to the antlers in the picture and asked her if she knew what these were on the girl's head. If she didn't know, I could have told her, so that she would have learned an important vocabulary word in the story. That would have meant that she might have used "antler" later in line 16 instead of "the thing."

In reviewing this transcript, I found that I wished I had done something different in lots of places. Another place might have been when I just accepted Teresa's approximation in line 10 about the brother doing his homework. I might have had her consider a different interpretation that made more sense and was closer to the meaning of the book (that brother might have been checking the book to figure out what was wrong with Imogene). I do think I did okay right after that spot, though, by getting Teresa to think about what was happening next in the book. She also did a good job in coming up with a good idea—"The mother fell out." The way of my accepting this was a good strategy, too, because I was able to repeat the same meaning by adding another vocabulary word for her ("fainted" for her "fell out").

Thus, I should have focused more on the meanings Teresa was expressing in her story inventions because that is where she was developmentally. Like Samantha, however, I missed some good opportunities to scaffold her pretend reading. It was so hard with many of the students because I had such a range of development and they were changing all the time. Anyhow, even with my successes, I struggled throughout my inquiry to assess where they were and to help them to get better in their pretend reading.

ADDITIONAL COMMENTS, REFLECTIONS, AND CONCLUSIONS

As time went by, I developed additional strategies to get students to stay involved in their pretend-reading routines. One was to let students continue Angel's idea of reading aloud to the class in the way I read to them. The demand was so great that I had to have a sign-up sheet to schedule them all in. A by-product of this was that students wanted to take books home to practice reading in preparation for their scheduled turns. I had not allowed that initially, but I did so when they seemed so motivated and excited. They were very good in bringing them back to school, too. In addition, students came up with the idea of reading to other classes, and even to the principal, which we did.

I decided to audiotape my students as they were reading their favorite books. However, I only taped the "advanced" students, and then it was a spontaneous activity that was utilized only a few times. In hindsight, I realize that I should have scheduled that opportunity into my daily routine. I could have set up a new kind of a listening center and created a format in which all of the children could communicate and listen to their interpretations of books. This might have quickened the pace by which they—even the more reluctant and very early emergent readers—saw themselves as readers.

Towards the end I also tried my own videotaping of children's reading (individually and out of the classroom), and although, in the beginning, some students were very nervous about it, they relayed so much excitement about the videotaping to the rest of the class that everyone immediately wanted to be taped. Thus, I discovered at the end of my inquiry that videotaping was another strategy that I could have used earlier. Besides giving me periodic assessments, it would have been an important tool in scaffolding, motivating, and giving them a visual awareness that they are truly readers.

My inquiry into pretend reading taught me that boys can be motivated to be readers even if they enter kindergarten with reluctance. One thing that helped was making sure I used high-quality literature that they would be interested in. Once my students got into pretend reading, motivating them became less difficult. The confidence of being able to read successfully several favorite books made them read the same books over and over again. Students leveled off from time to time in their own personal comfort zones and sometimes it was hard to nudge them to move on to more difficult books. However, this was not all bad because the students had different favorite books and taught each other how to read them. In short, reading became a prestigious thing in the classroom.

I also discovered that just because some students were not always pretend reading that much in school, it didn't mean that they were not reading at all. Students were reading their own personal books at home, and later school books that they borrowed to use at home. I got them to bring their home books to school, and involved them by my reading them at school.

As I already noted, I had ongoing struggles in my inquiry regarding how to figure out how to help students who were at so many levels in my classroom. Some students seemed to be stuck at a level longer than others, and I didn't always know what to do about it. Once they mastered a book, they clung to it and read it over and over again. I had to determine how and when to raise the ante by encouraging them to read a book a little harder than the previous one.

I lacked information books in my classroom. I was forced to use the school library's sources. These texts could not support their pretend reading well, even though students were really fascinated about the topics of these books and really wanted to read them. However, if I read them over and over, they did remember the content and did attempt to pretend read them.

My greatest regret was in my failure to develop a formal assessment tool to use. From the beginning of my inquiry I wasn't able to document and make valid comparisons during the year. I got started by taking my own fieldnotes, and by trying to write down the children's strategies and abilities in reading. As I said, I did the audio- and video-taping of their pretend reading at the end, so if I had used these in the beginning, I would have both motivated my playful boys and reluctant readers, and I would have had a better assessment picture.

Finally, I had trouble in being more diligent, consistent, and detailed in my notetaking. I did not realize that my inquiry would result in such dramatic improvement in my students' skills and in their abilities to construct meaning from the written word. I sometimes missed important data about their progress. All of the children—girls and boys—mastered directionality, one-to-one correspondence, began to pick up sight words, and at the end of the year could even read some books conventionally. They could all give close approximations of the language of books. I was proud of their accomplishments and their enthusiasm to learn and to read. Working with male students became a pleasurable challenge. My students took risks, and I learned to take risks also. Students forced me to totally rethink how best to motivate and scaffold them in seeing themselves as readers.

Finally, I learned that all students become readers in their own ways. I believe that they come to school capable of succeeding. I believe that it is up to the teacher to promote pretend reading by utilizing creative, innovative, interesting materials and strategies. Pretend reading is an important developmental step in the process toward conventional reading.

ABOUT THE AUTHOR

I attended Chicago State University for my undergraduate training, and received my bachelor's degree in June 1972. Although I interviewed in the suburban school districts around Chicago, I decided to teach in the city, starting that fall at Andersen. I returned to school several years later and earned a master's degree in urban teacher education at Governor's State University, with an emphasis in early childhood education. Andersen is the only school in which I have taught, and it has been both a challenge and a rewarding experience.

DEDICATION

I dedicate this chapter to my parents, Willie and Pauline, who instilled in me the importance of education. I also dedicate this chapter to my brother, Drewus C. Collier, who was my sidekick throughout high school and college.

REFERENCES

Carlson, N. (1988). *I like me!* New York: Puffin Books.
Greenspun, A. A. (1991). *Daddies.* New York: Philomel.
Hillman, J. (1989). *When I was sick.* Crystal Lake, IL: Rigby.
Merriam, E. (1989). *Mommies at work.* New York: Simon & Schuster.
Small, D. (1985). *Imogene's antlers.* New York: Scholastic.
Wood, A. (1984). *The napping house.* San Diego: Harcourt.

Chapter 4

Now I Know My ABC's, Plus a Whole Lot More! Using Alphabet Books With First Graders

Anne Barry
Jungman Elementary School

EDITORS' COMMENTS

Anne had already moved into creating collaborative read-alouds using a range of text genres when she started this new inquiry. Here, she focuses on her study of first-grade students' initiations of a new genre—ABC or alphabet books. Her intent was to see how her reading of these books would foster her students' phonemic awareness, but as she shows here, they learned this and much more.

Part of her inquiry was also learning about the various number of ABC books that are now available for sharing with children—ones that have the typical "A is for ..." format, as well as others that provide the alphabet information in very different ways. Thus, informing us about this genre is another thing that Anne's chapter contributes. Finally, Anne covers some of the difficulties—what she calls "bumps"—that arose in the course of her inquiry. One major bump had to do with how she could understand, appreciate, and evaluate the children's initiations as phonemic approximations in the quick pace of the oral read-aloud setting.

The introduction chapter of this book provides the theoretical and methodological background for the larger collaborative school–university action-research project and this chapter about Anne's inquiry on ABC books.

University researchers, Diane Escobar and Shannon Hart, collaborated with Anne in her inquiry.

BACKGROUND AND INTRODUCTION TO MY INQUIRY

For many years I have been a primary first-grade teacher in the Chicago public school system. Most of those years were spent being a very traditional teacher. There were certain views that I held as a traditional teacher. I believed that the children who I taught came to me without much prior knowledge, and that for the time they were with me in my first grade, I was the sole deliverer of all there was to learn in first grade. Things were pretty rigid in my classroom. Desks were always in straight rows with me up front doing most of the talking and imparting of knowledge. This made my classroom almost always quiet while everyone listened to me. I only had small-group instruction for round-robin reading from the basal readers, while the rest of the students engaged in lots of ditto sheets for drilling the skills. And, so it went for the rest of the school day, with lots of large-group direct instruction from the teacher and more purple ditto sheets for children to fill in the blanks.

However, as I look back over the last several years in my first-grade classroom, much has changed. Now, student initiations, inquiry, and choice are major elements of the everyday instruction in my classroom. Changes at Jungman, my school, and the fact that I embarked on a 2-year master's program certainly influenced my changing beliefs about student's knowledge and what my teaching practices ought to be. It became clear to me that students were active meaning makers, continually constructing their own knowledge (Wells & Chang-Wells, 1992). It meant that I needed to develop different instructional strategies in my interactions with my students.

About this time, I was asked by Celia Oyler (a research assistant of Chris Pappas, who met weekly with a group us at the school over the years about our ongoing inquiries into literacy teaching learning—see chap. 1) to be a collaborative participant in her doctoral dissertation. I felt that this was an exceptional opportunity in my professional career—to study with her what I was trying to develop and to figure out about my teaching. It was Celia who actually recognized during the 1991–1992 school year that the reading-aloud routine was the centerpiece of the literacy learning in my classroom. At the same time, Celia was looking at how my students and I shared authority in these new teaching practices and interactions (Oyler, 1993, 1996).

In the past, I had always read aloud to my classes. The students remained in their desks, which were grouped in traditional, straight rows, with me, the teacher, up front. I would read aloud only one book a day, primarily to quiet down my classroom after lunch. The books chosen to read were basically narrative fiction with a "Once upon a time ..." fairy tale-like beginning. Children never talked, made comments, asked questions, or offered opinions, ideas, thoughts, or feelings. If I wanted to know what they were understanding, I was the only one to initiate any kind of questions. Their responses to my questions were my evaluations of how they were doing.

However, reading aloud to my students drastically changed in my classroom. No longer are students sitting rigidly at their desks. Now read-alouds are enthusiastic literacy events with teacher and students nestled close and comfy together in a large area with all sitting either on the floor or in small chairs, in a kind of semicircle so that all can see the books being read. There is much social interaction among children and between students and myself that occurs during my teacher-led read-alouds where I immerse children in good literature. The literature that I share has meaning and purpose. I bring a wide variety of books throughout the course of the school year: picture books, Big Books, predictable books, poetry, riddle, and joke books, information books, stories, children's magazines (e.g., *Ladybug*), flap books, chapter books, children's newspapers (e.g., *Weekly Readers*), cartoons, books with children's recipes, and so forth.

During the 1994–1995 school year, I added the genre of the ABC or alphabet book. It was a genre that I had not included before in my growing array of different types and kinds of literature. Besides, I really wanted my students to have the knowledge of these books in their repertoires of good children's literature. Because I am always trying to be a growing teacher, defining, changing, and formulating inquiries under the whole-language umbrella, one of the bigger pieces of inquiry for me to fit was the question of phonics or knowledge of sound–symbol relationships. How do I help my students learn about sound–symbol relationships without drill-and-skill types of instruction? How do I make the phonics (sound–symbol) system as integral a part of language learning as the cueing systems of syntax (grammar) and semantics (meaning of language)?

I chose to read aloud alphabet or ABC books to see if this would foster my first graders' phonemic (sound–symbol) relationships as they became readers and writers, and to help me answer those questions that I had posed. I already had a few years of risktaking with my students, particularly when it came to allowing them to make their own initiations to books I read to them. I moved away from the transmission model and into the interactive-experiential model that Cummins (1989) described: "The instruction is automatically 'culture-fair' in that all students are actively involved in expressing, sharing, and amplifying their experience within the classroom" (p. 65). The classroom discourse of the everyday read-alouds was quite different from the common IRE pattern (teacher *i*nitiates, student *r*esponds, teacher *e*valuates) that is found in many classrooms (Cazden, 1988). Thus, I became intrigued by what the dynamic interchanges among students would be like when I read ABC books. What I found as a result of my inquiry was that my first graders certainly learned their ABCs—plus a whole lot more!

DEVELOPING PHONEMIC AWARENESS:
"ALLEYOOP? MOLLY, MOLLY, MOLLYOOP!"

Playing with language involves phonemic awareness because children
consciously attend to various phonemes. Many ABC books facilitate this
play and understanding and could be seen in many of the initiations my
students offered in the read-aloud sessions. For example, *Chicka Chicka
Boom Boom* (Martin & Archambault, 1989) is an all-time favorite alphabet book that fosters their wanting to experiment with the words they are
hearing. Many children were delighted with "alley-oop," the first part of
which they thought was word play on one of their classmates' name,
"Molly."

Example 1

1	Anne:	M is looped. N is stooped. O is twisted alley-oop.
2	Cs:	Alleyoop?
3	Anne:	Alleyoop.
4	Cs:	Molly, Molly, Mollyoop. [turning to look at Molly, who is sitting in the back]
5	Cml:	<Every book says "Molly.">
6	Anne:	Well, I said "alley"....
7	Cs:	Alley! Molly!
8	Anne:	But it reminds you of....
9	Cs:	Molly.
		{Fieldnotes, videotape 12/07/94}

Students first identified the word "alley-oop" from the book in a questioning tone, as if they weren't sure they had heard it right. After I confirmed it
for them, they began to chant Molly's name, then "Molly-oop." C1 states
that "every book has 'Molly,'" referring, I think, to the many times children have mentioned her name when we have come across the "M" in the
other alphabet books we have read. When I repeat the "alley" of the book,
students again let me know what they have discovered about the "sounds"
of these two words, which I acknowledge.

During Halloween, I couldn't resist reading *The Monster Book of ABC
Sounds* (Snow, 1991) because I knew it would encourage students to make
their own sounds. The format of this rhyming book has text on the top of
the page while the lower page is the spelling out of an alphabet letter
"sound," usually in a large dialogue bubble said by a creature depicted in
the illustration. In Example 2, as I read letter "O," children began to re-

peat "Ooooooh," and one student (Cm4) tried "m" at the end of that
sound word by attempting a different letter–sound relationship.

Example 2

1	Anne:	[raising my hand as a motion for students to stop their talk] Wait. We are going to go to 'O.' HE FLIES UPSIDE DOWN AND DOES OTHER BRAVE TRICKS. [points at print on the bottom of the page] OOOOOOH!
2	Cs:	Ooooooh.
3	Cm4:	Oooooom.
4	Anne:	Ooooooh.
5	Cm4:	Ooooooh.
6	Anne:	Okay? Oooooooh.
		{Fieldnotes, videotape, 10/26/94}

When I got to the letter "U," there was more experimenting with language
and then a student came up with her own new "U" word—"ugly"—from
"uuugh" sounds offered by the book.

Example 3

1	Anne:	The next letter is "U." [pointing to the letter as I read it] HE GOES TO THE CABINET, BUT RATS GOT THERE FIRST.
2	Cml:	U, U.
3	Anne:	UUUGH!
4	Cs:	Uuugh.
5	Anne:	Uuugh.
6	Cf2:	Like "ugly."
7	Anne:	Like "ugly." Yes! Uuugh!
8	Cs:	Uuugh!
9	Cf3:	Ugly, ugly. (...) "E" at the end.
		{Fieldnotes, videotape, 10/26/94}

Even more sophisticated phonemic awareness came through as one of the
girls responded to "ugly" by hearing and remarking that there is an "E" at
the end. For the next letter in the book, "V," (not provided in the above ex-

ample), the sound word is "Vrrroom." When several children said, "like a broom," I had an opportunity to give them credit for this sound connection and to extend their understanding by telling them explicitly that words are made out of sounds.

By December, I began to notice more advanced phonemic awareness in their initiations in a non-ABC book. In Example 4, I read from *What is Christmas?* (Hall, 1991). I chose this book because all of my students celebrate this holiday and because I wanted to show them certain physical format features of the book that they might use in the books they were writing on their own. As I tried to point out what is meant when words are boldly and largely printed, Casey commented on the "K" in "KNOW" and amazed me with his growing letter–sound knowledge.

Example 4

1	Anne:	Look what happens to the print in the book. All of a sudden it gets really big. "I KNOW!" SAID LITTLE MOUSE. Casey?
2	Casey:	Why did they put a "k" if it doesn't sound?
3	Anne:	Why did they put a "k" and it didn't sound? Really good question. There are some words in English——in English ... Oscar?
4	Oscar:	(。。。 。。。).
5	Anne:	Right. Just like some words in Spanish don't sound....
6	Cm1:	Like "H." Like "H" in Spanish doesn't sound.
7	Anne:	Doesn't sound?
8	Cm1:	Doesn't sound.
9	Anne:	So you see that there are some words in English that don't——some letters in the beginning that don't sound. You're absolutely right.
10	James:	But you still have to put them.
11	Anne:	But you still have to put it down when you spell it. Yep. So you still have to *know* it (pointing to the "know" word in the book).
12	Cm2:	Words that start with "N"?
....		[There is a distraction by one of the students that I quickly deal with.]
13	Cm2:	Words that start with "N." First you have to put "K" [pointing to the book and then making the letter in the air]. Then an "N," then an "O," then a "W."
14	Anne:	Then an "N," then an "O," and then a "W." Yep.
		{Fieldnotes, videotape, 12/07/94}

I immediately took up Casey's question instead of pursuing the point I had wanted to make about the size of the print in the book. Then, as I began to answer his question (in line 3), Oscar brought up the idea that there are some words in Spanish that "don't sound." (Note that Oscar's words are inaudible in line 4, but I repeat the meaning of his remarks in line 5.) Subsequently, another student initiated by giving an example—"Like 'H' in Spanish doesn't sound." Additionally, James stated his understanding that you still have to write these "silent" letters down when spelling or writing those words containing them. Thus, many of the students involved in this dialogue were becoming truly bilingual, functioning well in both the Spanish and English languages.

In sum, all of the children were, indeed, developing sophisticated phonemic awareness not only in their responses to the ABC books, but also in non-ABC books. This increasing knowledge is seen in the rest of examples in this chapter. However, in following sections, I try to highlight other overlapping dimensions of student learning that I think my reading of ABC books facilitated. I focus on how content knowledge, predictions, and intertextual connections were promoted, and then cover some of the other literacy activities that I provided as extensions of my reading of ABC books. I also talk about what I learned about the variety of ABC books available for young children. At the end I address some of the "bumps" that arose in my inquiry on reading aloud ABC books.

CONTENT KNOWLEDGE: "WHITE IS FOR SNOW, BROWN IS FOR SPRING"

The ABC book read-alouds not only fostered phonemic awareness, but also added to children's content knowledge. One of the most popular alphabet books that I read for my inquiry was *The Pop-Up Animal Alphabet Book* (Cerf, 1994). It was a book that had pull tabs and flaps on most every page. These attributes in books always seemed to intrigue my students. I have a lot of these books (including non-ABC books) and I really believe that this particular book feature invites children to physically interact with them by hooking them to books, which is an important step in becoming lifelong lovers of reading.

Example 5 shows some of the kinds of student responses to this book, which also let me know what they knew about various animals in the book—a valuable assessment tool.

Example 5

1   C: Radio.

2   C: Rake.

3	Anne:	R'S FOR THE RHINO, WHOSE TEMPER IS SHORT.
4	C:	What is "temper"?
5	Anne:	(... ...). [I give a short definition that is inaudible]
6	C:	People use horns for medicine.
7	Anne:	[nods in affirmation]
8	C:	He can go 30 mph....
9	Anne:	V'S FOR VARYING HARE, SOMETIMES WHITE, SOMETIMES BROWN.
10	C:	[Goes up to the book——which shows a white hare in snow——and pulls the tab——which now reveals a brown hare in green grass.]
11	C1:	It's like a picture.
12	C2:	It changes its hair.
13	C3:	White is for snow, brown is for spring.
14	Anne:	[nods in confirmation] W? WOLVES, WHO FORM PACKS TO HUNT GAME.
15	Cs:	Ooooooooooo.
16	C1:	Like a ghost, like a witch.
17	C2:	Wolves eat people and lions and leopards. I saw it on a program.
18	C3:	A dog looks like a wolf.
		{Fieldnotes, 10/12/94}

This example shows how the children demonstrated their content knowledge in their responses to this book. With respect to the rhino, they contributed, "people use horns for medicine" and "he can go 30 mph." When the varying hare was read and children saw the differences in the hare when the tab in the book was pulled, children connected these changes to seasons—"white is for snow, brown is for spring." Regarding wolves, students produced the sound that wolves make, which led to links to ghosts and witches (topics of books they read during this month of Halloween). They also included other information about wolves—what they eat and what they look like. Thus, ABC books like this provided opportunities to learn new information, and also enabled students to tie it to the prior knowledge they might already have on topics.

Because this pop-up book was such a favorite book, I followed my students' lead and reread their requests for this book. The next example occurred in February. My children always have lots of opportunities to read in the classroom (silently, in whole-group choral reading, in small groups, with a buddy), as well as at home because I allow books to be taken home from my extensive room library. The following classroom discourse is a wonderful example of the wealth of information students can acquire when they are given a wide variety of literature and are also given spaces to connect their ideas with a book being read. Casey, the child in this dialogue, showed us about his prior knowledge of snakes. I was aware of his interest in snakes because he often chose reptile books to read in the classroom or chose them to read at home. I think this example also illustrates how Casey was taking responsibility for his own learning and how empowering that was for him, which is what I wish for all of my students. In Example 6, I am about to read the "M is for Mongoose" page, which has a snake in the illustration.

Example 6

1	Casey:	That's the king of all of the snakes. That's——that's a cobra.
2	Anne:	That's a cobra. You know about the cobra?
3	Casey:	It's the strongest of all the snakes.
4	Anne:	The cobra is the——how did you know that? Did you read that in a book?
5	Casey:	Yes. In this book. [getting out of his chair and pointing to books on the side of the room]
6	Anne:	Oh. Maybe you can find it.
....		[Casey has gone to look for the book; most of the children turn in their chairs to watch what he is doing.]
7	Anne:	Okay. While he's looking——oh see how you can find lots of good things in books? He knew that and we didn't——I didn't know that. Did you know that?
8	C1:	(••• •••).
9	Anne:	They have a flap on the side? Why? You know what?, I don't know. Maybe the snake book will help us.
10	Cf2:	(•••) snakes.
11	Casey:	I found it.
12	Anne:	Okay. You can bring it over. Yes, in the *Zoo* book.
....		[There is a long pause as Casey looks for the cobra in the book. Children are very quiet. Casey finds the page and holds the book up over his head for classmates to see.]
13	Anne:	[looking at video camera operator] See, he knew exactly. [addressing Casey] Come over here to the middle so everyone can see, sweetheart. Oh I am so proud of you. You did——want me to read it? Would you like to read a little bit about it?
....		[Casey gives the book to me and sits down.]
14	Anne:	[holding the book open in front of me, pointing to the picture of the cobra] Look, here's the cobra. [C1] was just talking

about the big flaps at the sides. Right here. [pointing to the picture again] That's what he was talking about. The flaps.

{Fieldnotes, videotape, 02/22/95}

Although it wasn't indicated in the text, Casey recognized that the snake in the picture was a cobra—"the king of all of the snakes," "the strongest of the snakes" (lines 1 & 3). Moreover, when I asked how he knew that, he could find another book in the room that told all about it.

In this case, Casey could extend his knowledge of snakes for the benefit of all of us. In fact, many ABC books allowed students to learn new content knowledge in this way, by linking it to other information they may have already had on the topic.

PROMOTING PREDICTION: "C IS FOR HEN. WHY? CHICKA, CHICKA."

In the middle of the school year, I purposely brought to the read-aloud time an alphabet book that was like a guessing game, *Q Is for Duck: An Alphabet Guessing Game* (Elting & Folsom, 1980). I was curious about how my students would respond to an alphabet book that didn't begin with the "A is for ..." kind of format. I wanted the ABC books to become more thought provoking and challenging. Because students had to answer the question, "Why?", for each letter of the alphabet being read, they also had to associate that particular letter with an appropriate attribute of the animal being read about. For example, the format "Q is for duck" would be on one page, then the "Why?" would ask them to guess what the next page's answer might be, namely, "because a duck quacks." So, before we turned the page for the author's answer children had some wonderful opportunities for making predictions.

As Smith (1994) explained, we all predict all of the time, and that means children do also. Smith's formal definition of *prediction* is "the prior elimination of unlikely alternatives. It is the projection of possibilities" (pp. 18–19). I find that my students are making predictions constantly, but this book explicitly called for them in their responses. The following excerpts in Example 7 show that my students' predictions even surpass the book author with their originality and humor.

Example 7

1   Anne: C IS FOR HEN. WHY?

2   C: Chicka, chicka.

....

3	Anne:	G IS FOR HORSE. WHY?
4	Peron:	Run.
5	Anne:	That's how horses go [nodding in affirmation]. Perhaps gallop.
6	C1:	They graduate.
7	Anne:	Where do they go? [laughing]
8	C2:	To the farm school.

....

9	Anne:	L IS FOR FROG. WHY?
10	C1:	Lick.
11	C2:	Lily ponds.
13	C3:	Because they *love* flies.
14	C4:	They have a *long* tongue.

....

15	Anne:	N IS FOR CAT. WHY?
16	C:	Scratch.
17	C:	They eat rats.
18	C:	They have nails.
19	Karen:	They *nip* milk.
20	Anne:	Let's get the "N" words.
21	C:	Maybe his name is Nicky?

....

22	Anne:	P IS FOR CHICK. WHY?
23	C:	They *pop* out of their egg.
24	Peron:	[Makes gesture of pecking with his fingers.]
25	Anne:	[Nods with affirmation.]
		{Fieldnotes, 01/30/95}

It is readily apparent that my students loved to propose possibilities in answering the why questions in this book—for example, horses graduate from the farm school was offered for "G is for horse"; frogs love flies and have a long tongue was provided for "L is for frog"; cats nip milk was given for "N is for cat"; and so forth. Also, note the first prediction in the above example—"chicka, chicka" for "C is for hen"—which of course has its connection to the *Chicka, Chicka Boom Boom* book found in Example 1. All of their predictions reflected higher level thinking. Prediction here and in response to all books promotes children's comprehension and understanding in complex ways.

INTERTEXTUAL CONNECTIONS: "KING KONG. 'KING' STARTS WITH 'K'"

I always noticed during my numerous teacher-led read alouds that my students' initiations were often linked to other texts. What do I mean by other texts? A few years ago, I collaborated with Celia Oyler (mentioned earlier in the chapter) to study what first graders' intertextual connections were around informational books (Oyler & Barry, 1993). We defined *intertextuality* as students juxtaposing two texts, which we meant their reference to other books, songs, movies, filmstrips, poems, chants, and student writing.

While reading alphabet books, students likewise made wonderful intertextual initiations. There were some already illustrated in the previous examples; that is, when a child said "chicka, chicka" in the Example 7 in the previous section, or when Casey brought the book about cobras to the mongoose page the in the *Pop-Up Animal Alphabet Book* in Example 6, or when a child brought in the fact that wolves eat people, lions, and leopards from a TV program in response to the wolves' page in that same book (see Example 5), and so forth. In the following example, during reading the classic *Alligators All Around: An Alphabet* book by Sendak (1962), students came up with wonderful ones, even though it was early in the school year and I had not as yet read from a large number of alphabet books, and had never encouraged these kinds of remarks in any explicit way.

Example 8

1	Anne:	P PUSHING PEOPLE
2	C:	Peter Pan.
3	C:	Pinocchio.
4	C:	Peanut butter.
5	C:	Popeye.
6	C:	Penguin.
7	C:	Bat.
8	Anne:	"Pat," "bat," "bat" is a "B" word.

....

9	Anne:	Q QUITE QUARRELSOME
10	C:	Queatiful.

11	Anne:	[smiling] Queatiful.
12	C1	Queen.
13	C:	King Kong. "King" starts with "K."
14	Anne:	"Quiet" is a "Q" word....

....

15	Anne:	RIDING REINDEER
16	C:	Robin Hood!
17	Reyn:	Reynaldo. "R" is for me.
18	C:	Riding on a bus!
19	Peron:	Peter Pan.
20	Anne:	Does "P," "Pa" [emphasizing the "P" sound] Peter Pan start with "R"?
21	Cs:	#No.#
22	Peron:	#[shrugs his head side to side]#
23	Anne:	Peron, I think you're thinking of your name.
24	C:	Rice-a-roni.
25	Cs:	Ricky Lay. [referring to a large gorillalike stuffed animal in the classroom that children frequently lean on when they read in the classroom]
26	Anne:	What comes after "R"? S SHOCKINGLY SPOILED

....

27	Anne:	Let's go to "U." U USUALLY UPSIDE DOWN
28	C:	Youth Center.
		{Fieldnotes, 10/05/94}

These urban first-grade children have their own vast experiential back-grounds, and if given the opportunity, will let you know how they con-nect these texts of the real world. By reading aloud from these various ABC books, I was interested in finding out what intertextual links my students will make and how I can connect what my students already know to what they don't know. As Example 8 demonstrates, the children connect to literary characters (Peter Pan, Robin Hood, Pinocchio), to foods (Rice-a-roni, peanut butter), to their own names, and cartoon characters (Popeye). They even make up new words, such as "queatiful." When someone mentioned "queen" for a "Q" word, King Kong was offered. Then, sometimes, my students connect me to words in ways that I had never thought of before—for example, when a child mentioned the "Youth Center" in their community when I read about the letter "U." Thus, the intertextual ties these children constructed were pervasive and helped to make our reading of ABC books a complex, rich experience.

OTHER CONNECTED CLASSROOM LITERACY ACTIVITIES AND ROUTINES: "R IS FOR ME!"

Early in the school year, most of the ABC books that I brought to the teacher-led read-alouds had the very familiar pattern, "A is for—" "B is for —," etc. It wasn't long before the children were initiating and connecting the letters of the alphabet with the first letters of their names. As the children connected more, this made them become very interested in the spelling of their own names as well as in the names of their friends in our classroom. Consequently, this led to more classroom alphabet-literacy activities and routines through out the school year.

One of the earliest ones was to take a letter of the alphabet that began the name or names of children in the classroom and create texts telling all about them. The following is the one that was composed for Reynaldo:

> R is for Reynaldo.
>
> His favorite color is white.
>
> Reynaldo likes ABC soup.
>
> His favorite animal is a horse.
>
> Reynaldo likes his mom and dad.
>
> He wants to be 18 years old.

Each child was able to have a designated day at school that was a special day for his or her first name. As a whole-class experience the child for that day dictated to me whatever was important to him or her, which I wrote down on the board for all to see. Most of these texts ended up being five to six lines telling of favorite colors, foods, animals, friends, and wishes. After this was completed, the rest of the other students wrote a special message for the child. These were usually written in a range of different genres (letters, poems, messages). Then I created a take-home folder that included these writings, plus a note from me and a copy of the text we wrote down on the board. This was something that the child could keep as something special from all of us.

While we progressed through the school year, my students began writing more and more of their own books. As I saw this happening, I felt they were ready to write their own alphabet books as a whole-class project. Students were encouraged to use whatever theme or format of ABC book they wished. I tried to brainstorm with them lots of general, big ideas or themes, which were listed for handy reference in a pocket chart on the wall.

The finished alphabet books showed much of the standard "A is for —" format, but some also reflected more sophistication by inclusion of tables of contents, glossaries, and chapters. Also, their books covered a variety of subject matter and used a range of sentence structures and vocabulary.

Whole-class writing of Big Books has always been a very popular literacy activity in my classroom. During December, my class composed a *Christmas Alphabet Big Book*. What made the writing of it so interesting was that it encouraged students to brainstorm together and then to come to a consensus about what Christmas words they really wanted to use in their book. Sometimes, because all of the children celebrate this holiday at home and are exposed to so many Christmas-related experiences in their everyday lives (TV shows, family traditions, etc.), there were difficult choices to make, but considering all of the possibilities made many opportunities for higher level thinking.

Finally, I encouraged the alphabet book writing to be continued in their at-home writing journals. On most school days, my students loaded up their backpacks with good literature from our class library and their at-home writing journals. Students returned the next day with the books read and the journals written in. Often, I would find that my students' ideas from this at-home writing would include responses to the ABC books I had read or would refer to possibilities to consider for their individual books or the Big Book. Thus, reading and writing both were fostering phonemic awareness specifically around the ABC activities. In fact, phonemic awareness, reading, and writing all go together as children travel down the road to becoming literate.

"MAYBE THIS IS AN ABC BOOK": FORMAT AND SELECTION OF ABC BOOKS

I believe most of us consider ABC books to be rather simple kinds of books with a good deal of the same format, "A is for ———," etc. As I was searching and choosing which alphabet books I would bring to my read alouds, I found much sophistication and variety in what I had to select from. Books were not always in that pattern, so this provided important challenges for my students as they began also to learn with me what this range of ABC books offered us.

The next example includes some responses to an ABC book that had an alternative format, namely, *Old Black Fly* by Jim Aylesworth (1992). In fact, when I first began to read it, one student was quite tentative about its identification—"Maybe this is an ABC book."

Old Black Fly is filled with wonderful rhyme, rhythm, and repetition as an old black fly causes chaos wherever it goes, for example: "He ate the crust of the Apple pie. He bothered the Baby and made her cry. Shoo fly! Shoo fly! Shoooo." In this book, the "A" of "apple" and "B" of "baby" are capitalized, in bold, and in different colors (red and blue in this case, respectively) to highlight the letters of focus.

As I read how the old black fly flies through the alphabet, students and I chanted the "Shoo fly" refrain of the book. In addition, this book enabled my students to initiate wonderful and varied responses. In the following dialogue, I have already read up to the letter "L." Immediately, a student notices that the illustration has a list and that becomes a topic to pursue further.

Example 9

1	Anne:	HE LIT ON THE LIST FOR THE GROCERY STORE. SHOO FLY! SHOO FLY! SHOOO.
2	Oscar:	Paper! [standing and pointing at the book——there is a grocery list in cursive writing in upper right-hand corner of the page]
3	Anne:	What's that paper for?
4	C1:	School?
5	Anne:	School, huh?
6	C2:	For the grocery.
7	Anne:	[rereading part of the text] HE LIT ON THE LIST FOR THE GROCERY STORE.
8	C1:	What does it say on the paper?
9	Anne:	Would you like me to read the list? See this is what mom does. You can help her——you can write lists in your journals. We write lists for all different reasons. Mom needed a grocery store list. I'll read it. CHOCOLATE, EGGS, APPLES, OLIVE OIL, HONEY, MILK, SALAMI, JELLY....
10	C3:	What are noodles? ["noodles" is the last word on the list that I had not yet finished reading]
11	C1:	A kind of soup.
12	Anne:	Like soup? Do you get noodles in your soup?
13	C2:	Sometimes they're green.
14	Anne:	Sometimes noodles are green. Absolutely right! [turning to show the "M" and "N" page]
15	C:	And yellow.
16	C3:	Instead of mostaccioli, it's "mostanoodles"!!
17	Anne:	I like that! You got both things in the word. I like that! I'm so glad you asked about noodles because ... [skipping the "M" page and reading] HE NIBBLED ON #NOODLES# IN THE CASSEROLE....
18	Cs:	#NOODLES#
		{Fieldnotes, videotape, 02/01/95}

Just as I was about to read "noodles," the last item on the grocery list, C3 asked the question, "What are 'noodles'?" Others provided their own additional knowledge about noodles, "a kind of soup," as well as the fact that noodles come in different colors. Then in line 16, C3 provided a great example of sophisticated word play that incorporates both the "M" and "N" of the upcoming page. This is the kind of thing that I am always amazed and fascinated about regarding my students' responses—in no way would I ever come up with "mostanoodles"!

Thus, during my inquiry I learned that ABC books were quite diverse—they covered many topics and were structured in various formats. The different formats found in the genre offered different opportunities for students to respond in unique ways, and I learned a lot as they met the challenges of this diversity.

THE BUMPS: "NO, THAT WOULD BE 'YIRE.'"

Thus far in my story I told and illustrated what I think are great examples of my students' responses to the numerous ABC books that I read during the year. I argued that their initiations, questions, and comments reflected what they learned about phonemic awareness and other important understandings.

However, there were also bumps along the way in my study of my sharing ABC books. There was still a small number of children in my classroom who, at the end of the school year, just were not connecting with literacy learning the way I had hoped they would. There were four students who weren't independent readers as yet and had not developed a stable, strong understanding of letter–sound relationships. This was apparent in many of the reading and writing activities in which they engaged, as well as in their responses to the ABC read-alouds.

Another kind of a bump throughout my study was that I had trouble trying to decide the extent to which I should accept children's various approximations. When should I correct what they offered with more accurate information? When should I just ignore them? When do I accept and value them? These were all difficult to answer.

Other bumps occurred when particular ABC books I chose to read were so stimulating that they caused my students to lose sight of the content of the books. The class would get so involved in either pulling tabs, lifting flaps, or putting the stickers on the map that a book included that I found it hard to control the read-aloud in a collaborative way. Sometimes, I actually had to stop the read-aloud altogether. However, I remained committed to include these books in the read-aloud sessions at other times. I found that when these more exciting books were used later during self-directed reading or at-home reading, the novelty of the physical features of the books wore off. Or, sometimes, I could solve this dilemma by only reading half of this kind of an ABC book that continued to cause behavior problems, and come back to it during the next read-aloud.

In addition, there were times during read-alouds when I just didn't "get" what my students were trying to tell me about letter–sound relationships. Frequently they were hurling so many ideas so quickly at me that I couldn't appreciate what they reflected regarding their understandings, and therefore I don't think I always provided the best feedback or response to their initiations. Example 10, taken from the my reading the "Y" page from Sendak's (1962) *Alligators All Around* book, shows the nature of these difficulties.

Example 10

1	Anne:	Y....
2	Cs:	Yak, yak, yak.
3	Anne:	In our alphabet book, it is YACKETY YACKING.
4	Cs:	Yak, yak, yak.
5	Anne:	The book says "yackety-yacking."
6	C:	Hawaii.
7	Anne:	You hear "Y" in the middle. Say the word "Ha-wa-ii." There is a "Y" sound in the middle of "Hawaii." Oh, this is interesting.
8	C1:	Yes.
9	C:	Why.
10	Anne:	The question word.
11	C:	Wife.
12	C:	White.
13	C:	Wire.
14	Anne:	No, that would be "yire." You are getting "Y" and "W" mixed up. We'll have to do something with this.
		{Fieldnotes, 10/05/94}

In the beginning, children brought in the "yak" as a response to "Y," which is a popular animal that many ABC book authors use for that letter. I accepted those, and at the same time had them note what was presented in this book. In line 6, when a child offered "Hawaii," I appreciated and got that contribution as representing a "Y" sound, as well the "why" word (see lines 9 & 10). However, it wasn't until I had a conversation with one of the university researchers did I appreciate what phonemic knowledge the responses of "wife," "white," and "wire" represented. I did realize there was confusion, but that was mostly mine because I didn't seem to recognize how these student efforts also reflected a letter–name strategy. That is, these children used the *name* of the letter (the name of "Y" is "wye") in coming up with these words, and I just didn't get it fast enough to "see" it. This means that I couldn't respond more appropriately. Maybe if I had gotten it, I might have been able to acknowledge the phonemic knowledge they were showing, and then might have been able to add extra and better information to extend their present understandings. As I reviewed classroom transcriptions subsequently, I realize that this was an ongoing challenge in this inquiry. I had several years of deciphering children's written invented spellings that reflected their letter–sound knowledge, but a teacher has much more time to respond to writing than he or she does in whole-class read alouds.

"A, B, C, D, E, F, G ...": A WHOLE LOT MORE

My first graders approached learning their ABCs by singing the popular ABC song often during this school year of inquiry. However, this year this song was always a reminder to them that we were focusing more on the awareness of letter–sound relationships as we read aloud from ABC books.

Reading aloud ABC books certainly did foster letter–sound phonemic awareness in my students. This is readily apparent from all of the examples of classroom discourse I provided in this chapter. Thus, I was able to get away from drill-and-skill types of instruction to support these understandings. However, reading this genre of books also fostered word play, vocabulary, sophisticated predictions, content knowledge, and intertextual connections. Moreover, this and critical thinking are the "whole lot more" that emanated as a result of this inquiry.

Phonics does not stand alone as the only cueing system used by students as they become readers and writers. *Syntax* (grammatical structure) and *semantics* (meaning, context, background knowledge) are intricately woven together with phonics as readers make meaning from print (Mills, O'Keefe, & Stephens, 1992). Thus, the read alouds of ABC books was an instructional approach that embedded the fostering of phonemic awareness in a contextualized reading activity (Richgels, Poremba, & McGee, 1996).

Finally, I learned "a whole lot more" specifically about the genre of the ABC book. There are many ABC books that are appropriate and enjoyable for first graders. As always, I was not disappointed by my students initiations and responses to ABC books. They continued to astound, delight, and amaze me as they engaged deeply into the text world of good literacy experiences. These become occasions of envisionment, which Langer (1995) describes as "dynamic sets of related ideas, images, questions, disagreements, anticipations, arguments, and hunches that fill the mind during every reading, writing, speaking, or other experience when one gains, expresses, and shares thoughts and understandings" (p. 9). I think that this is what happened in my inquiry—in the reading aloud of ABC books, we really shared together our thoughts and understandings of the ideas these books evoked.

ABOUT THE AUTHOR

After teaching for 20 years, I received a master's degree in curriculum and instruction from National-Louis University. Subsequently, with additional graduate study, I received an ESL endorsement from the state of Illinois.

At the present time, I am teaching first grade at Jungman School. I continue to be interested in teacher research, and especially in collaborating with the University of Illinois at Chicago. I believe that by opening my classroom to my students' questions, comments, thoughts, ideas, and feelings, I can better understand how they are connecting their world to the larger world around them. Figuring out how to do this best remains one of my greatest challenges in teaching.

DEDICATION

I dedicate this chapter to all of the members of my family, with thanks for their patience, understanding, and love.

REFERENCES

Aylesworth, M. J. (1990). *Old black fly.* New York: Henry Holt.

Cazden, C. B. (1988). *Classroom discourse: The language of teaching and learning.* Portsmouth, NH: Heinemann.

Cerf, C. B. (1994). *Pop-up animal alphabet book.* New York: Random House.

Cummins, J. (1989). *Empowering minority students.* Sacramento: California Association for Bilingual Education.

Elting, M., & Folsom, M. (1980). *Q is for duck: An alphabet guessing game.* New York: Clarion.

Hall, S. T. (1991). *What is Christmas?* Racine, WI: Western.

Langer, J. (1995). *Envisioning literature.* New York: Teachers College Press.

Martin, B., Jr., & Archambault, J. (1989). *Chicka, chicka boom boom.* New York: Simon & Schuster.

Mills, H., O'Keefe, T., & Stephens, D. (1992). *Looking closely: Exploring the role of phonics in one whole language classroom.* Urbana, IL: National Council of Teachers of English.

Oyler, C. J. (1993). *Sharing authority in an urban first grade: Becoming literate, becoming bold.* Unpublished doctoral dissertation, University of Illinois, Chicago.

Oyler, C. (1996). *Making room for students: Sharing teacher authority in room 104.* New York: Teachers College Press.

Oyler, C. J., & Barry, A. (1993, December). *Urban first graders' intertextual connections around information books in the collaborative talk during teacher-led read-alouds.* Paper presented at National Reading Conference, Charleston, SC.

Richgels, D. J., Poremba, K. J., & McGee, L. M. (1996). Kindergarteners talk about print: Phonemic awareness in meaningful contexts. *The Reading Teacher, 49,* 632–642.

Sendak, M. (1962). *Alligators all around: An alphabet.* New York: Harper & Row.

Smith, F. (1994). *Understanding reading.* Hillsdale, NJ: Lawrence Erlbaum Associates.

Snow, A. (1991). *The monster book of ABC sounds.* New York: Penguin.

Wells, G., & Chang-Wells, G. L. (1992). *Constructing knowledge together: Classrooms as centers of inquiry and literacy.* Portsmouth, NH: Heinemann.

Chapter 5

My Journey to Create a Writing Workshop for First Graders

Pamela Wolfer
Formerly at Andersen Elementary School

EDITORS' COMMENTS

Pam's inquiry involved developing her own version of a writing workshop for her first graders. It had two major emphases: how to help her students write with voice, and how to teach them skills in the process. Her writing workshop was an hour long and included various subactivities; she explains all of these in her chapter. There were many ups and downs in her journey and she explains these as well.

She concentrates especially on how she helped her students consider the content of their texts, providing examples of her individual conferences with Julissa and share times around Alan's spider text. As students began to publish their texts, they also began to be readers, usually with the help of their classmates, which Pam illustrates too.

She had 28 students that year, many of whom had limited literacy skills and were reluctant to write. Despite this, she had high expectations for these emergent learners. She ended up creating writing-workshop contexts in which they became confident writers *and* readers.

The introduction chapter of this book provides the theoretical and methodological background for the larger collaborative school–university action-research project and this chapter about Pam's inquiry on writing.

University researchers, Jane Liao and Dian Ruben, collaborated with Pam in her inquiry on writing.

My inquiry began with how I might teach writing to 28 first graders so that they would enjoy it. I wanted a writing program where students could bring their personal experiences and voices into our classroom. I wanted children's writing to be "theirs," so they would be able to share their personal feelings and educate not only me, but also others in room.

I did not want to transmit information to them, but instead wanted to try to use their current knowledge as something they could build on and be transformed. The classroom would be a place to belong, a place where it would be okay to explore without negative consequences. Thus, I hoped to create writing experiences in which they would not be afraid to take chances and where their efforts would be accepted.

Throughout the year, as I began to try to answer this inquiry, very cautiously at times, many interrelated subquestions arose. I briefly sketch out some beginning steps, and then describe how I created my own version of a writing workshop for first graders, which continually changed as I addressed emerging new issues and questions in my inquiry.

FIRST STEPS IN MAKING WRITING "FUN"

I began by having group-composed writing sessions every day wherein we would write a story as a whole class. Students volunteered suggestions and dictated ideas for the story, which I wrote down. Hence, they felt that it was safe to voice their opinions. Even if other students didn't like particular suggestions, it was made clear that all would be used for the story. I felt that promoting mutual respect in this way was a very important part of making it okay. We did these group-composed texts for all of September and for the beginning of October.

Then I took the step to actually publish one of the stories to make it special as a permanent Big Book to be used in the class. Again, the dictated writing was easily done as students volunteered their suggestions because they had lots of practice in the process. They worked in groups to illustrate its pages. It was then laminated and shared with other first graders. The students and I both thought this book was just great.

Then I thought, wouldn't it be great if they could simply copy the book so they could each have one? How proud they would be, and what an accomplishment! Well, many problems emerged. Students did not have enough knowledge of written language or the fine-motor skills to copy the text. Although the text consisted of only several sentences, most found the task difficult. Some of children did not have the concept of "word." Their knowledge to form letters in conventional ways was so limited that they became very frustrated and confused. Although I knew implicitly that students' written language understandings were limited, it now became clear to me that they needed more experience in writing their own texts. Within this context—not by copying our class texts—they could gain practice in writing letters and words. Thus, my inquiry to have children write with voice began to include questions about how I could also incorporate these "skills" dimensions in my writing program.

EARLY ATTEMPTS IN CREATING A WRITING WORKSHOP

After this experience of whole-group book making, I found the book, *Joyful Learning*, by Fisher (1991). I decided to use some of the writing workshop ideas from it. Fisher's writing workshop format offered a minilesson time where skill-oriented topics could be addressed. This writing workshop method was also something that my school and I were becoming very interested in developing.

My writing workshop started with the *minilesson* period (10 minutes), and then included a *group assembly* where our group- composed writing occurred. After that, there was a *work time,* in which students had some kind of written task to be completed either individually or in small groups. Finally, a *share time* capped the workshop where students shared a part or a whole piece of their writing from the day's workshop.

I also went to the teacher's store for supplies. I filled a place in the room with markers, crayons, and different types of paper. Most of the paper was without lines so as not to restrict the students. In the beginning, students' assignments consisted of one-page, one-day tasks. However, as the writing workshop progressed, students had opportunities to expand their projects by working on texts for more than 1 day. Each child was given a writing folder in which to keep daily work. This enabled them to keep their works in progress for several days.

The Halloween Project

One of the first writing projects that occurred after this transition centered around Halloween, and illustrates how this early, workshop format worked. During minilesson and group-assembly time we met to discuss ideas about Halloween. This represented a brainstorming activity in which they talked of what costumes they were planning to wear, and of scary things, like bats and witches. We also discussed trick or treating, the food we eat, and some safety precautions to consider during Halloween. Before leaving the rug, I gave an open-ended assignment. I instructed them to use the paper shapes (different sizes of triangles, circles, ovals, squares, rectangles, and trapezoids) at their tables to make a pumpkin patch. I encouraged them to be creative, with hints that the patches could be happy, scary, or silly patches. Students then returned to their seats for work time, and as they worked on their designs, I met with children (whose desks [4–6] formed a table). My role as I roved around the room was to inquire about their designs and encourage discussion among peers. I also wanted them to be able to verbalize their thoughts as they worked to prepare for the task of telling what was happening in their pumpkin-patches pictures later on. Share time that day was simply showing their designs to each other.

The following day, the students joined on the rug for minilesson and group-assembly time. Once again, displaying their pumpkin patches was highlighted. Now as we informally discussed them, we tried to brainstorm descriptive words to explain them. They wrote these words on large paper posted in the room. At work time, I instructed students to write some words from the list, which told about their pictures. They were also able to come up with some of their own. Share time today was reading their word choices that best described their designs.

Throughout this week and into the following, students slowly formed short stories about their patches. They had use of the word lists that were developed, but I also encouraged them to use their current knowledge of letter–sound relationships to form different words through invented spelling. Many of the children's inventive spellings were very primitive because of their underdeveloped skills in the English language (many were learning English as a second language).

However, through experiences like the Halloween project, the students and I both became more comfortable with the workshop process. I think the slowness of each step in the writing process was responsible for this feeling. I did not expect a story to come about in one or two class periods. A lot of review each day during group assembly was also a plus.

As I used a similar approach through the following weeks, I had several questions I still wrestled with:

- Were they learning their skills?
- Were they learning reading through writing as much I had hoped?
- How do I document their progress?
- How do I encourage peer cooperation at groups without having discipline difficulties?
- How do I get reluctant students to produce?
- How will students' writing foster their skills as readers?

Reexamining My Writing Assignments:
Conferencing With Julissa Over a Story Starter

At this time, although I thought I was providing openness for children, I was still controlling the topics that children wrote about. To support many of my reluctant writers, I frequently gave them *story starters* to do during work time. My conference with Julissa illustrates some of the difficulties that arose as I attempted to resolve some of current questions I had in my inquiry.

In January I began a Community thematic unit and both sets of Julissa's writings had to do with neighborhood. In Example 1, I wrote a two-sentence story-starter assignment on the board. Children were to copy and then complete them with their own ideas:

My neighborhood is special because ————.

My neighborhood is fun because ————.

I hoped that such writing experiences would help the reluctant writers like Julissa. Also, I hoped that students' reading would also be facilitated by such tasks, and that as I conferenced with students individually, I would be able to provide specific guidance on their skills, especially spelling skills. As you will see, few of these goals were being accomplished.

Before Example 1 took place, Julissa had already written her version of the first sentence starter when I came to her desk. When Julissa was unable to read the word "neighborhood" in her sentence, we went back and forth between the board sentence and her sentence at her desk. I kept trying to help her read that word with little success. As Example 1 began, we returned to Julissa's desk and were still at it.

Example 1

1	Pam:	What word doesn't belong?
2	Julissa:	[Points to the word "neighborhood."]
3	Pam:	[I reread what Julissa had written.] I LOVE THE MY NEIGHBORHOOD IS SPECIAL. Do you want to write this? What word doesn't belong?
4	Julissa:	[Points to "is."]
5	Pam:	What word doesn't belong? I LOVE THE MY NEIGHBORHOOD IS SPECIAL. Does that make sense?
6	Julissa:	[Points to the word "neighborhood."]
7	Pam:	I LOVE THE MY NEIGHBORHOOD IS SPECIAL. What word doesn't belong? Does "love" belong?
8	Julissa:	[Shakes her head "no."]
9	Pam:	I LOVE THE MY NEIGHBORHOOD IS SPECIAL. How about the word "my"?
....		[Other children interrupt with questions and then I return to working with Julissa.]
10	Pam:	How about the word "my"? I LOVE THE MY NEIGHBORHOOD IS SPECIAL.
11	Julissa:	[Continues to point to "neighborhood."]
12	Pam:	That stays. [referring to "neighborhood," which I underline] That is a whole word.
		{Fieldnotes, 01/17/95}

At the end of the session (the rest is not included here) I erase both "is special" and "my" from Julissa's writing, telling her that they "don't belong." When I left Julissa I felt frustrated, and I was sure that Julissa felt the same.

Thus, although I tried to help my students connect their real life experiences in their communities with the reading and writing activities in the classroom, the rigidity of the sentence-starter assignment did not foster this connection. Such a task certainly did not offer ways for students to find joy in their writing or to write with their own voices, which were the primary purposes of my inquiry in the first place. Thus, my workshop format began to change once more as I looked for new solutions to my inquiry questions.

MORE PROBLEM SOLVING IN THE WRITING WORKSHOP

One of the major changes I made was to have students choose their own writing topics. This also coincided with changing the format of the writing workshop. I eliminated group assembly time so that students had more time to write on their own, which also meant that I now had more time to conference with individual students.

I took two other steps at this time. I tried different ways to facilitate the children's letter–sound relationships so that they felt more confident to use invented spelling, and I attempted to make explicit the writing process for the children.

Using Alphabet Books to Foster Phonics and Invented Spelling

I taught phonics lessons with the basal series that the school had adopted years before. I never thought of changing this practice because this is what they told me to use when I began my career at Andersen. One day, a university researcher asked about one of alphabet cards that are posted high on the front wall. She had trouble figuring out how the picture (a man in shorts) represented the "H" "sound." I explained that it was supposed to stand for a man running, whose panting ("huh huh") was supposed to trigger the idea of "H" sound. She was dismayed with this explanation and wondered if children really knew what these symbols on the wall cards meant. So, I began to find more enriching ways to portray sound–letter relationships. Every day during minilesson time, I read an alphabet book, which gave us a context to talk about letter–sound relationships. Table 5.1 shows 10 of our favorite books.

I also hung new alphabet cards whose pictures seemed to show a closer depiction of sound–letter relationships. These pictures were of animals, which were frequently found in the alphabet books I was reading. Hence, the children seemed to make the connections more easily. I kept the old wall cards just in case there were a few children who were relying on them as a resource.

TABLE 5.1

Ten Useful ABC Books

Aylesworth, J. (1992). *Old black fly*. New York: Holt.

Brown, J. (1976). *Alphabet dreams*. Englewood Cliffs, NJ: Prentice-Hall

Ehlert, L. (1989). *Eating the alphabet: Fruits and vegetables from A to Z*. San Diego, CA: Harcourt Brace Jovanovich.

Gag, W. (1933). *The ABC bunny*. New York: McCann.

Gundersheimer, K. (1984). *ABC say with me*. New York: Harper & Row.

Lobel, A. (1981). *On Market Street*. New York: Greenwillow.

Musgrove, M. (1976). *Ashanti to Zulu: African traditions*. New York: Dial.

Sendak, M. (1962). *Alligators all around*. New York: HarperCollins.

Watson, C. (1982). *Applebet: An ABC book*. New York: Farrar, Straus & Giroux.

Wild, R., & Wild, J. (1977). *The bears' ABC book*. New York: Lippincott.

The students were very active in their responses to the ABC books and looked forward to them every day. Some students used the books during writing time for beginning sounds. In the beginning, they did not yet find the relationships to the letters at the ends or middles of words. They also became preoccupied with "How do you spell —————?". I consistently reminded them that they were first graders and that they were not supposed to know how to spell all these words. We would worry about their spelling another time; they were to try their best on their own, or to use their table partners' brains to help them. The interesting thing is that the students did not worry about their spelling during share time when they read their stories. They could read what they had written using their inventive spelling. As we talked more and more about letter–sound relationships in the minilessons, and in my conferences with them, they became better in their spellings and increased their confidence as spellers.

Making Explicit the Writing Process

Along with the reading of alphabet books and learning strategies for letter–sound relationships to use in their spelling (and reading), I introduced the features of the writing process in an explicit manner. It took me 4 months to finally decide what steps I would use so that my students would understand them. Actually the class and I already had the steps in motion. Now was the time for me to provide *name tags* on the steps and bring them to students' attention—that is, this is what this is called, and this is how we will talk about it. For first graders, I condensed the process into four very simple steps: brainstorming, first draft, conferencing (consisting of revising and editing), and publishing.

Brainstorming is simply coming up with an idea and telling everything one knows about it. *First draft* is writing knowledge of the topic in sentence form, using invented spelling to write down the words to express ideas. *Conferencing for editing and revising* is the time to ask for help with content or mechanics. For example, this is the time to "worry" about spelling. In this way, I was able to give them the message that skills are important and were not be overlooked, but that understanding this step also lifted the burden of getting everything right the first time. The final step, *publishing,* in which the piece would be formally shared, would be the ultimate goal. The published piece, a booklet that I typed on the computer, used conventional spellings and was complete with their illustrations. In the week during which I introduced the writing process, each step was summarized and discussed during one minilesson time. Then, much time was spent on each step in future minilessons as was needed.

Many new problems and issues emerged throughout the year, regarding these steps of the writing process. For example, finding different ways of brainstorming that might aid students' diverse ways of communicating on paper became a key goal of mine. Drawing pictures, followed by oral expression of each picture, seemed to be the most logical first brainstorming technique I explained to the children because it was something we had already in place. Because students were comfortable with verbally telling stories about their pictures, the objective was merely relating the idea that this is brainstorming.

Once they orally expressed their stories they were then ready to move on to step two—first draft. Here they were to write the story they had just told aloud. This brainstorming technique enabled many students to produce their initial texts. However, they also sometimes forgot the details or transitional parts that gave sense to the stories. The class and I struggled with this oral brainstorming method for many weeks. I realized that my original intention of introducing the steps of the writing process was now expanding into many more content issues along with skill development. I was becoming overwhelmed with the number of content topics I was trying to cover during the minilesson time of the workshop. I was frequently challenged with the question: "How do I choose what is most important?" I made the decision to separate my skill development lessons, which were the ABC books and spelling issues, from writing workshop minilessons. I moved the sessions to the morning reading sessions. This way, I could refer to the ABC books later on in the writing workshop, and have fewer topics to juggle within the workshop itself.

In summary, by January I had a writing workshop structure that was working and that the children understood. However, many ongoing problems still emerged for me to resolve. I discuss and illustrate some of the ones that focused on the content of children's writing next.

ADDRESSING THE CONTENT OF CHILDREN'S WRITING

Content issues were addressed throughout all of the steps of the writing process, but attention to individual students and their texts mostly occurred during work time (approximately 40–45 minutes) and at share time. I cover another conference with Julissa (who you met in Example 1) and then discuss how content was addressed during share time in the next section.

Conferencing to Promote Revision

During my individual conferences with children, students read their works in progress and I asked many content-oriented questions. Example 2 is another interaction with Julissa, who was one of my reluctant writers. However, now that she could choose her own topic and was getting more confident in using invented spelling, I could help her understand the idea of revision, which became an important goal of my inquiry.

Example 2

1	Pam:	What is the main thing the story is about?
2	Julissa:	My dad told me to buy food. [reading from her text] I BOUGHT VEGETABLES AND COOKIES. I BUY SOME FLOWERS. I BUY SOME MILK. I SAW GENNA AT THE STORE. I SAW RONNIE. I SAW ALBERTO. I SAW ELENNA.
3	Pam:	Okay and so that's the end. I loved the beginning.
....		[At my request, Julissa rereads the first part about the grocery shopping.]
4	Pam:	Who did you buy the flowers for?
5	Julissa:	For my mother.
6	Pam:	Could you tell us that maybe on this page? On the next page? Could you tell us that?
7	Julissa:	[nods slightly]
8	Pam:	Yeah? Do you think we could add a page here and you can write who you bought the flowers for? And what would you say? How would you write it?
....		[With my help, Julissa orally creates: "We bought flowers for our mother." I begin to help Julissa figure out how to spell this addi-

tion to her text. Julissa has written "We" and is beginning to tackle "bought."]

9 Pam: How do you spell "bought" here? Okay, now you're writing the word "bought," right? [pointing to Julissa's already spelled version of the word in her text] This is the word "bought." I want you to write that word right here [referring to her new sentence]. That's how you spelled "bought" before. That's how you're going to spell "bought" now. Can you write that down?

10 Julissa: [writes down the word, using her previous spelling]

11 Pam: Unhuh. Okay, let's read it. [pointing to the two words written so far, and then to the next space]

12 Julissa: WE BOUGHT ... ... flowers.

13 Pam: Okay. Where did you write "flowers" before?

14 Julissa: [points to the word in her text]

15 Pam: Okay. If you wrote it like that before, it's going to be spelled and——you're going to use the same letters you used there.

16 Julissa: [adds "flowers" to her sentence: "We boutt Flrs ...."]

{Videotape, 03/22/95}

In contrast to what happened in Example 1, this time when I addressed the message or content of her text, Julissa is quite able to answer my question about it and then to reread it. After favorably responding to the first part of her story and having Julissa reread it once more, I try to get her to revise it by writing more about the person the flowers were for (lines 7 & 9). Julissa creates a new sentence to add to her text, "We bought flowers for our mother." During the rest of the conference, I showed her that she could easily add this to her text because she already gave reasonable invented-spelling approximations for "bought" and "flowers." Here, Julissa was much more confident about her writing, and I felt much more confident in being supportive of her efforts.

Example 2 worked with a final first draft. However, during my conferences I addressed the content of children's texts in many ways. For example, if children had only come up with their topic (or maybe title), but had not written the first draft yet, I might have them talk through what they planned to write about. I might even help a child with a webbing map, another brainstorming technique I introduced to them. Or, I might ask questions about what was going to happen next when they had only partial drafts. I kept notes on what we did in conferences. I also checked students' folders at the end of the day or early the next day before school to monitor the progress of their writing so I would know when to have another conference. This was important because I had so many students, who were at different writing development levels and who were at different places in the writing process.

Addressing Content at Share Time

I set up the rules for share time, but the children primarily ran this part of the writing workshop. Two or three authors read their work. After a text (or partial draft) was completely read, the illustrations were shown. Children raised their hands if they wanted to comment or ask questions about an author's work, and the writer could select three of them for responses. After the third exchange, we would applaud. I did join in as another member of the audience, but I tried to have my comments to emphasize some idea or meaning that children raised.

Alan shared his story, *I See a Spider,* during two separate share times. Alan initially worked on creating a web for his topic. I had modeled this technique using a "spider web" during several minilessons. We completed a spider web together as a whole class and wrote a story from the information. Throughout the weeks, we experimented with this new brainstorming method of writing down notes about the content, right on a spider sketch. The students, however, continued to use the previous technique of pictures and oral storytelling. Alan was the first student who took the plunge to try the new spider-web method on his new topic—"spider." I was not sure if he had mixed up the meaning of the "spider web" with choosing a topic about a spider; I decided not to overanalyze his thoughts, but to merely accept his willingness. Hence, we forged ahead with his idea. During our conference, he came up with the following ideas to place on the "legs" of his spider web—pet, John, play games, bought (pet store), and eat flies. Example 3A is an excerpt of the share time of his first draft based on that web. Alan's story entertained his classmates and also initiated discussions around various content issues.

Example 3A

1	Alan:	*I SEE A SPIDER.* I SEEN A SPIDER. HIS NAME IS JOHN.
2	Cs:	[giggling]
3	Cm:	What's so funny?
4	Cf:	A spider named John.
5	Alan:	I SEEN A SPIDER. HE WAS JOHN.
....		
6	Alan:	JOHN IS MY PET. JOHN AND ME PLAY HIDE AND GO SEEK.
7	Cs:	[giggles from several children]
8	Alan:	I FEED JOHN WITH FLIES.
9	Cs:	[laughter from audience]
10	Cm:	Spiders don't like flies!

11	Alan:	They——they suck flies. So that's why I give him flies. I BOUGHT JOHN. THE END.
....		[Alan shows the pictures he drew to accompany the story. There is some consternation on the part of the other children about how tiny his pictures are. Alan defends them by saying that the picture seemed small to them because "It was too far." I bring them back to the share-time structure by asking Alan if he is ready for questions. The first question is asked by Manuel.]
12	Manuel:	Was your spider a daddy longlegs?
13	Alan:	Huh?
14	Manuel:	Was your spider a daddy longlegs?
15	Alberto:	What?
16	Alan:	[shakes his head negatively]
17	Pam:	What kind of spider was it then, Alan?
18	Alberto:	[interrupting] Alan, let me see up the pictures, *si*?
19	Pam:	*Shhh!* Alberto! Let Alan think of the question! Alan, what kind of spider was John?
20	Cf:	A nice (...).
21	Alan:	A nice spider!
22	Pam:	A nice spider. Do you know what type of spider he was though?
23	Alan:	[nods, but does not answer]
24	Cs:	[a group in front trying to clarify the question for Alan] Color! What kind? Kind!
25	Pam:	What kind? What type of spider was he?
26	Alberto:	[whispering to Alan] Tarantula? (...) a tarantula spider.
27	Alan:	[to the class] A tarantula spider.
		{Video, 03/23/95}

The children thought that several parts of Alan's story were funny—that he named the spider John, that they played hide-and-go-seek, and that Alan fed him flies. Children frequently complained that Alan's pictures were too tiny, but it was also clear here that they were very interested in his tale about John.

Manuel brought up the major content issue when he asked, "Was it a daddy longlegs?" When Alan nodded negatively, I followed up on the question (in line 17). A classmate suggests "nice" as a possibility, which I accept, but still have Alan consider the *type* of spider it was. Other children in the front near him chimed in to encourage him to respond, and then Alberto whispered a possibility to him, "tarantula," which Alan then agrees on.

In a share time in April, Alan reread his story, now published, and new questions about some of its events arose. Example 3B began after Alan read and showed the pictures of his book, and chose Victor for comments.

Example 3B

1	Alan:	Victor.
2	Victor:	Why did you catch John?
3	Alan:	I didn't catch him!
....		
4	Alan:	I bought John. I didn't grab him. If I grab him then he'll be bad to me....
....		
5	Cm:	How you bought John?
6	Alan:	I went to the store——the <department> store, and I bought John.
7	Cm:	With what money?
8	Alan:	I had money. [opens his book looking for a picture] I just forgot to make [draw] the money.
		{Videotape, 04/11/95}

In this second share time, other students wanted to know how Alan obtained the spider. Alan explained that he bought John, saying that if he had grabbed him, he might hurt ("be bad to") him. Further questions focused on how Alan bought the spider, and when Alan looked at his illustrations again, he commented that he forgot to include the money in his pictures.

Thus, in both occasions of share time, Alan gained useful feedback to make his text better. He and his classmates also learned that the content of their texts should be interesting and have important information in them.

Examples 3A and 3B were successful share times, but it is important to emphasize that there were many rocky paths on the route before the children arrived at this place. In the beginning, I really had difficulty getting them to attend to content, because they only wanted to talk about their pictures. For example, right before Clarissa was to share her story about playing Power Rangers with her brother in January, I urged, "Remember, think about the *story* and what questions you can ask about the story." {Videotape, 01/24/95} However, after Clarissa read her text, my reminder was lost on the children, who were still asking questions only about the pictures. I tried asking questions of my own to change the tide, "How many were you playing with, Clarissa? ... You were playing with six people? ...

You're going to add on and draw it tomorrow? {Videotape, 01/24/95} This really didn't change the course of that share time, but I just kept at it. What I think finally seemed to make a difference was when I began to stress the "what, when, where, how, and why" questions of their writing. I did that in a couple of minilessons. They used these ideas first by focusing only on the pictures, but then after a couple of weeks I started getting really good questions and comments about the content.

FINAL THOUGHTS ON THE WRITING WORKSHOP

My journey in creating a writing workshop for first graders included many ups and downs and detours, and I was able to mention only parts of that trip here. Throughout the year, I had to figure out many things, so changes occurred frequently. For example, I went through many ways to document individual children's progress—from post-it notes and check lists, to keeping a journal with pages for each child. Also, I had to help children learn to write on their own during work time. I wanted them to talk and assist each other, but I wanted that talk to be *on* their writing and to be quiet enough so as not to disturb other writers in the room or to disturb my conferences with individual students.

More on Share Time

Share time was probably the facet of the writing workshop that developed the most during the course of the year. Students valued this time and worked to achieve success as writers because of this time. Not only did they want to be one of the featured authors, they wanted to voice their opinions and to assist the writer in decision making. I already talked about some of the struggles (e.g., addressing the content of texts, not just pictures) that occurred before the students reached this constructive, common goal. Students began to ask more pertinent questions—"Where did you get the idea?", and "Why did you ———?"

Share time provided me with an individual assessment of the author. The feedback that peers provided also became an integral part of another ongoing evaluation. I not only documented the author focus of the share time, but also documented the questioning and participation of the audience. Besides a good time for documentation, share time was a major motivator for reluctant writers and for those who were between texts. When I began the writing workshop, share time was at the end of the hour session, and students shared what they produced during work time that day. They were allowed to sign themselves up to share. Later, I changed this because too many were reading the same story with little changes, and we just didn't have the time for all to share. I chose those who shared by evaluating my conferences of that day or by noting who I had seen making progress. I began with six authors and decreased the number to three.

In addition, by the end of the year, share time had moved to the beginning of writing workshop. This actually happened by chance. It was health week and students were being pulled out of class to have their vision, hearing, and dental tests. Because I didn't want students to miss share time, I moved it so that it launched the writing workshop. I noticed the difference in attention and feedback given by the audience immediately. Share time was so much more productive. Moreover, it was more of a motivator for writing for the rest of the workshop. Students seemed to go to work time with a vengeance to produce and publish.

Publishing Books for Readers and Using Computers for Writing

When the student produced a story and took it through the complete writing process, it was ready to be published. In the beginning, I took each finished piece and typed it in book form on the computer. Students then illustrated, and the book was laminated for binding. The books were displayed in their own spaces in the room. Students checked out these books to take home to read in the same fashion as were real published books. Children also read the student-authored literature during Sustained Silent Reading time. At the end of the year, besides writing new texts during work time, children were also reading the many published books they had authored. Peer cooperation and tutoring helped many children learn how to read these books independently.

Example 4 shows Leon's reading of his published book, *The Rainbow*. Leon loved to read his books to his classmates. As you will see, he still needed help in reading his book. Ana, a more adept reader, was available and eager to help him.

Example 4

1	Ana:	[to Leon] Read it! Read it!
2	Leon:	THE RAINBOW. BY LEON [LAST NAME].
3	Ana:	Read it louder.
4	Manuel:	[stands behind Leon who is seated, looking over Leon's shoulder]
5	Ana:	[pointing to the words in the book] THE RAINBOW.
....		[Leon seems initially to resent Ana's help, and as he tries to get the book more under his physical control, pages get loose from the binding. They sort out the book and how to get going on the reading. Ana once more begins by reading the title page, with Leon quietly "shadow" reading after her. Then Ana relinquishes

		control to Leon by turning the page, pointing to the first word, and waiting for Leon to read.]
6	Leon:	[pausing briefly before uttering each word] MY ... MOM ...
7	Ana:	WAS ...
8	Leon:	WAS IN THE HOUSE.
....		[They briefly exchange glances at each other and turn the page together.]
9	Ana:	[pointing to the word, almost whispering] SHE ...
10	Leon:	SHE ...
11	Ana:	#LOOKED OUT THE WINDOW# ...
12	Leon:	#LOOKED OUT THE WINDOW# ...
....		[They both turn the page and point at each word.]
13	Leon:	[begins to read this new page on his own] ME AND MY MOM SAW A RAINBOW.
14	Ana:	[turns the page]
15	Leon:	THE RAINBOW ... DIS ... A ... PPEAR.
16	Ana:	Now the pictures.
17	Leon:	[holds up the illustrations, turning the pages one by one]
18	Ana:	The end. [briefly applauds]
		{Videotape, 05/10/95}

Leon seemed a little upset with Ana's initial efforts to help him, but later he seemed to appreciate her help. I was happy that students read their own books. They seemed to learn sight words easier. As writers, they used words that were part of their oral vocabulary, and as they read the books, they learned some really difficult words, ones that are rarely found in most first-grade readers, for example. Even when they might have problems in figuring out some words, it was easier for them to get the words because they had used their own language, they wrote as they spoke. Because their classmates knew their language too, they were able to be great helpers in this reading. They could help each other many more times than I could possibly have been able to. Thus, as they grew confident in writing, they began to become more confident in reading, which was another goal of my inquiry.

Toward the end of the year, I introduced the computers as a tool for writing. Students began to take off and type their own published books. They also used some of the graphic designs the software provided, alleviating the need to illustrate manually. Peer tutoring again played a significant role in this final aspect of my inquiry because students who were more computer literate helped other authors learn how to use the computer in all of the steps of the writing process.

SUMMARY

We frequently traveled a rocky road during the year of inquiry on writing, and I still had many new questions still to tackle (e.g., how to get children to write more genres, or forms of writing, and how to better facilitate their skills in spelling). Nevertheless, the major goals of my inquiry were accomplished: Children enjoyed writing; they thought of themselves as writers; they understood the writing process and what it meant to be an author; they published books in their own voice, and they became adept as readers in reading these books.

ABOUT THE AUTHOR

I received my bachelor's degree in education from the University of Illinois at Chicago in June 1989. I completed my student training sessions in three Chicago public schools. I found great hope and desire to make a difference in our urban communities among many of the staff members and decided to join in their efforts. I was hired at Hans Christian Andersen and remained there for many years. My teaching experience has been very rewarding and challenging. I have since retired to raise my family. My future involvement in education will be as a parent and community member. I hope my past experience in teaching will make this new role an understanding and productive insight into our community's scholastic needs.

DEDICATION

I dedicate this chapter to my best friend and husband, Michael, who always lends his support and encouragement and to the loves of our lives, our daughters, Tori Jo and Haley Rose. And I thank my sister Donna, who taught me how to write.

REFERENCE

Fisher, B. (1991). *Joyful learning: A whole language kindergarten.* Portsmouth, NH: Heinemann.

Chapter 6

Learning How to Scaffold Second Graders to Become Authors in a Bilingual Classroom

Sarah Cohen
Formerly at Jungman Elementary School

EDITORS' COMMENTS

Sarah had a new position—teaching in Spanish in a bilingual second grade. On the very first day of school, she gave these second graders the task of writing a sentence to go with their picture of an adventure they had during the summer. One girl responded to the assignment, "I don't know how to write." This became the impetus of Sarah's inquiry on writing—trying to help these young children see that they *could* be writers, and *could* be authors.

In her inquiry, Sarah set up many contexts and purposes for writing. Especially emphasized in her plan was having children think and talk about the meanings of their texts. In this process, she struggled with the "right measure" of explanation in author's chair and mini-lesson sessions. She struggled with how and in what ways she should be explicit in fostering revision and other aspects of writing. Despite the difficulties that arose, her efforts were successful, however, because these Latina and Latino second-grade students did become avid authors.

The introduction chapter of this book provides the theoretical and methodological background for the larger collaborative school–university action-research project and this chapter about Sarah's inquiry on writing.

University researchers, Liliana Barro Zecker and Caitlyn Nichols, collaborated with Sarah in her inquiry.

It was my first year teaching in a bilingual classroom. I was back teaching in the Chicago public school system (CPSS) after living in Mexico for a year and teaching English in a private bilingual school there. For the 4 years before that I taught in the CPSS in monolingual classrooms. One of the reasons I had originally decided to go to Mexico was to learn Spanish, so that I would be better able to communicate with the parents of the students I was teaching. I also wanted to better understand the culture from which the majority of my students came.

In this new position, I taught in Spanish, a language that at this point I knew well enough to be called fluent, but it was not my native language and this added a new dimension of self-consciousness to my teaching. I was deemed qualified to teach a bilingual class, not because I had ever completed a degree program in bilingual education, but because I spoke the Spanish language. As I sense then, and as I saw with more clarity as I began the school year, speaking and understanding the language are very different from teaching all subject areas in that language and having the resources in Spanish at hand to create the curriculum. I was also to teach ESL to some extent, but exactly how that was to be accomplished was still not clear to me. Thus, there were many things for me to learn and inquire about during this year teaching Spanish-speaking second graders.

THE IMPETUS FOR MY INQUIRY ON WRITING

My inquiry focused on studying the development of my second-grade students' writing. Specifically, I was interested in observing the relationship between students' potential to see themselves as writers and in their development of greater proficiency as writers. I knew that developing better mechanical skills was a necessary part for the students to become more fluent writers, however it seemed important first that they think of themselves as writers. Then the acquisition of any of these skills would have meaning for them and truly influence their writing.

On the first day of school I asked the students to write a sentence to go along with a drawing they completed about an adventure that they had during the summer. Julia, faced with the task, looked at me and said flat out, "Maestra, yo no se escribir." ("Teacher, I don't know how to write.") I admit that I felt the impact of that statement with some level of shock—not so much from the awareness that she was ill-prepared to accomplish what I had expected that she (and her classmates) would be able to do, as from the finality and lack of presumption with which she conveyed her lack, or perceived lack, of skills. In fact, as it turned out, Julia initially possessed few reading or writing skills, but it seemed equally obvious to me that somewhere along the way she had been told this, and had also been told, that for this reason she could not write. This was exactly the kind of logic that I wanted to turn upside down—have students write first, and in doing so, they find the need for the spelling of words. I knew that I needed first of all to convey to my students the essence of writing as communication. I tried to make most of their writing as personal as possible to increase their investment in the work and to show them that I as their teacher wanted to read their writing and know them through their stories, both real and made up.

CREATING PURPOSES AND CONTEXTS FOR WRITING

I set out to encourage writing in as many different contexts as possible. My first priority was for the students to become accustomed to writing on a daily basis. I introduced them to journals. I told the students that this would be a place for them to tell me about themselves; they could write about their families, what they did after school, how they were feeling, or any other thing that they wished to include. I said that I would read the journals every day and respond to what they said.

When I taught sixth grade, my students also kept journals, and I had a system for reading what they wrote and for writing back to them twice a week. When I began the journals with this second-grade class, however, I was unprepared for the students' desire for an immediate response. I found myself surrounded all of a sudden, on that first day that they wrote in journals, by a group of eager children all wanting me to read at once what they had written. Their desire to share their work was great and, although I soon found myself wrestling with how to control the whole group and see each child during journal time, I did not want to dampen their enthusiasm.

I also discovered that it was useful to have them share their writing with me, as closely as possible to the time of their writing, for a couple of other reasons. Many of the students still relied heavily on invented spelling that reflected varying degrees of readability. Thus, it made it easier on me if I heard their texts, read by the children first. Reading aloud their own writing meant that they had to sound out their words, often being forced into the awareness of having left out letters or whole words. Thus, this practice served as a method of self-correction in their writing, a reading exercise, as well as enhancing their sense that their writing was serving a form of authentic communication with me. This last point is significant because for the students to learn to write, they had to see themselves as writers—they had to understand that what writers do is to communicate—expressing ideas, thoughts, and feelings to others.

Beyond Journals: Establishing Other Contexts for Writing

As I already noted, I felt that I had to provide many contexts for writing. I figured out a system for journals—students worked on journals, read books, or created illustrations for their writing, while individual students met with me to read and hear my response to their journal entries. This system worked moderately well, and 4 weeks later I was ready to introduce another context and purpose for writing—writing books. I called these "libros de cuentos" (story books) to distinguish them from their journals.

As I introduced the idea of writing books, I talked to them about becoming authors. I cited examples of books that we had read, reminding them that real people had to think of the stories and develop the material. I insisted that they, too, could learn to do that. However, they were not so sure. Raul expressed their common, skeptical sentiment, "Pero, nosotros no somos autores!" ("But, we are not authors!") I kept emphasizing that each *could* be an author—someone who writes, who tells stories, and who learns how to make people want to read what he or she writes. They could do all of those things even though their books would be published just within our classroom.

Although I set up out opportunities for other kinds of writing (e.g., reading logs in which children wrote about the books they were reading) much of my inquiry revolved around routines that supported the writing and publishing of the books. I set up two kinds of individual conferences, content and editing, and had author's chair sessions in which children shared their texts and received audience feedback for revision. Relying on what I observed in their writing, I also instituted minilessons to cover emerging issues with them. Throughout my inquiry, I especially struggled with how best to explain to my students the various facets of making meaning in a written form. Next, in this chapter, I cover discourse examples in which I provide explanations about revision and differentiating fiction and nonfiction to illustrate my efforts to support my students as authors.

EXPLAINING REVISION

I had short roving conferences with students daily in which I attempted to address the content of my students' texts. They would quickly read their writing in progress and I would ask one or two questions to provide more details, elaborate on an idea or theme, and so forth. My intent was to help my students make their writing more clear to the reader and, when possible, to include more detail.

Promoting revision was a big issue in author's chair sessions as well. During this time, one or two students read their texts to the whole class and heard various questions that other classmates had about their writing. I explained the purpose of audience feedback and set up guidelines for participation on many occasions.

> "Vamos a dar nuestros comentarios, sugerencias, preguntas, ummm, comentamos como siempre y vamos a platicar en grupo después, cómo se pueden usar esos comentarios para cambiar el cuento, para desarrollar el cuent. … Lo que pasa es que muchas veces escribimos un cuento y ya pensamos que ya está terminado pero a veces le faltan detalles en alguans partes, o se podría desarrollar mucho mas."

"We are going to give our comments suggestions, questions, ummm, we comment like always and we are going to talk as a group, how those comments can be used to change the story, to develop the story. ... What happens is that often we write a story and we think that it is already finished, but sometimes it is missing details in some parts, or it could be developed much more."

{Fieldnotes, 11/02/94}

However, although all students participated and all—the author and the audience—seemed to enjoy the discussions that were designed to promote and model revision, students' products rarely showed any changes based on these ongoing sessions. Information from the author's chair session with Lorena illustrates the difficulties that arose regarding revision.

Lorena's Author's Chair Session

In this session, Lorena read a story about a girl named Julia who liked to draw, to color, and to make books. Julia also had a friend who enjoyed these same activities. After reading her text before the class, Lorena chose the students who had raised their hands to offer feedback. Lorena responded to their questions with short comments having little elaboration. I wrote the questions students raised on the board (I have included only the English translation):

- What was the girl's name?
- Why did she like to make stories, books, and pictures?
- Why did she like to color them?
- Why did the books have pictures?
- Did her friend like to color too?
- Did her friend help her to make the stories?
- Did she go out?
- Did she like to do other things besides making books, like going out?

I added the last question as an elaboration of the last one that a student offered. I then explained that Lorena could use this feedback to revise her story. In doing so, I even tried to model possible ways that Lorena could actually change her text.

Example 1

1 Sarah: Estas preguntas pueden ayudar, okay? Te preguntaron, "¿Por qué le gustaron los cuentos a la niña?" y "¿Por qué le gustaban los dibujos?" Eso es una cosa que no está en el cuento. Podrías poner estos detalles en tu cuento. Parece que la gente que lea tu cuento le gustaría saber mas sobre la niña. ¿Me entiendes, Lorena?

2   Lorena: Sí, entiendo.

3   Sarah: Y si pones esos detalles, sería mas completo, entiendes? También te preguntaron, "¿Por qué los coloreó, los cuentos y los libros? Y si lo hacía sola o con su amiga. Si su amiga la ayudaba, okay? Parece que tus compañeros, Lorena, están diciendo que quieren saber mas; podrías darnos un ejemplo. Podrías darnos una escena entre la niña y su amiga haciéndolo. lo que hacían. ¿Entiendes? Eso es diferente que decir, "A la niña le gustaban los dibujos." Podrías decirnos, umm, "Una niña, Julia, y su amiga un día estaban haciendo unos dibujos. Julia hacía eso y … después dijo su amiga, '¿Por qué no ponemos el color rosa en el conejo en el cuento?'"

4   Cm1:   (... ...).

5   Sarah: Uh, huh. Puedes darnos una perspectiva sobre cómo se portan las niñas. ¿Entiendes?

6   Lorena: [Nods.]

7   Sarah: Hay otras cosas que podrías decir sobre la niña. ¿Cómo es su vida? A parte de que le gustaba hacer dibujos y cuentos, podrías decirnos si va a la escuela, si sale, cómo es su familia, cosas así, verdad? Okay? Entonces si tu crees que te gustaría hacer el cuento mas grande, cambiar un poquito, contesta algunas preguntas que te hicieron tus compañeros, okay? Esas preguntas, Lorena. [pointing to the board]

Translation

1   Sarah: These questions can help, okay? They ask you, "Why did the girl like stories?" and "Why did she like the pictures?" That is something that is not in the story. You could put those details in the story. It seems as if the people that read your story would like to know more about the girl. Do you understand me?

2   Lorena: Yes, I understand.

3   Sarah: And if you put those details, it would be more complete, do you understand? They also asked you, "Why did she color the stories and the books? And if she did it alone or with her friend. If her friend helped her, okay? It seems that your classmates, Lorena, are saying that they want to know more; you could give us an example. You could give us a scene between the girl and her friend doing that … what they did. Do you understand? That is different than saying, "The girl liked pictures." You could tell us, umm, "A girl, Julia, and her friend, one day were drawing pictures. Julia was doing that and … then her friend said, 'Why don't we color the bunny in the story pink?'"

4   Cm1:   (... ...).

5   Sarah: Uh, huh. You can give us a perspective about how the girls behave. Do you understand?

6	Lorena:	[Nods.]
7	Sarah:	There are other things that you can say about the girl. What's her life like? Besides liking to make drawings and stories, you could tell us if she goes to school, if she goes out, what her family is like, things like that, right? Okay? Then, if you think that you would like to make the story bigger, change a little, answer some of the questions that your classmates asked you, okay? Those questions, Lorena. [pointing to the board]

{Fieldnotes, 11/02/94}

As you can see, I took some of the actual questions that Lorena's classmates asked, and tried to show how she could add more details into her story. I was sure that Lorena was now ready to revise. However, after a few minutes of having the students back at their desks, I noticed that Lorena was busy on a completely new text quite unrelated to the story we had just discussed at author's chair. When I reminded her about the audience feedback she received and how she could use it to revise her story, her only response was to copy the questions from the board. It is possible that Lorena was copying the questions so that she would have them later to revise her story, but my conversation with her did not indicate that this was her intention. Even with all my explicit explanations about what to do and my oral composition of a part of the text to add to her story, Lorena never changed her story in writing.

Looking back, I think that during these times I did all the talking: Collaborating with them as I tried to model these changes was difficult. I ended up taking over, and it was hard to decide how much to say and how much was too much. I often struggled with the "right measure" of explanation. They seemed to understand when we were talking about these issues, but then they had trouble applying the ideas or ways of writing that I explained to them. It was possible that while my students understood what I meant by adding details and clarifying, talking about possible changes and giving the information as it was requested by the audience on the spot was sufficient for them. I wish I had spent more time showing them how to actually introduce changes in their writing, and modifying a real written product so that they could see how to do it. I also began to wonder just how much of these ideas were developmentally appropriate to the students' ability to conceptualize this task of revision. I came to understand that it was a task that was more abstract than I originally thought.

I kept the author's chair sessions, however, and I kept encouraging revision. I thought it was important to them to hear these ideas and to participate in these discussions. Just discussing these ideas was enriching for them. It was as if they could do the revisions at the oral language level, perhaps at that stage it was all we could afford. I got them used to thinking about writing, even if it did not show up in their products.

STRUGGLING WITH THE RIGHT MEASURE
OF EXPLANATION ON THE TOPIC OF FICTION
VERSUS NONFICTION

The challenge to find the right measure of explanation was often seen in
my minilessons as well. In the next example, I use Felipe's text to explain
the differences between fiction and nonfiction writing. He was very involved in writing about the Bulls basketball team. Although I had always
emphasized that they could write anything in their "story books," it was a
rare occasion that a student deviated from the fictional style of writing.
Thus, I decided to bring it to the students' attention.

Example 2

....		[I am standing in front of the class, addressing the students while holding Felipe's piece.]
1	Sarah:	Felipe no está haciendo exactamente un cuento.
2	Cm1:	(... ...).
3	Sarah:	Está escribiendo algo——algo que no es ficción. Es sobre la ciudad de Chicago.
4	Cm2:	¿Cómo?
5	Sarah:	¿Mande? ¿Cómo? Dice cómo es Chicago ... es lo que está escribiendo. Eso no es un cuento. No es ficción.
6	Cm2:	Yo no quiero hacer eso.
....		[I am interrupted by students telling her what they are writing about. There is lots of overlapping talk.]
7	Sarah:	Ummm, lo que estoy diciendo es que no tiene que ser un cuento. Si quieren hacer——escribir otra cosa, otro tipo de cosa, cómo son los animales, las plantas ... otra cosa que no es——que no sea ficción. Kara, tú pronto vas a Puerto Rico. Podrías escribir cómo es Puerto Rico. Hacer no exactamente un cuento sino una descripción, como hemos estado haciendo descripciones sobre monstruos, sobre tu persona, sobre tu casa. Podrías hacer otro tipo de descripción sobre otra cosa, animales, o lugares, lo que sea....
....		[Children talk about the stories they have written.]
8	Sarah:	¿Mario? ¿Entienden la diferencia entre ficción.....
9	Cm2:	[completing my sentence] Y cuentos?
10	Sarah:	Cuentos y cosas que no son cuentos, que no son ficción. ¿Qué entiendes Vicente?
11	Vicente:	Que no debo hacer cosas de ficción.
12	Sarah:	No, no ... no que no debes sino que——no que no tienes que hacer cosas de ficción. Puedes hacer cosas de ficción pero

		también puedes si quieres hacer cosas que no son ficción. ¿Qué es ficción, Alma? ¿Qué es ficción, Raúl? ¿Franco?
13	Franco:	Como de eso de … de brujas
14	Sarah:	Okay, brujas sí, si escribes sobre brujas generalmente … generalmente es ficción. ¿Por qué? [addressing the class]
15	Cm3:	Porque es mentira.…
16	Sarah:	Mentira … o también se puede decir que no exactamente es mentira sino que no es real, okay? Una cosa que.…
….		[There is an interruption as a child yells at Mario and I need to spend some time asking them to quiet down. Then I go back to the discussion.]
17	Sarah:	Franco, una cosa que escribes sobre algo que no es real es, es como ficción. ¿Entiendes?
18	Franco:	¿Como básquetbol?
19	Sarah:	¿Mande?
20	Franco:	¿Como básquetbol?
21	Sarah:	¿Como básquetbol? Bueno, puedes hacer un cuento de ficción sobre básquetbol pero.…
22	Cs:	(… …).
23	Sarah:	Un cuento, por ejemplo, de ficción es como diciendo cosas que no——que realmente no han pasado, okay? Inventado, una historia.
24	Cs:	(… …).
25	Cm1:	(…) cuento de básquetbol (…).
26	Sarah:	¡Claro! Un cuento sobre cualquier cosa, de básquetbol, de pescados, todas esas cosas son reales. Solamante cuando hacen cuentos, usan esas cosas para inventar una historia. ¿Entiendes Vicente?
27	Vicente:	Sí.
28	Sarah:	¿Bien? ¿Sí? ¿Pablo?
29	Pablo:	¿Cómo un pescado que juega básquetbol?
30	Sarah:	¿Cómo qué?
31	Pablo:	¿Un pescado que juega básquetbol?
32	Sarah:	Bueno, eso sería como muy, muy irreal, como fantasía. Ficción no tiene que ser fantasía. Ficción puede ser un niño jugando básquetbol, o un hombre, o una mujer jugando básquebol. Ficción no tiene que ser fantasía, Pablo, okay? Solamante la diferencia entre ficción y fantasía es que——si no es ficción, tiene que haber pasado … haber pasado en la vida. Ummm, por ejemplo, una descripción sobre la vida de Michael Jordan es una historia sobre su vida, es real, okay? Pero si tú quieres escribir un cuento sobre.…

33	Cm1:	¿Michael Jordan?
34	Sarah:	Sobre tu ... siendo una estrella de basquetbol, no sería real....
35	Cs:	(... ...).
36	Sarah:	Sería algo que estás creando en tu imaginación.
37	Pablo:	(...) pero (...) puede ser real.
38	Sarah:	Puede ser en el futuro. [turning to Franco] Franco, me molesta que estés haciendo ruido! [returning to the class] Puede ser real en el futuro pero ahorita no es real, okay? Es algo que estás imaginando, Pablo, para escribir como un cuento, okay? ¿Felipe?
39	Felipe:	Maestra, lo que escribí, qué es? [pointing to his text that Sarah is holding up]
40	Sarah:	¿Esto? Lo que estás escribiendo, algo sobre Chicago, de cómo es Chicago en tus ojos, verdad? ¿Es algo real o irreal?
41	Cs:	Algo ... real.
42	Sarah:	Real? Sí ... es algo muy real ... estás haciendo como un librito explicando cómo es la ciudad....
43	Felipe:	Como (...).
44	Sarah:	No estás inventando una ciudad, verdad? Entonces es real, no es ficción. ¿De acuerdo? [to the entire class] ¿Otras preguntas?....

Translation

....		[I am standing in front of the class, addressing the students while holding Felipe's piece.]
1	Sarah:	Felipe is not writing a story exactly.
2	Cm1:	(... ...).
3	Sarah:	He is writing something——something that is not fiction. It's about the city of Chicago.
4	Cm2:	What?
5	Sarah:	Pardon? What? He tells what Chicago is like ... that's what he is writing. That's not a story. It's not fiction.
6	Cm2:	I don't want to do that.
....		[I am interrupted by students telling me what they are writing about. There is lots of overlapping talk.]
7	Sarah:	Ummm, what I'm saying is that it does not need to be a story. If you want to do——write something else, other type of thing, what are animals like, plants ... something else that is not——might not be fiction. Kara, you are going to Puerto Rico soon. You could write about what Puerto Rico is like. Write not exactly a story but a description, like we have been writing descriptions about monsters, about yourself, about your house.

		You could write a description about something else, animals, or other places, whatever....
....		[Children talk about the stories they have written.]
8	Sarah:	Mario? Do you understand the difference between fiction....
9	Cm2:	[completing my sentence] And stories?
10	Sarah:	Stories and things that are not stories, that are not fiction? What did you understand, Vicente?
11	Vicente:	That I should not write fiction things.
12	Sarah:	No, no ... it's not that you shouldn't——it's not that you shouldn't write fictional things. You can write fiction things but also, if you want you can write things that are not fiction. What's fiction, Alma? What's fiction, Raúl? Franco?
13	Franco:	Like that about ... about witches.
14	Sarah:	Okay, witches yes, if you write about witches generally ... generally it's fiction. Why? [addressing the class]
15	Cm3:	Because it's a lie....
16	Sarah:	A lie ... or we can also say that it's is not exactly a lie but it is not real, okay? Something that....
....		[There is an interruption as a child yells at Mario and I need to spend some time asking them to quiet down. Then I go back to the discussion.]
17	Sarah:	Franco, something that you write about something that is not real, it's like fiction. Do you understand?
18	Franco:	Like basketball?
19	Sarah:	Pardon?
20	Franco:	Like basketball?
21	Sarah:	Like basketball? Well, you can make a fiction story, you can write a....
22	Cs:	(... ...).
23	Sarah:	A fiction story, for example, it's like saying things that——that have not really happened, okay? Making up, a story.
24	Cs:	(... ...).
25	Cm:	(...) basketball stories (...).
26	Sarah:	Right! A story about anything, about basketball, about fish, all those are real things. It's only that when you write stories, you use those things to make up a story. Do you understand what I am saying, Vicente?
27	Vicente:	Yes.
28	Sarah:	Good. Yes? Pablo?
29	Pablo:	Like a fish that plays basketball?

30	Sarah:	Like what?
31	Pablo:	A fish that plays basketball?
32	Sarah:	Well, that would be like very, very unreal, like fantasy. Fiction does not have to be fantasy. Fiction can be a boy playing basketball, or a man, or a woman playing basketball. Fiction does not have to be fantasy, Pablo, okay? It's only that the difference between fiction and fantasy is that——if it's not fiction, it has to have happened——have happened in real life. Ummm, for example, a description on Michael Jordan's life is a *story* about his life, it's real, okay? But if you want to write a story about....
33	Cm1:	Michael Jordan?
34	Sarah:	About you ... being a basketball star, that wouldn't be real....
35	Cs:	(... ...).
36	Sarah:	It would be something that you are creating in your imagination.
37	Pablo:	(...) but (...) it can be real.
38	Sarah:	It can be in the future. [turning to Franco] Franco, it bothers me that you are making noise! [returning to the class] It can be real in the future but now it is not real, okay? It is something that you are imagining, Pablo, to write as a story, okay? Felipe?
39	Felipe:	Teacher, that, what I wrote, what is it? [pointing to his text that Sarah is holding up]
40	Sarah:	This? What you are writing, something about Chicago, about what Chicago is like in your eyes, true? Is it something real or unreal?
41	Cs:	Something ... real.
42	Sarah:	Real? Yes ... it's something very real ... you're making like a flyer explaining what the city is like....
43	Felipe:	Like (...).
44	Sarah:	You are not making up a city, true? The——it's real, it's not fiction. All right? [to the entire class] Other questions?....

{Fieldnotes, 06/02/95}

This was a long session. I initially brought up the idea of *nonstory* by referring to Felipe's text about Chicago (lines 1, 3, & 5). Then I commented on other students' ideas about basketball, about Michael Jordan, and about witches to further elaborate on the distinction between fiction and nonfiction. We had already done some work on description and I attempted to connect this to the possibility that Kara might write an informational piece about Puerto Rico when she goes there (line 7). I also tackled the difference between fantasy and realistic fiction in line 32. Students were eager participants in this discussion, asking questions and offering various comments, despite the fact they didn't seem too sure how my explanations might be related to their writing (see, e.g., Felipe's remarks in line 39).

I often felt somewhat like a lawyer arguing her case regarding fiction versus nonfiction. It certainly went much longer than I anticipated, and I certainly didn't plan to get into a fantasy and realistic fiction distinction. Also, I got all snarled in that explanation when I tried to talk about what could happen in "real life" and what is "very, very unreal" (line 32). It got somewhat worse because I used the word "story" to describe both nonfiction and fiction: "A description on Michael's life is a 'story' about his life, it's real. ... but if you want to write a 'story' about ... you being a basketball star, that wouldn't be real" (lines 32 & 34).

Even though things were confusing at times, I think that students benefited from these sessions and my explanations. Again, it helped them think more about the complex nature of writing. For example, at the end of the session (discourse not included in Example 2), Jorge jumped in to state that his text was nonfiction. When I asked why he thought that, he said that it was because he saw a fish in Acapulco like the one in his book. I argued that it couldn't because his fish had a shiny nose because the fish's mother ate a worm from outer space when she was pregnant. I suggested that maybe the fish looked like the one he had seen, but that he had developed a whole complicated story about this fish. Then, when I once again asked Jorge if that story was real, he persisted that it was "in his head." I agreed with that it could be real in his head, but asked if it had actually happened. He finally admitted that he couldn't say that, but he also worked to be sure to leave open the possibility that he believed that it *could* happen.

I think my challenges were good for Jorge (and the other students in Example 2). I also believe that his (and other children's) challenges were useful for me, forcing me to try to articulate clearly, including various examples to make the points I was trying to make. The whole class was riveted while Jorge and I went back and forth getting more specific in our reasoning as we went. Several other children occasionally interjected their points of view or further questions, which enriched the discussion more. This discussion, like others, again made me reflect on the developmental issues and the importance of taking into account students' ability to conceptualize different genres of writing when their understanding of the difference between reality and fantasy is still fluid.

FINAL THOUGHTS

I took a maternity leave in the middle of February and came back to the classroom 12 weeks later, about 6 weeks before the end of the school year. When I left, the substitute teacher indicated to me that she would not be including the kinds of writing activities I implemented. Therefore, I set aside the story books (and the journals) that the children had written. Students were so excited when I gave those books back to them on my return. I asked them to take a look at them to see if they wanted to change or add anything. Students reread their old work to their peers, often changing spelling and adding words, so they began to revise, if only at a low level. Perhaps all of our sessions on audience feedback and revision were starting to sink in.

The students had always been very social; they loved working together. Some groups got more done than others did, but I could see how they thrived. Their collaboration often took different forms. Some children wrote a piece together, although one of them once commented to me that "writing with another person was really hard." Many took advantage of the opportunity to work together to solve mechanical aspects of writing, and of spelling in particular. Some of them were better spellers and the children were aware of their different levels of expertise in this area. Some took the role of editors; others liked to become the illustrator of someone else's piece. I am not sure they worked together as well as I had envisioned in terms of the kind of feedback that they were able to provide to each other, or in the ways they understood what to do with it, but the most amazing thing was to witness their growth as writers. That same student who had announced her inability to write so categorically at the beginning of the school year now composed stories with others, and explained what and how to do it to less skilled students. These children were still struggling with many aspects of learning to write, but they had certainly become authors!

Thus, I have learned that treating students as authors—even though they aren't exactly sure of it themselves—is crucial. I also believe that making opportunities to have explicit talk about the meanings expressed in their writing is significant, even though it might be an ongoing struggle for a teacher to come up with the right measure of explanation in these sessions. Even though students' understandings or developmental ability to make sense of the explanation may lag somewhat, the exposure to the kind of discourse and terminology I offered them is the very kind of cognitively challenging talk that is sometimes absent from classrooms with a high percentage of students from low-income, cultural-minority families. Teachers must take the risk if they want students to take a risk themselves in looking at their writing more critically.

ABOUT THE AUTHOR

I have taught in the CPSS for many years. I left for 1 year to live and teach in a private bilingual school in Cuernavaea, Mexico.

My teaching career began in Vermont when I studied in the teacher education program at Prospect School and Center for Higher Education, a unique program that combined a year-long internship in the Prospect

School (a progressive school with a multiage, activity-based curriculum) with intensive site-based coursework in the history and philosophy of education and in methodologies.

I currently teach first grade at Inter American Magnet School, a dual language (Spanish and English) program where I have been fortunate to be able to combine my interest in children and teaching with my love of languages. I am also the parent of Abraham, who is a preschooler and who relishes books, language play, and stories as much as I do.

DEDICATION

To Abraham.

Chapter 7

Creating Safety Zones in Reading Aloud to Empower Second Graders as Readers

Hawa Jones
Jungman Elementary School

EDITORS' COMMENTS

This was Hawa's first year teaching second graders, and she was having troubles of adjustment. Many students didn't seem to be that interested in reading and her inquiry was to turn this around—to provide *safety zones* in her read-alouds so that her students would participate more in reading and would become critical readers.

She describes her early management difficulties as she tried to create contexts where students' voices were encouraged and heard, as well as covers the many successes that she and her students achieved in her inquiry. She also talks about the ongoing monitoring strategies she developed to track students' contributions. Then, at the end, she discusses how her new way of reading aloud led to student-run read-alouds that encouraged parent involvement in their children's reading.

The introduction chapter of this book provides the theoretical and methodological background for the larger collaborative school–university action-research project and this chapter about Hawa's inquiry on read-alouds.

University researchers, Shannon Hart and Diane Escobar, collaborated with Hawa in her inquiry.

113

BACKGROUND TO MY INQUIRY

The fall of the 1994–1995 school year began unusually hot and humid. Irritability and lack of responsiveness were reflected in the behavior of my second graders. Much reading time consisted of my being seated at my desk, dryly reading aloud, as my students sat wearily at their desks, barely keeping their eyes open. I felt I was a major problem, but did not know what to do.

I had taught fourth grade for 4 years at Jungman, but this was my first year teaching second grade. This was a challenge for me because many of my students were emergent readers, as opposed to the fourth graders who had come to me as experienced readers. I felt that I needed to do something quickly to get my students even interested in reading. I asked for ideas from my colleagues as to how I could get my students involved more into reading. They gave me lots of advice, which ranged from my using a more animated voice when I read to them, to using round-robin style reading, to having students hear stories on audio cassettes. I tried all of them, but all met with various degrees of failure. Because many of my Latina and Latino students were also ESL learners, the routine of my students taking turns to stumble over the words, as they tried to read one or two paragraphs at a time, ended up as a very long and drawn out process. All of this was causing even more listlessness in the students.

One day I was in the teacher's lounge and began to tell one of my colleagues, Sue Jacobson, about how second grade was more difficult than I had realized. She suggested that I join the teacher-researcher group at the school and think about how I could study how I might motivate my students' reading. In the beginning, the focus of my inquiry was pretty vague, but I did begin with the decision that whatever I came up with would involve using quality children's literature. Because I was new at second grade, I had to do some work finding good titles that would get my students addicted to reading. As I visited local libraries and book stores, I discovered that there were all kinds of children's literature available in a wide array of genres for this grade level. I spent numerous hours in the children's literature sections of the library and book stores reading and taking notes. I began to share these ideas with my students and we brainstormed and drew up many webs to identify books of all of our interests that could be read aloud.

I began, also, to get more clear about the purpose of my inquiry. I wanted my students to take more ownership for their reading experiences. I wanted them to feel empowered during our read-aloud sessions by initiating questions, responding to each others' comments, as well as giving me feedback about what I might bring up. Before, when I read to my students, they were quiet, and then I would just ask them to answer some literal, yes and no questions to "check" their comprehension. Now I wanted to promote critical readers. I hoped that if my students knew that they were allowed to say anything during the read-aloud time, then reading might become more of a part of their lives. Thus, I wanted reading to become a safe zone for them where anything was possible.

EARLY DIFFICULTIES WITH PROCESS AND MANAGEMENT

One first step in my inquiry was changing where we did the read-alouds. I called my students to the carpeted reading area that is located in the southwest corner of the room. They were surprised by this change and there were some rocky times getting there and then back to their desks afterwards. There were problems once we got to the carpet, too, because they had not ever had a time before where we all sat together. There was a transition time when they had to learn not to fool around with the books that are housed there, and to respect each other's space.

I began to encourage the children to speak up during the read-alouds, to interrupt my reading to bring up their ideas. For example, I stopped and asked them if they had questions about a page, or about what I had just read. I really wanted everyone to participate, so I said things such as, "I want to hear from you today," or "I want to hear what everybody is saying." {Fieldnotes, 10/17/94}

Quite soon many students participated in the discussions. Then, that became a big management problem for me. Everyone was trying to talk at once and no one could hear anything. We discussed this issue in one of teachers' meeting in the middle of October. Someone suggested that I might consider a counting, nomination system, which I decided to try. Example 1 is an excerpt from my reading of *Mufaro's Beautiful Daughters* (Steptoe, 1987), which is one of the first times I used this technique I called the *1, 2, 3, routine*. When there was more than one student who wanted to share or initiate a comment, I called out a number to represent the sequence in which I saw them raising their hands, indicating their turns.

This book is about two beautiful daughters, Manyara and Nyasha, who go to meet a great king, hoping that one of them might be chosen for his queen. At different times in the discussion, students voted or predicted which daughter—the "bad" or "good" sister, as they called them—would end up being successful in this goal. Example 1 begins with my reading the part of the book where Manyara, the bad girl, met an old woman, who tried to give the girl some advice.

Example 1

1   Hawa: … THE OLD WOMAN SPOKE. "I WILL GIVE YOU SOME AD-
                  VICE, MANYARA. SOON AFTER YOU PASS THE PLACE WHERE
                  TWO PATHS CROSS, YOU WILL SEE A GROVE OF TREES.
                  THEY WILL LAUGH AT YOU. YOU MUST NOT LAUGH IN RE-
                  TURN. LATER, YOU WILL MEET A MAN WITH HIS HEAD

UNDER HIS ARM. YOU MUST BE POLITE TO HIM." "HOW DO YOU KNOW MY NAME? HOW DARE YOU ADVISE YOUR FUTURE QUEEN? STAND ASIDE, YOU UGLY OLD WOMAN!" MANYARA SCOLDED, AND THEN RUSHED ON HER WAY WITHOUT LOOKING BACK.
[holding up the book for students to see the illustrations, I seem to be addressing a student who might not be attending to the book] Tara, I hope that you're enjoying the story.

2	Cf1:	She's not going to be a queen.
3	Hawa:	[still focusing on Tara] It's one of my favorites. You want to see it.
4	Cf1:	She's the bad girl.
....		[Several children are talking at once. A girl in the front row raised her hand, and I called on her, but unfortunately the girl's talk is inaudible.]
5	Cf2:	(... ...)
6	Hawa:	Oh, she might see her sister there already? [Then when two children begin to talk at once, I give each a number] One, two.
7	Cf3:	Have you read that story, but on your own?
8	Hawa:	Yes.
....		[There is more discussion on how many times I have read the book and then I call on Jonathan.]
9	Jonathan:	Um, by the time ... she thought that when she left her sister——left before the sister ... her sister probably left before her ... and she's still going to ... (...) before she took off.
10	Hawa:	Okay. Three, four, five. [assigning turns to three other children by pointing to those with their hands raised] Speak louder so that the people in the back can ah ... hear us ...
....		
11	Hawa:	[I am now at another part of the book, showing another page of the book, and call on a student who has a comment.] Yes?
12	Cm4:	You see that (...) right there?
....		[There is a short interruption as I ask students to listen to their classmates.]
13	Cf5:	[pointing at the picture] You see like that house right there?
14	Hawa:	Right.
15	Cf5:	Maybe she has to go over there.
16	Hawa:	Could this be the——where the king lives? Or the prince?
17	Cs:	Yeah.
18	Cf6:	It looks like it's not far but the (...) line that you could go through, the path....

19	Hawa:	C, are you listening to what she's saying?
20	Cm6:	It looks like a street, Teacher. It looks like a street.
21	Cf6:	You go——you go….
22	Cf5:	Like a path.
23	Hawa:	Like a path, a street.
24	Cf5:	And the other girl didn't——the other girl didn't.
25	Hawa:	(…), Can you hear what she's saying up here? If you three have something to share, please share with all of us.
26	Cf2:	And the other girl, she's not going to know where the prince lives.
27	Hawa:	Vera, I haven't heard from you. Maria, I haven't heard from you today.
28	Cm4:	Maybe the evil sister probably took the wrong path.
29	Hawa:	She took the wrong path?
30	Cs:	Yeah.
31	Hawa:	Okay, maybe.

{Fieldnotes, Videotape, 10/24/94}

You can see my use of the counting system in the beginning of the example, as well as at other times later on. I also addressed process or management issues at other times, for example, when I asked students to talk louder or to listen better to their classmates. There was also an interest in whether I had read the book on my own and how many times I had read it. I think that was due to the fact that I am an African American and children thought I somehow especially liked the book because it was an African folk tale.

Anyhow, you can see that, because I was dealing with these process problems so much, I didn't spend effort on responding to student comments. I did check what students had said a couple of times, letting them know that I was accepting them. Also, when students tried to figure out the paths in the illustration, I extended C5's idea by suggesting that path might lead to the king. Towards the end, different children considered different ideas about these paths. In line 26, C2 thinks that the good girl might have taken the wrong path, and therefore may not get to the prince, and in line 28, C4 thinks that the evil sister might have taken the wrong path. Many students seem to agree with this latter possibility, which I do too, but I seem to do it tentatively.

Thus, I felt successful in getting many students participating in the read-alouds, but this led to management problems for me. However, I was also learning how to resolve them, but seemed to be caught up too much with these process issues. Better collaborative talk would occur as I began to figure this out, that is, to be better able to address the content or meanings of what students said. This is where I could add my expertise and my ideas to extend their ideas.

SEEING OUR WAY CLEAR: COLLABORATING ON CONTENT

Students became more and more comfortable in offering their own questions and comments—we were indeed creating safety zones to become critical readers. This was apparent in the next example when I was reading the story *How I Captured a Dinosaur* (Schwartz, 1989). As I read the book, Jorge asked a question that began a discussion about the fate of dinosaurs.

Example 2

1	Jorge:	Why are there no dinosaurs here in this time?
2	Hawa:	Why do you think?
3	Jorge:	They ate everything there was and so they died.
4	Hawa:	I'm not going to tell you the answer because if I do, you won't be interested in it. Instead I'm going to bring in some books for you to find out for yourself. Why does anybody else think there aren't any dinosaurs here?
5	Emmaual:	There's a time to live and a time to die.
6	Donia:	Yes, he said it was time for them to die.
7	C1:	Maybe because they were killing others so they died.
8	C2:	Maybe because we were born.
9	Hawa:	Maybe we, people, were born so the dinosaurs had to die?
10	C2:	[nods agreement]
11	Hawa:	Hmmm, that's an interesting idea.
12	C3:	The rock hit the earth and there was a fire and they died.
13	Hawa:	Remember what you're saying, so when we do our research you can see if you were right.
14	Jorge:	Teacher, I know why dinosaurs—that a meteor hit Earth and they went extinct.
15	C4:	What's "extinct"?
16	Jorge:	Dead.
17	Hawa:	No more, gone forever and ever.
		{Fieldnotes, 11/03/94}

Jorge posed the questions about why dinosaurs do not exist now, which I used to set up as an inquiry for him and others who would be interested in pursuing it. When I asked him what he thought the answer to his question was, he thought it was because they ate everything. Then, as I opened it up for other ideas, several students gave interesting hypotheses—from Emmauel's simple statement that it was just time for them to die, to ideas that the dinosaurs had killed each other off, that people had been born and that situation somehow caused the death of dinosaurs, and that a rock hit the Earth causing a fire that ultimately did them in. Then, apparently sparked by the latter idea, Jorge remembered a television show about dinosaurs and offered a revision of what he had earlier said. He then built on C3's statement by suggesting that a meteor caused them to be extinct.

All of this critical thinking about the ideas of books occurred more frequently because I learned better how to share my authority during read-alouds by providing spaces for my students to initiate their own responses to books. Students were talking to each other more, too—for example, when C4 asked Jorge what *extinct* meant, he then answered. This does not mean that I didn't have an important role to play in these discussions. I nudged Jorge to think about an answer to his question; I made sure that checked and clarified C2's contribution about people being born. Finally I built on Jorge's definition of extinct, adding that dead meant that dinosaurs were "no more, gone forever and ever." Thus, I paid more attention to content, and shared my teacher expertise in our talk.

Another major way that my students and I collaborated in the read-alouds was when *intertextual links* were made. These occur when students connect other books, songs, movies, prior curricular information they had studied, personal stories from their homes or communities, and so forth, with the book we are reading. In Example 3 I had been reading *The Vanganee and the Tree Toad* (Ardema & Weiss, 1983) when I noticed that a boy had a comment.

Example 3

1	Cm1:	Why does he have to (...)?
2	Hawa:	Why does....
3	Cm1:	[pointing to the picture] The——whatever it is.
4	Cf2:	Toad.
5	Hawa:	Yeah, why does the toad have to sing?
6	Scs:	Or else they won't go to sleep.
7	Hawa:	They won't go to sleep. Oh, Clarissa, Clarissa. Maybe Clarissa will have some answers.
8	Clarissa:	The frog looks like the book——the book that last we read——that we read last time.
9	Hawa:	*The Lion and the*....

10	Cf3:	No, *The Mouse and the Toad.*
11	Hawa:	*The Frog and the Toad?*
12	Cf3:	*The Horse and the*....
13	Clarissa:	*The Horse and the Dog.*
14	Hawa:	Ok, Clarissa, you made a connection there. Good thinking....
		{Fieldnotes, Videotape, 3/21/95}

Initially, a student asked why the toad was singing in the book. As I had done in the previous example, I turned this question back to the students. Some students suggested that it was because it was because "they won't go to sleep." Then in line 8 Clarissa brought up that the frog was like another book we had read. Then several of the students and I tried to identify what book that was. I really valued those connections, so that's why I told Clarissa that she had "good thinking" on that connection.

Example 4 shows another intertextual link. This time I brought it up, but it happened because I was building on a student initiation having to do with certain wordings used in the book *Magnet Magic* (Adams, Mitchner, & Johnson, 1987).

Example 4

1	Hawa:	[I am in the middle of reading the book] "LET'S SEE. IT'S SOMEWHERE ON THIS TABLE," SAID MR. SMITH. HE STARTED MOVING THINGS ALL AROUND. "OH, HERE IT IS," HE CRIED. HE HELD UP SOMETHING SHAPED LIKE THE LETTER U.
2	Cf1:	Teacher, why did he cry?
3	Hawa:	Why did he cry?
4	Cm2:	[laughs]
5	Hawa:	Cm2, why are you laughing?
6	Cm2:	Because she said——said——why did he cry?
7	Jeanna:	[putting her hand to her throat with sound coming out of her mouth] He——he like screamed out. Screamed out like crazy. Not cried but screamed.
8	Hawa:	Not cry, like cry, Jeanna's saying. Like when we're writing, you know how I told you sometimes you can use different words to ah.....
9	Jeanna:	You don't have to just put, "I screamed." You could put, "he cried."
10	Hawa:	So it is just an expression.

11	Jeanna:	It's just another word for——it's just another word for um "screamed."
12	Hawa:	"Screamed," okay. Or "I said." Instead of the writer——the author saying, "I said," all the time or, "Mr. Smith said," he said, "he cried."

{Fieldnotes, videotape, 02/02/95}

Cf1's question had to do with why Mr. Smith in the book "cried." So, when I turned the question to everyone, Jeanna told and showed how the author's meaning was really "screamed." That's when I came up with my intertextual connection—tying in an earlier minilesson in writing where I tried to show students that their stories might be more interesting if they used other words for "said." So again, my students and I worked to share our knowledge to make new meanings.

Many wonderful intertextual connections occurred when I read the book *Family Pictures/Cuedros de Familia* (Garza, 1990) in January. This book had both English and Spanish text, and I read the English version. This is a book that tells about various traditions or celebrations of the author's family. When I read the part about a birthday party, children told all about how about birthdays were celebrated in their various homes. Also, there were lots of discussions about games that they played when that topic was brought up. The author mentions a game called Cake Walk, with which I was not familiar. Because many of my Latina and Latino students knew it and had even participated in it, they offered explanations of it. It was one where the music starts and you walk around until you stop on a number. If you happen to stop at the right number, you win a cake. Then, two other girls and I thought that it sounded like Musical Chairs. I selected this book to read aloud because I thought it would touch my students' culture, and it did indeed! Students were definitely the experts when we read this book, teaching many things about themselves and their family events and traditions.

STRATEGIES TO MONITOR STUDENTS' CONTRIBUTIONS IN READ-ALOUDS

In my inquiry I learned a lot about good literature to share with second graders. I also learned how to share my power so that our read alouds could be collaborative. We created safety zones to learn from each other and the students became critical readers. I had some rocky times doing this, as I tried to show in the examples. However, overall, my goals of my inquiry led to great success.

I never anticipated that read-alouds would give me so many insights into students' capabilities, but they did. I jotted many of these assessments into the research journal that I kept during the year. Next to the date and the book being read, I noted my interpretations of how every read-aloud went, and also how each of my students contributed to the discussions. To save time, I copied my students' names in the margin of my journal ahead of time, then it was easy for me to write brief comments next to their names. For example, when reading about dinosaurs, my student asked, "If Barney is a dinosaur and dinosaurs are extinct, why is he still alive?" Another student replied, "Remember the theme song, Barney is from our imagination." Thus, I was able to capture memorable contributions of students that were made during read-alouds afterward.

After several months keeping my research journal, I began to review my notes. I detected an interesting pattern. I realized that the children who were engaged during our read-aloud deliberations were the students who were reading more in class and at home. They were participating in buddy reading in their free time, and they were fascinated by books of various genres. This seemed to encourage them to write more about the many things that they read about.

Those who were not participating in the read-alouds, according to my notes, were also not engaged much in the other reading and writing activities in the classroom. When I discovered this, I quietly talked to these students to find out what the problem was and how I might help them to improve their levels of participation during read-aloud time. In my conferences with these nonparticipants, I learned that some were just shy and did not find it comfortable expressing their thoughts in front of a large group; others did not think their English skills were good enough to hold meaningful conversations. I really empathized with them. We worked out a deal where I showed these children the books before I read them to the class. We sort of had a miniread-aloud where I would tell them where I would pause for comments when I read the book the next day. We would then brainstorm ideas of things they could say at these points, and I told them that I would expect to hear their responses the next day. This worked quite well, and students began to participate more and more and as they came to have more self-confidence.

I continue to keep a research journal and I also frequently audiotape my interactions during my reading-alouds and other interactions in the classroom during the years subsequent to this year-long inquiry. Both are valuable tools to assess both the students and myself.

CREATING STUDENT-LED READ-ALOUDS
AND PARENT INVOLVEMENT

Parent involvement, too, became very important as a result of my read-aloud inquiry. I think it started when we began reading several of Tomie dePaola's books. The children really enjoyed these books and made many initiations during our reading of them. They were so excited about this author that some of the students asked their parents to take them to the local library so that they could read more books by him. Also, they began to bring in other books of various genres, and books of the same author, to class to share. It got to the point that we had to change the design of our read-alouds—instead of my reading everyday, two of the days were set aside for their own student-led sessions. Parents had to be involved by helping their children with their reading the night before, if the children were to read in front of the class.

This desire to run their own read-alouds also occurred, I think, because I frequently turned student questions or comments back to the students themselves when I read. Also, besides the 1, 2, 3 system, I started using another technique to handle those occasions when many students wanted to give comments at the same time. I called it the "Share With a Friend" technique, which I had learned from seeing a video featuring a Harlem second-grade teacher. This is where I would just stop the reading and children would talk to someone next to them about their ideas. Also, when students began to read to the whole class, we set up rules that they had to be able to write up open-ended questions for the audience to answer, and also to be prepared to answer any questions that students might ask them as readers. I could not believe that these were same children who had come into my classroom in September, but then, again, I was not the same teacher either. We were all becoming empowered learners!

FURTHER REFLECTIONS

I felt in my inquiry that I was really taking notice of the population of students I was teaching. I *was* serving their needs. I think that children who are in urban classrooms like mine may be struggling to achieve academically, but by no means is it because they are not intelligent. I certainly witnessed that when I shared my power with my students, they became more involved in their own learning. I am extremely proud of myself because my inquiry made a difference in my teaching. I think urban teachers like me have to empower themselves with strong, pragmatic teaching approaches that allow for students' input. Students can provide us with so much information as to what they know if we use more holistic ways to teach. I discovered this when I shared my power with my children. Teachers have the power to be in charge, but when we do share, something wonderful happens to students. They create safety zones that foster critical and empowered readers.

ABOUT THE AUTHOR

I am originally from Liberia, in western Africa. I enjoy living in the United States because of the freedom I have here. I have four sisters, and am married with one child. I enjoy sewing, reading, and "shopping."

I always wanted to teach. I grew up with teachers. My father taught school for a while before he went into the medical field, and my Aunt Ella is also a teacher.

I hope when you read my chapter, you realize that I enjoyed working on my inquiry. My students were the real heroes in it—they were the ones who became in charge!

DEDICATION

With love to my understanding husband, Ray, and my sweet daughter, Rayna. To my beloved parents, Joseph and Maggie Vincent. To my cherished sisters, Yeama, Kona, Nyandabeh, and Margaret, and to Leslie, who is also like a sister to me.

REFERENCES

Aardema, V., & Weiss, E. (1983). *The Vanganee and tree toad.* New York: Puffin Books.

Adams, P., Mitchner, C. P., & Johnson, V. (1987). *Magnet magic.* Cleveland, OH: Modern Curriculum Press.

Garza, A. L. (1990). *Family pictures/Cuardros de familia.* San Francisco: Children's Book Press.

Schwartz, H. (1989). *How I captured a dinosaur.* New York: Orchard.

Steptoe, J. (1987). *Mufaro's beautiful daughters.* New York: Lothrop, Lee, & Shepard.

Chapter 8

Fostering Second Graders' Participation in Literacy Activities Around a Novel Study

Renuka L. Mehra
Andersen Elementary School

EDITORS' COMMENTS

Renuka's teaching practices, and her inquiry, were influenced by her own educational experiences as a child. Student participation and collaboration with others were important goals as she attempted to set up various literacy activities for a novel study. After her first missteps, she used read-alouds, reader response journal writing, and small-group extension activities as ways for students to respond to a novel study of *Ramona Quimby, Age 8*.

Renuka provides examples of all three to explain her efforts in creating these three routines for her students, who were very diverse in their literacy understandings. In doing so, she illustrates both her successes and her vulnerabilities in fostering her students' participation in these experiences.

The introduction chapter of this book provides the theoretical and methodological background for the larger collaborative school–university action-research project and this chapter about Renuka's inquiry on collaboration in reading.

University researchers, Jane Liao and Dian Ruben, collaborated with Renuka in her inquiry.

PERSONAL ROOTS

The way I teach—including how I attempted to teach in my 1994–1995 year of inquiry—has been influenced by my educational experiences as a child. I went to school in India, and in ninth grade I even failed. Since then, I thought about this experience and am still trying to answer the why of this failure. I realized that I did not fail because I lacked the intelligence or ability to read or write. I was an avid writer and reader (except that I was not always a reader of the school's textbooks!). I failed because I was unable to conform to the conventions of that particular education system and its unrealistic requirements. My memory failed me on that annual event known as the final exam. I could not quote or show what I learned from the books I hid inside my textbooks and read on the sly. I could not show the knowledge of endless short stories that had spun off from my readings, logs, and character analyses I had done during recreational reading. The information that I was supposed to memorize at school seemed unrelated and disconnected from my world, and I did not make the effort I was expected to. I also realized that the texts we were supposed to memorize did not enable us to make necessary connections to the world.

Thus, school reading during my childhood, and in ninth grade, was viewed as a process of memorization and regurgitation of what others had said. The assumption was, that if we read and memorized at least portions of the text, we had mastered the basic skills that we needed at that level. We were never encouraged to learn and construct meaning for ourselves from materials that were most relevant to our lives. At that time, I did not have the capability and confidence to understand that one learns from reading per se, not just from reading in order to memorize a text. All of this personal scrutiny, I think, affected my efforts to teach many years later. My present teaching practices are a reaction to those experiences I felt as a child. I don't want my students ever to be treated the way I was taught.

BACKGROUND OF MY INQUIRY

In my second-grade classroom during the 1994–1995 school year, there were 28 students (mostly Latina and Latino children with small number of African Americans). They were clustered and seated in groups of four or five. These groups were heterogeneously formed because I always felt that collaboration encourages us to see others in terms of their potentials. It opens up new possibilities for everyone to work together through a shared process of inquiry. Throughout the day, we engaged in a variety of individual and group activities. This gave students personal time and space to explore their own interests and it also allowed time for interacting with their peers.

This was a far cry from how things were done in the school I attended in India, and I enjoyed the challenges presented to me as a teacher in my school. I realized that teaching required me to be sensitive to the needs of the students. It would be easy to do the same thing year after year, but that does not do my students any justice. Moreover, they are dynamic learners and provide much input in the classroom. A classroom is a "happening" place where I try to have them determine and set the pace for their own learning. I want them all participating.

I frequently had a group of children of diverse ability in my past years of teaching, but nothing was like this year. My inquiry was tied to my desire to hear my students' voices, their participation in reading—even though I had such a range of reading abilities in the class—from very emergent readers to third-grade level. In providing these experiences I also wanted to be sure that I would have opportunities to give my students feedback to sustain and extend their ideas and interpretations of texts.

Unfortunately, my first efforts ended up being a huge misstep. Although I do have a classroom library and have access to the school library for books, I do not have multiple copies of books. At first, I guess I wanted to do some version of group reading similar to literature circles. However, because of the lack of materials, I ended up using basal stories. The stories were okay, but the groups ended up like dreadful, traditional round-robin reading groups, with me acting out a lot of the teacher-directed procedures of these basal manuals.

My vision had been one of collaboration, because this process was important to me. Being grouped, to me did not imply being the same. It meant becoming effective and contributing members. It is a process of learning where individual students can accomplish various tasks by contributing their talents, knowledge, and ideas to a community. It would also mean a reciprocity in the classroom between students and myself. Well, my first attempts were definitely not what I hoped for, so I abandoned this approach for other possibilities.

I subsequently tried three kinds of literacy activities that could realize my goal of high student participation and opportunities for me to meet the needs of my mixed group of readers. Because of what I thought was a failure in my first step, I decided to work with a smaller group of students (18, who were still quite diverse in ability) who remained after 10 students left each day to attend a computer class. I decided that the focus of my new inquiry would be around a novel study of *Ramona Quimby, Age 8* by Beverly Cleary (1981). It seemed relevant to the age group represented in the classroom and I felt it would provoke a significant response from the students. Literature like this book could help my readers discover that others may have the same problems, as well as give life to new meanings. We would have great conversations in which we shared and learned to value others' opinions. I try, in the next section, to describe the trials, tribulations, and successes as I plunged into three major activities of this novel study—creating collaborative read-alouds, reader response journals, and small-group extension projects.

FOSTERING STUDENT PARTICIPATION IN READ-ALOUDS

I read aloud to the students each day. This is important because it provided an opportunity to share our own thoughts about texts; it further established that feeling of community. Also, in this context I was able to model strategies to tackle the reading of a text. By participating in these read-alouds, students learn different ways to refine what they know about responding to text, and they move toward the ultimate goal—becoming reflective and critical readers themselves.

My reading aloud to this smaller group of students, then, was an extra session. During the preceding year, many of our teacher-researcher group studied how to make our read-alouds more collaborative, so that students' voices could be heard, and so that one could respond to their meanings and ideas to sustain and extend them. I think I was becoming pretty successful in that, but was still working on the best ways to accomplish this as I took on the literature study of the *Ramona* book.

I introduced this book on the day that one of the students was celebrating her eighth birthday, which is the same age as the main character in the book. Before I showed them the book, we discussed celebrating birthdays and what it feels like to be a year older. When I showed them the book and read the title, they were excited to find out that a whole book could be written about a kid their age. We mused over the character, I shared some facts about the author, Beverly Cleary, and told them other titles by her.

It was an important ritual for us to sit together on the rug and discuss Ramona. The students seemed to relate to the character whose experiences were similar to their own. For example, she had an older sibling (Beezus) like many in the class, she rode the bus to school (Kenneth was an authority on that), she scraped her knee on the bike when the training wheels were not there (Marisol told us that her dad had just taken off the training wheels from her bicycle and that she too had fallen off her bike), and Ramona's school anecdotes were fascinating to them.

"What Is 'Dreadful' Mean?"

Students eagerly initiated their own comments and questions about the book. They also asked about particular vocabulary words that they didn't know, as Example 1 shows. In this example, I read chapter 6, which is about halfway through the book. It is about an incident where Ramona goes to school not feeling well. She had oatmeal for breakfast, so when she saw the jars of blue oatmeal that housed fruit-fly larvae in the classroom, she began to feel even worse. I interrupted the reading to ask students to predict what they thought would happen, when a student asked, "What is 'dreadful' mean?"

Example 1

1	Renuka:	GO AWAY, BLUE OATMEAL, THOUGHT RAMONA, AND THEN SHE KNEW THE MOST TERRIBLE, HORRIBLE, DREADFUL, AWFUL THING THAT COULD HAPPEN WAS GOING TO HAPPEN. What might that be?....
....		[I then ask this of a particular child, Ana, who does not respond; I then ask the class in general.]
2	Renuka:	What could that possibly, possibly be? That she is thinking something is dreadful ... awful is going to happen.
3	Cm1:	What is "dreadful" mean?
4	Cm2:	She (... ...).
....		
5	Renuka:	What do you think is going to happen to Ramona? (...), what do you think is going to happen? Why don't you help each other here, (...)?
6	Cm:	It's gonna happen for.....
7	Renuka:	Something dreadful she thinks is going to happen.....
8	Cm:	Something bad.
9	Renuka:	And yeah.....
10	Cm1:	Something awful?
11	Renuka:	[reading the text again] AND THEN SHE KNEW THAT {SOMETHING}——THE MOST TERRIBLE, HORRIBLE, DREADFUL, {AND} AWFUL THING THAT COULD HAPPEN WAS ABOUT TO HAPPEN. What was——what might that be? (...).
12	Cf:	Maybe what you just said, that what she thinks will happen *will* happen. Maybe it will happen to her.
13	Cm:	(... ...).
14	Renuka:	What do you think that might be, (...)? What do you think that might be?
15	Cf:	The teacher might call her a nuisance.
16	Renuka:	Oh, again?
17	C:	Again.
18	Renuka:	Do you think that will be awful for Ramona?
19	Scs:	Yeah.
20	Renuka:	I think she is going to feel terrible about that.
....		[There is a student interruption that is dealt with.]
21	Cf:	I think I know why the teacher maybe wants to call her that. Because she said, "go away blue oatmeal" right now.
22	Renuka:	Oh, she's——actually it's——you know what? When you look at——look at the line. [showing the actual print in the book

		and everyone moves in to see the book] Do you see that GO WAY, BLUE OATMEAL? Is that in quotation marks?
23	C:	Yeah. No.
....		[There is a discussion about the fact that there aren't any quotations marks, which includes examining the function of quotation marks versus exclamation marks, and then I return to how to interpret the text that lacks the quotation marks.]
24	Renuka:	When you are saying something. But she's obviously not saying something because I don't see any quotation marks. So what do you think she's doing, "go away, blue oatmeal"?
25	Cs:	(... ...).
26	Renuka:	She's thinking it because see what it says after that. GO AWAY, BLUE OATMEAL....
27	Kenneth:	Let me see it.
28	Renuka:	....THOUGHT RAMONA.
29	Cs:	[Students are all looking at the book, talking at the same time.]
30	Renuka:	Right here. [holding up the book] GO AWAY, BLUE OATMEAL, and there's no quotations marks there, THOUGHT RAMONA. So she's——what is she doing? [pointing to my head]
31	Cm:	Thinking.
32	Ramona:	Okay. Let's see what happens.
		{Videotape, 02/02/95}

I began by asking for predictions of what they thought might happen next, when a student asked the meaning of "dreadful." I sometimes go over vocabulary ahead of time, if I think that it is significant in getting the gist of the text, and I am quite sure that most students would not know it. However I also encouraged my students to ask about words in the book when they seem important to their understanding. As you can see here, someone else in the class usually can come up a good answer (in line 4, which is inaudible, but must have had something to do with bad, as other responses show).

Other parts of Example 1 also show successful ways that I supported students' predictions. For example, in line 15 a student suggested that the dreadful thing that may happen could be that Ramona would be called a nuisance. This is a reasonable idea because in the preceding chapter Ramona overheard her teacher calling her this, and because the title of the chapter we were reading was "Supernuisance." Thus, I accepted this prediction, and then another student (in line 21) tried to provide a good reason for the other girl's idea—"I think I know why the teacher maybe wants to call her that. Because she said 'go away blue oatmeal' right now." I then worked with the students to assess this explanation. I tried to go back to the author's words, even the punctuation, to show how important it is to make predictions and also evaluate them. Thus, in these read-alouds I tried to respond to their ideas in ways that modeled strategies they could use subsequently in their own reading.

Barriers to Participation—Pushing My Agenda Too Much

As I already said, I think I did a good job in fostering student participation and providing useful feedback in Example 1. Sometimes, however, as I reviewed transcripts, I realized that I wasn't always so helpful. In the next two examples, I seemed to push my own agenda too much, trying to get students to get to my "correct" answer. We were reading chapter 2 where Ramona's mother tells Ramona to be nice to Willa Jean, who is the 4-year-old sister of Ramona's friend, Howie. Ramona stayed at their house after school each day until Ramona's parents picked her up. Here I attempted to have students consider a "big problem in the story." To save space, I summarized students' responses in the example and focused more on how I talked to them.

Example 2A

1	Reunka:	AND EVEN THOUGH HER FAMILY UNDERSTOOD, RAMONA STILL DREADED THAT PART OF THE DAY SPENT AT HOWIE'S HOUSE IN THE COMPANY OF MRS. KEMP AND WILLA JEAN. Is that a big problem in the story? So far, does that seem to be a big problem?
2	Cm:	Yes!
3	Renuka:	Yes? Because what? How do you know it's a big part in the story? Or a big problem in the story? How do you know?
....		[Students venture a number of guesses that all seem to answer my question. They say that it's a problem because Ramona has to take care of Willa Jean; that people get tired and can't do that; that Ramona hates to do all the jobs she has to do now that she's 8 and particularly that she has to be nice to Willa Jean. None of these answers seem to satisfy me.]
4	Renuka:	I know she [Ramona] says that but how do we know that it's such a big problem for her? How does the author convey this to us? How does the author convey that to us?
....		[This question again draws responses similar to the ones summarized above——namely, Ramona has a problem about going to Howie's house because she has to take care of people and has to do all the jobs.]
5	Renuka:	[interrupting and shaking my head negatively] You're repeating the same thing I just finished saying, again and again and again. You're not listening. Yes, it is a problem for her, she's already

said that, and so have five others. But how does this author tell us, other than saying that [Ramona] has to take care of Willa Jean? How do we know that this is a big problem of Ramona?

{Videotape, 12/08/94}

In this example I told the students they were not listening, but I think it was more my problem. They were trying to attend to my questions, but I just didn't do a good job in expressing exactly *what* I wanted them to consider. Students were not put off by my approach, though; they continued to persist with their ideas. I just kept taking what they said, but then repeated over and over about the author's craft. Finally, I stated the answer I was hoping that the students would "discover" by saying it myself.

Example 2B

1	Renuka:	How does the author tell us that it's irritating for Ramona to be taking care of Willa Jean? How do we get that message from her?
2	Cm:	Willa Jean——I think Willa Jean is bad and is——she gotta ummmm … tell her how to learn things.
3	Renuka:	Okay. And one time we learning a little bit about Willa Jean's personality, not an easy personality. But does the author bring it up again and again and again?
4	Cs:	Noooooo!
5	Renuka:	From the first chapter to this chapter, how many times have we heard that she does not like Willa Jean? A few times? Is she trying to convey that to us by telling us repeatedly?
6	Cs:	[agreeing with me as they shake their heads in a yes] Yes!
7	Renuka:	Yes. She tells us in about three or four places in one chapter and now we're starting the second chapter and we hear about it again. So she is trying to tell us by writing about it again so that we don't forget what problem it is that Ramona is facing with Willa Jean.

{Videotape, 12/08/94}

I think that my intent here was good—I was again trying to demonstrate a good strategy for them—but this time I just let it go way too long. It is hard to juggle and negotiate the many student responses at the same time. Being aware, however, of the challenges that the last two examples show, I was better able to make my read-alouds ones where all students could feel comfortable in expressing their own questions and ideas, as well as have them hear my ideas to help them be better readers.

HELPING STUDENTS MAKE READING–WRITING CONNECTIONS

To give students more opportunities to respond to the book, I implemented reader-response journals in which they wrote down their comments and ideas. I did this kind of thing before, but it was a very short-term activity for them. I never gave students the responsibility to write after the read-alouds in an ongoing manner. Because of the diverse abilities of my students, I provided them with the prompts, which I changed all the time. Again I thought these journals would allow for everyone's participation, and at the same time would provide me with ways to assess and respond to students individually.

I initially tried small-group discussions in which group members would share their responses, which was something I was learning about in my master's degree program. The format I brought in to extend the reading I hoped would serve a practical (assessment) purpose and a personal purpose (the students' insights). I thought if it worked so well for us in the graduate class, it couldn't possibly go awry in our classroom. The criteria for forming groups for this activity were to include both readers and emergent readers and to have both quiet versus talkative students. I tried out different roles that various students would take, but the roles or jobs themselves became too important, and few good discussions occurred. As the activity progressed, I realized that it was not working well. Thus, I ended up just roving around to students or tables of students as they wrote their responses, meeting with them to support and extend their work. I tried to maximize my time with individual students. I listened, observed, and assisted. I became a participant and shared my ideas about strategies the students could use.

Examples 3 and 4 show my interactions with two students who were at the ends of the developmental continuum regarding their writing skills. We had just read chapter 7, and the prompt that day was to tell the parts of the book that they liked so far. With students having more advanced abilities, I tried to go beyond just identifying a favorite part. In Example 3, for example, Chandra kept just summarizing an event from chapter 2 that related to Ramona's day-care experiences at Howie's house, and I tried to get her to tell *why* she liked it.

Example 3

1	Renuka:	Okay, that's something you want to talk about. What are you going to say about that part? What is it that you liked about that part?
2	Chandra:	When I say....
3	Renuka:	That was the part you liked. What did you like about it?

4	Chandra:	I liked when they're playing dress up, but the mother said, "What are you doing on (...)?" Then Willa Jean said, "Dress up!" And she brought her some clothes and let Ramona have a ripped-up shirt and then the boy have some slippers on so he could <swim> and he had on a suit and her dad's old hat and she had on a dress.
5	Renuka:	And the last part was what?
6	Chandra:	And they were getting married and she said, "Will you marry me?" and then she said, "You have to...."
7	Renuka:	Now you've told me the story, actually you've told me——summarized the story for me. But what was it that you really liked about that part?
....		[The interchange continues with Chandra describing more about the story and my asking yet two more times why she has chosen this part of the story.]
8	Renuka:	But why did you like that part?
9	Chandra:	Because I——I was laughing about when he said that cause he said it funny.
10	Renuka:	He said it funnily? So you liked that part because it was <stated> funny. So you're going to write about, briefly, about the part and then why you liked it, okay?
		{Videotape, 12/08/94}

So, when Chandra continued to summarize her favorite part (which I thought was well expressed), I tried to have her think about her rationale for choosing this part as her favorite part.

Evaluating Different Prompts: Two Examples from Dennis

In Example 4, however, I had to respond differently. Dennis was a student who entered my class as an emergent reader and writer, using mostly invented spelling. Here I simply helped him to write a summary or description of his favorite part.

Example 4

1	Renuka:	Okay, what is it that you're going to write about? The part that you liked best in the story?
2	Dennis:	Willa Jean.
3	Renuka:	Willa Jean? Okay, but what about Willa Jean?
4	Dennis:	Uhmmmm ... The part——here's a story that I did about Willa Jean that I couldn't finish.

....		[Dennis reads haltingly from what he has written. What he reads does not seem to be very coherent and he has difficulty reading it. I have him find words that are familiar to him to facilitate his further reading and then my discussion with him.]
5	Renuka:	Okay, point to some words that would tell me about something about the story. [waiting about 30 seconds while Dennis looks for words]
6	Dennis:	[points to a word]
7	Renuka:	Okay, what's that word?
8	Dennis:	Dad.
9	Renuka:	Okay, what about Dad?
10	Dennis:	The dad came in and says (...) and then he says that he's going to medical school....
11	Renuka:	Okay, that he's going back to school again?
12	Dennis:	[nods affirmatively]
13	Renuka:	Okay. And what was he going to do at school?
14	Dennis:	He was going to be an art teacher.
15	Renuka:	Okay. He was going to be an art teacher. Was that one of your favorite parts though?
		{Videotape, 12/08/94}

Here I tried to help Dennis his writing, which he did with great difficulty. My feedback for him was quite different from that which I gave to Chandra—I followed up by asking if that was really a part that was important to him.

I varied my prompts and some were better than others in eliciting children's ideas. One of the richest journal responses was when I asked students to write about a time they had been punished after we read chapter 4 ("The Quimby's Quarrel"). In this chapter, when Ramona and her sister refused to eat the tongue that their mother made for dinner, their parents told them that they would be responsible for making dinner the next day. At the end of the chapter, the two sisters talked about how this was unfair and tried to think that they might avoid this punishment if they were very good the next day.

At the end of the writing session, we usually shared as a class what the individual students worked on. That day, many wanted to volunteer to read their ideas. I chose six students, and Dennis was the third one to read his journal entry, which is Example 5. Once again he used mostly invented spellings, but this time he could easily read what he wrote, even though it was only about a month or so after the time of Example 4.

Example 5

1 Dennis:	[beaming and looking pleased with himself] I did both things. [meaning both parts of the assignment, writing about his experience being punished and making a prediction for the next chapter]
2 Renuka:	You did both things? Oh, wonderful, Dennis, oh!
3 Dennis:	Should I read both?
4 Renuka:	Yeah, please!
5 Cm:	Yeah, Dennis!
6 Dennis:	[reading word by word, pausing briefly between each word, but reading fluently without repeating or misreading the words] THE LAST TIME I WAS PUNISHED THAT WAS IN NOVEMBER AND I WAS PUNISHED FOR BEING BAD IN SCHOOL AND I COULDN'T PLAY MY NINTENDO.
7 Renuka:	How did you feel about that?
8 Dennis:	Um, I felt sad and I was crying.
9 C:	#I cried.#
10 C:	#I cried.#
11 C:	#I never cry!#
12 Renuka:	#Did you think about what you need to do about (...).# Sh—h—h! I cannot hear Dennis, but I hear other voices! [redirecting my attention to Dennis] Yes?
13 Dennis:	Um, I couldn't play with nothing because I was put on punishment. And then I had to sit down so I couldn't play with none of my toys. I couldn't watch TV. (... ....) I think that the fifth one [fifth chapter] is going to be about the good Sunday [title is "Extra-good Sunday"] and they may not fight no more.
14 Cs:	[agreeing and appearing to cheer him on] Yes!
15 Renuka:	So you're thinking about a day when they don't fight. [sounding very impressed] That's very good, Dennis, for thinking of that.
	{Fieldnotes, videotape, 01/19/95}

Everyone supported and cheered Dennis on about his work this day. Although the prompt I had given the children was not one that explicitly asked them to connect their own punishments and those of the characters, it did have them think about their own punishments as Ramona did in the book. Thus, this prompt was very effective in allowing for *all* of the students to be successful in expressing their responses. As I reviewed my data in my inquiry, I became aware how student participation was tied to the kind of prompt I chose.

PARTICIPATING IN SMALL-GROUP CULMINATING ACTIVITIES

All of us have the need to make sense of, and then communicate, the meaning of what read to others. Each student, as a reader, interpreted the book his or her way, and the culminating extension activities of the book offered another opportunity to see each other's perspectives. Thus, these culminating activities were important events, not only because they showed students that the possibilities in presenting a book could be endless, but also because they brought everything we had worked on toward a neat whole or toward a memorable closure to our novel study.

As a community, the process of collaborating, participating, and sharing was always an ongoing issue. We continually negotiated the meaningfulness of working together. Also, by now, we (myself and my student teacher at the time) had ample opportunities to observe students engaged in reading, discussions, and writing activities; we were familiar with their strengths and weaknesses. In forming the small groups, we took some risks and hoped that any glitches would smooth themselves out if everyone was given an equal opportunity to perform tasks in groups. It would have been the most democratic to let students form their own groups, but there are some pros and cons associated with that process—there would always be some students left out of the process, some groups would be too large and unmanageable, and some groups would not be diverse enough in their membership.

Thus, I formed the four small groups of 3–4 members, but the students brainstormed various project ideas. We ended up with four possibilities, and a member from each group picked from a hat to decide which activity they would be involved in and perform—a poem, TV show, puppet show, or play. Students debated and decided what and how they would present the activity. Many hours were spent to get the groups started and to keep them going to accomplish their tasks.

For space reasons, I focus on the poem group. Although this group ended up doing a wonderful performance, which you will see, it also was perhaps the most vulnerable group regarding issues of collaboration and participation. It highlighted my struggles regarding my role in their group dynamics as well.

The Poem Group

I wanted these small groups to be student directed as much as possible. The poem group consisted of four members: Dennis and Tomas, who were very beginning readers and writers, and Angel and Marisol, who had higher abilities in literacy. Initially, in creating their poem, students wanted to limit their focus to one chapter, but when members disagreed on what chapter that would be, they ended up considering multiple chapters in their writing. During the very first session, I asked the students of the group about how they were planning to write the poem. When there was no response, Dennis talked about the part he would play in reciting the poem, but I reinforced the group nature of the project.

When I heard that they were going to look at the whole book, I suggested that they reread chapters and come up with some main points that could be incorporated in their poem. Unfortunately, my suggestion led to very little collaboration within the group for a period of time. The two more academically skilled members had to do much of this work. In spite of their persistence and good ideas, Dennis and Tomas often seemed to be ignored and ostracized by Angel and Marisol. Another problem was that the group decided that they wanted their poem to rhyme, yet they had major difficulties in doing that. Example 6 shows one of my efforts to help on this front. Dennis suggested that they take a look at the main ideas they had written down and then come up with a rhyme for them. In the excerpt, I tried to get them to think about what word could rhyme with "eight" to go with the first line, "Ramona Quimby, Age 8."

Example 6

1	Renuka:	What's the word that you want to rhyme with "eight"?
2	Tomas:	She was eight years old?
3	Cs:	Ummmm. [all appear to be thinking]
4	Renuka:	Oh, I can think of some.
5	Cs:	What?
6	Renuka:	But I'm not telling you. You tell me.
7	Angel:	[smiles]
8	Dennis:	Eight?
9	Angel:	<Six.>
10	Renuka:	[bringing my fingers to my ear and then drawing them away as I speak] Rhyming words mean words that sound similar.
11	Angel:	Eight, eight....
12	Renuka:	It's like "cat," "hat," "mat," "pat," "rat." All those sound similar.
13	Angel:	"Ate," "eat," (...)....
14	Renuka:	#No-oo, "eat" and "eight" don't rhyme. And you decided that your group wants a rhyming poem, right?#
15	Dennis:	#"Cat" ... ... "hat" ... ... "at"....#
16	Angel:	Yeah.
17	Renuka:	How about I help you with one line and then you go for it yourself. And I don't know if I can come up with this. You have to help me. "Ramona Quimby, Age 8, Never came to school late."

18	Angel:	#[begins to write] What is it again? [looking at me]#
19	Dennis:	#[rests his chin on his hand on the desk, putting his head close to Angel's arm to get a look at the paper that is nearly covered by Angel]#
20	Renuka:	Never ... came ... to ... school ... late. That's how you got it? "Never come to school ... late." Now what should the next line be? Did she meet somebody on the bus?
21	Cs:	Yeah.
22	Renuka:	Another word that rhymes with "late." Do you know another word?....
23	Angel:	"Eight"? "Eight"?
24	Dennis:	(... ...)
25	Renuka:	Do you know another word?
26	Angel:	"Eight"?
27	Renuka:	Another word for "friend." Do you know another word for "friend"?
28	Angel:	Ummm.
29	Renuka:	Because who does she meet on the bus?
30	Angel:	That kid.
31	Renuka:	Who.....
32	Dennis:	#Ummmm.#
33	Angel:	#Danny.#
34	Dennis:	The one they called the super foot.
35	Renuka:	Okay. Let's see, "Ramona Quimby, Age 8, Never came to school late" ... ummmm. "On the bus, she met a mate."
36	Tomas:	A "mate"?
37	Renuka:	A "mate." Means it's a friend. Okay. Now ... I'm leaving you to that. I did my part, which got that started. Now all you're doing is writing this because that's going to take a while. We already have a clue right here. This is telling us what those chapters are about. Take those and use one line to say something about them ... in a poem. And use that rhyming. Stick to that.

{Videotape, 03/15/95}

I realized in retrospect that, although the group members decided to have the poem rhyme, keeping to that when they found it so hard made it feel too much like a teacher-directed assignment for them. Little progress occurred on the poem until they came to know that they need not have this rhyming constraint.

However, once the group finished its poem and members began to work on their performance, more equal participation occurred in the group. Here is their final poem:

Ramona Quimby age 8

Never came to school late

After school she went to Howie's house

She played dress up

Willa Jean wants Ramona to be a dog

The next day Ramona went to school

She got a egg in her lunch box

She tried to crack the egg everywhere

But she cracked it in her hair

When Ramona heard that Ms. Whaley said, she was a nuisance

It hurt her feelings

Then Ramona was mad at her mom for giving her a raw egg

When they were cooking they made a mess

And they looked in the frigerator

But they forgot the butter

Ramona thought that the terrible, horrible, dreadful,

awful thing was going to happen

And then the terrible, horrible, dreadful, awful, thing happened—RAMONA THREW UP!

Students decided they wanted a larger audience than just the class, so they wrote and delivered invitations to the principal, a computer teacher, other second graders, and a special education class. Our classroom was buzzing with activity. During the actual presentation, members of the poem group were introduced by Dennis, who said, "'Ramona Quimby Age 8' … Just watch and act like you're at home. Marisol, Tomas and this is me. Angel is absent and the group requests someone to come forward to say his part."

After the introduction, members read and played out each designated part of the poem. Tomas showed pictures as he recited (very quickly), Marisol zipped through her part, and then Dennis, the African-American member of the group, said his part to a rap beat (his own innovation). Finally the whole group ended in a chorus by saying, "RAMONA THREW UP!"

CONCLUSIONS

When I looked back at that year it seemed incredible how much we learned from each other. Every step was challenging and exciting. We did a lot that year. We incorporated extended discussions around reading and writing. I tried to give glimpses of the three major ways I tried to have students be active participants in our novel study. In the read-alouds I encouraged all of their voices—their own questions and comments. In their reader response journals students could participate again by writing to my prompts, which we then shared as a group. Finally, in the culminating, extension, small-group projects, students had another opportunity to participate and negotiate with others regarding their interpretations of the book. Also, in all three activities I had many occasions to model strategies for my diverse learners, which was an important goal in my study. As Vygotsky (1978) asserted, and I tried to keep in mind, everything children can do with help one day, they can do by themselves another day.

Although I think all three of these activities were very successful in promoting my students' learning overall, I also tried to show some of the rocky parts in my teacher research. As a teacher, it is so tempting to impose and create a classroom that suits me just fine. Instead, I tried to facilitate, observe, and be an active participant *with* the students in my inquiry enterprise.

ABOUT THE AUTHOR

I was born in the United States of Indian parents. I am the second of four girls. My parents returned to India shortly after my birth so that my elementary and secondary school education was completed there. I returned to the United States when I was 20. I completed my undergraduate degree in education at the University of Illinois, Chicago, and recently finished my master's degree at Northeastern Illinois University. All of my teaching has been at Andersen. I am currently the Reading Coordinator at Andersen.

DEDICATION

To my family.

REFERENCES

Cleary, B. (1981). *Ramona Quimby, age 8*. New York: Avon.
Vygotsky, (1978). *Mind in society: The development of higher psychological processes*. Cambridge, MA: Harvard University Press.

Chapter 9

It Is Never Too Late to Change! Rethinking Read-Alouds for Third Graders

Dorothy A. O'Malley
Formerly at Jungman Elementary School

EDITORS' COMMENTS

Dorothy's teacher inquiry involved studying her third-grade students' responses to multicultural literature. However, for her to understand her students' understandings of their own ideas about these books, she had to study her own beliefs about what she felt were her teacher responsibilities. This meant changing her teaching practices after many years of teaching.

We think you will enjoy her candid story of this journey as she shares examples of discussions around her reading aloud of various multicultural literature books. She examines the ways in which she poses questions to her students; she explores the ways in which she and the students offered intertextual links with the books they read.

The introduction chapter of this book provides the theoretical and methodological background for the larger collaborative school–university action-research project and this chapter about Dorothy's inquiry on the reading aloud of multicultural literature.

University researchers, Shannon Hart and Diane Escobar, collaborated with Dorothy in her inquiry.

I was a teacher for the Chicago Public Schools for more than 20 years. My life has revolved around my large family, and many family events were frequently reorganized because of my teacher obligations. I truly love my profession and I take my teacher responsibilities very seriously. I once thought that these responsibilities included: imparting knowledge to my students, making sure to take the time to repeat and revise my instruction until most of my students had learned it; covering grade-level curriculum; respecting my students and expecting their respect in return—in the guise of a quiet, orderly, noncollaborative classroom setting; being a role model in both word and action; and being actively involved in school and community programs.

An additional self-imposed responsibility is that it is important to continue to grow as a person, as well as a professional. I believe that growth comes through change. You change, I think, when you put yourself in learning situations. This principle led to my joining the teacher-researcher group at Jungman. Even though I ended up retiring from teaching the year after my inquiry, this teacher research caused me to rethink some of the tenets of my profession mentioned in the first paragraph. Thus, my title, "It Is Never Too Late to Change ..." is a banner for my change and for other teachers who might be in a similar place in their professional lives.

BACKGROUND OF MY INQUIRY

Because I used thematic units as a method of teaching, which I learned many years ago from my teacher-education program, I was of the opinion initially that I need not make any drastic changes to my teaching methodology. I came to realize, however, that a whole-language perspective, which many teachers at my school were attempting to implement, is not a *method* of teaching, is not just using thematic units, but is a philosophy of education.

During the years since 1989 I gradually began to look at my teacher responsibilities in a different light as I participated in various in-service activities, as well as in routinely scheduled staff, grade level, and subject-area meetings. I participated in the teacher-researcher group when it first began. We teachers had opportunities to both bare our souls and to pick the brains of colleagues, while we examined issues about teaching and learning.

Because whole language philosophy argues that students come to school with prior knowledge from many learning experiences, not as empty vessels just waiting to be filled, I began to listen to my students more attentively. I began to hear and to take notice of what they knew, what they wanted to share, and also what they seemed most interested in. Just thinking about this made me realize that changes were going to have to take place in my classroom. Perhaps memorization and repetition of lessons were not always appropriate. Perhaps respect for me and others could still be shown, even when students are allowed to share their ideas more freely. Perhaps there even should be more peer coaching and collaborative activities going on in my classroom.

During the spring preceding my year of inquiry, I convinced my principal to put bilingual Mexican students (those whose first language is Spanish) as well as monolingual Mexican students (those whose first language is English) in my upcoming third-grade class. (Until then, I had mostly monolingual students.) I began to think about "Homelands" as one of my themes for my language arts program for that next year. I received a grant to purchase more multicultural literature to enhance the curriculum. In the fall of 1994, I chose as my inquiry to investigate my read-alouds of this literature. I was specifically interested in students' responses to these books and how these book-sharing experiences (and extension activities of these readings) might enhance their English language development more generally. Because I acquired many books having Latina and Latino themes, I also hoped that my sharing of them would give my students knowledge about, and a sense of pride in, their cultural roots—their homelands.

THE SHAKY BEGINNINGS OF MY READ-ALOUD INQUIRY

My teaching day always included read-alouds. My purposes varied: to provide a wrap up of the day, to fill time waiting for a resource teacher to arrive, and to furnish a quiet and a relaxing time for my students. However, as I embarked on my inquiry, I wanted read-alouds to begin to take on a more important and different place in the daily curriculum. Unfortunately, in the beginning I still expected my students to sit and listen attentively. I still rarely asked their opinions of the selection read, or allowed any time for reflection or discussion. I asked all of the questions, listened to students' responses, and then evaluated them to determine if their answers were correct. I was perfectly satisfied that these first steps would lead to a good learning experience. I clung to my old ways.

As time went on and I began to reflect more about the questions on my chosen inquiry, I realized that if my goal was to try to understand *my students'* responses to the literature read, I would have to implement changes. I started by asking for my students' ideas on how they would like to respond to the literature. This ended up including a range of extension activities—the use of pantomime, art, drama, retelling, and small discussions. I also accepted the fact that perhaps, at times, they might not like to respond at all, but how was I going to alter how I was structuring the read-alouds?

Even though I was committed to try other practices, it was still very difficult after more than 20 years thinking and doing based on a different set of beliefs. It was always important for me to see growth in my students, and I guess I thought that this was due to how my methods met their needs. I always concentrated on change of method or change in student, but never a change *in* me. It never occurred to me to review my beliefs or my teacher responsibilities, as I saw them, and to consider alternatives. For example, I could look at sharing some of my teacher responsibilities with my students. I could listen carefully and follow through on some of their ideas. Thus, my inquiry began to concern how to accomplish this new agenda when I read aloud to my students.

In the rest of the paper I share examples from my reading of four books to illustrate the nature of my journey to conduct read-alouds in a new way—by my trying to better hear students' responses.

READING-ALOUD IN A NEW WAY: *ON THE PAMPAS* DISCUSSION

It was October and read-aloud time had "loosened up" a bit. Students seemed more comfortable because of being allowed to arrange their own seating. That seemed to make me more relaxed, too. Also, I was working hard not to ask so many questions that had right or wrong answers, but instead to try to use more open-ended ones. In this first example, that was my intention, but as you see I still struggled to achieve that intention.

I just finished reading *On the Pampas* (Brusca, 1991) to my students. This is a story about a young girl who lived in Buenos Aires, Argentina, but spent her summers at her grandparents' ranch, hoping to learn all about gauchos. Although I started with a question I hoped would lead to a great discussion of the book, I ended up with one of those that would lead to right or wrong answers from students: "What are some of the things that Maria learned from her grandparents?" Maribel then commented on the fact that the girl in the story liked to learn from grown-ups. Now, this could have been a good opening to what I hoped for, but, instead of affirming this student's response to encourage her to talk more about the topic, I went off on some tangent by asking the class if they knew what "grown-up" meant. You can see that I still felt that I had to fulfill my teacher responsibility of making sure that my students understood every word or phrase in a book (or that another student might use). Rather than waiting to see if it was in fact a problematic term for them to understand, or if it might be clarified in the context of our discussion, I felt I had to "check their comprehension" of it. I still struggled and was not trusting enough to share my responsibility.

Thank goodness for Jimmy, who saved the day, so to speak. He didn't directly answer my question of what Maria learned from her grandparents, but instead built on Maribel's remark by relating what he liked and learned from his grandmother. Example 1 begins with the end of this response, after which Carlos told about some of the "stuff" his grandmother brought him from Mexico. Subsequently, the beginning of a fairly long discussion about the distinctive features of a poncho (versus a sweater) arose.

Example 1

1	Jimmy:	…. On Christmas Day she sings us Mexican songs and then she makes us Mexican food.
2	Carlos:	My Grandma when she was uh——she was born in Mexico. She brought like uh stuff from Mexico and she gave me a lot of….
3	Dorothy:	What kind of stuff?
4	Carlos:	Like….
5	Ana:	Carlos, what you're wearing. That is from Mexico. [referring to the striped sweater jacket he was wearing]
6	Carlos:	And she got me a Mexican hat.
7	Dorothy:	Something like what we have back there. [pointing to the sombrero on a back table]
8	Carlos:	Yeah….
9	Dorothy:	[pointing to Carlos] Did you get what you are wearing from your grandparents?
10	Carlos:	Yes.
11	Dorothy:	What is it?
12	Ana:	It's a jacket from Mexico that they use….
13	Miguel:	A poncho.
14	Carlos:	[shaking his head "no"] Not really, Teacher.
15	Dorothy:	Is it a poncho?

{Fieldnotes, videotape, 10/26/94}

Thus, Jimmy got us off my grown-up tangent by bringing in a personal story of what he learned from his grandmother. His account, then, apparently spurred Carlos to talk about what his grandmother brought him from Mexico. I then asked him to elaborate. Actually, my question, I came to realize as I reviewed a transcription of the conversation, might not have been necessary because Carlos was probably just about to tell us more details. Anyway, as Carlos began to answer, Ana remarked to him that he was wearing a sweater jacket from Mexico, and then Miguel thought it was a poncho. Carlos didn't think so, and then when I asked if it was a poncho, a long debate occurred (not provided in the previous example) where Carlos and many other children went back and forth with arguments as to why his sweater was or was not a poncho.

Thus, once I moved away from my own agenda about how my students should respond to the book and allowed them to reinterpret my question, they eagerly told of what their grandparents taught them about Mexican traditions and artifacts. I also felt that, in this renewed awareness, they seemed proud of their heritage. I think that Example 1 exemplifies some of my first steps toward allowing children to initiate. It would have been better if I had not posed the question I did—for example, I might have just asked them to give their thoughts about the story. This is how I would better understand my students' understandings of this and other books I read.

During the reading of this book, students loved teaching me the Spanish words in the book because I have limited knowledge of the language. We discussed words, such as *carbonade,* a thick stew made of corn and peaches, whether *siesta* meant just sleep or sleep at a certain time of the day, and how to dance the *zamba.* I brought in a mate cup I bought on a trip to Buenos Aires, and explained how, where, and when Argentineans drank this tea. This discussion, then, ended up very collaborative where I validated students' own language and their knowledge, and where I also contributed information that they didn't yet know. However, I was aware that I had to still think of other approaches that would lead us to create more collaborative talk.

READING-ALOUD IN A NEW WAY: *THE LITTLE BAND* DISCUSSION

In the next example, students willingly responded to a story without any urging. It showed that they can ask and answer their own questions, constructing their own understandings of what the author wrote. Here we are reading *The Little Band* (Sage, 1991), which is a short story about a mysterious little band who travels through a town playing music. Its members (depicted in the illustrations as six young girls of diverse ethnic backgrounds) don't stop to talk to people in the town who don't know who they are, why they are there, or where they are going. In their discussion, students puzzle about these questions themselves. I think I did a much better job in facilitating their efforts.

Example 2

1	Dorothy:	Does anybody else have a question about the book?
2	David:	Why didn't they want to talk to people?
3	Dorothy:	Oh, why didn't they want to talk to people?
4	Cm1:	They were just marching.
5	David:	(… …) the people were asking them (… …). I don't——I don't understand that.
6	Dorothy:	Okay, but he's saying——can I repeat this and you tell me if it's right?
7	David:	[nodding yes]

8	Dorothy:	So they can hear you. Why didn't this marching band who was expressing themselves——why didn't they answer the people? People actually——can you give an example?
....		[David helps me find a page where the major wants to give a speech of welcome to the little band. I read this part and then ask the whole class if they have any ideas to David's question. Students provided several possibilities—"maybe they were in a rush," "maybe they were concentrating on their work," "maybe they wanted peace." Then, an extended discussion took place between several of the students and me around this latest idea of wanting peace, and then Jeremy initiated another question to consider.]
9	Jeremy:	How come they picked *that* town (... ...)?
10	Dorothy:	How come *who* picked that town?
11	Jeremy:	The band.
12	Dorothy:	The band. The little band. What do you think?
13	Jeremy:	How come——how come they only went through ... through that town? How come they didn't go somewhere else?
14	Dorothy:	Maybe they have ideas. Maybe your classmates have ideas.
15	Cm2:	Maybe they didn't know (... ...).
16	Dorothy:	They might not have known of another place?
17	Cm2:	Yeah.
18	Dorothy:	Jeremy, where did you think this band came from?
....		[There is a short discussion away from this question and then I reiterated my question for Jeremy.]
19	Jeremy:	From another town because the people were shocked.
20	Dorothy:	Oh, so you think they didn't come from that town. They came from someplace else. So you want to know——what did you want to know again?
21	Jeremy:	Why did they only go to that town?
22	Dorothy:	Okay. [picking up the book] Let's look at this back page for a moment.
23	C:	Where did they come from?
24	C:	Where did they go?
....		[I hold up the book and point out on the back how the band must have come on the path between two hills. I follow the path with my finger to the place where the band is depicted on the front of the book. I pose a question for the whole class.]
25	Dorothy:	Do we know where they come from? Like Jeremy asked.
26	Cs:	(... ...)
27	C:	Mrs. O'Malley, Mrs. O'Malley, why did they go *only* to that town?

28   Dorothy: Do we know if they only went to that town?

29   Jason: No. I have a (...).

30   Dorothy: Okay, Jason.

31   Jason: (... ...) another town (... ...) Who *are* they? Because (... ...).

32   Dorothy: Good point! He was establishing the fact that even though we
                don't know where they come from ... the exact specific name of
                the town ... we know that they were from another town be-
                cause——why, Jason?

33   Jason: Because (... ...).

34   Dorothy: Oh, they [the people from the town] wouldn't be asking those
                questions. Good for you. But that still doesn't settle that ques-
                tion for Jeremy.

     ....

35   Cm3:   Why didn't the author tell the names of the kids?

36   Dorothy: Why didn't tell the names of the children?

37   Cf4:   Maybe he didn't think of it.

38   Dorothy: Maybe he didn't think of it.

39   Jeremy: [standing up] Maybe they are from another country. Maybe they
                are from a different country. They talked to them in English and
                so they didn't understand them.

40   Dorothy: Oh, he doesn't have them coming from a different town, but he
                has them coming from a different country. That's a point....

                {Fieldnotes, Videotape, 03/29/95}

It was interesting to note how involved students became in this book, considering it was such a short story. It fostered a lot of cross discussion
among students. They questioned why the little band played and marched
for the townspeople. They wanted to know why the band members didn't
talk to the people in the town, why the police officer didn't greet them, why
the band didn't play in another town, and why the author did not give
names to the kids in the band. I felt good about this read-aloud. By changing my habits of interaction with them, and making students feel comfortable to express their ideas and concerns, students began to think more
about what they were reading rather than trying to give correct answers to
my questions.

READING-ALOUD IN A NEW WAY: EXAMPLES OF INTERTEXTUALITY

The next two examples illustrate the *intertextual links* that students in-
creasingly made during the read-alouds. This happened when they con-

nected something in the book being read to other books, songs, movies, personal stories, prior things we had studied, and so forth. Example 3 shows two intertextual links in our reading of *Diego* (Winter, 1991)—the first initiated by me, and the second offered by a student.

Example 3

1	Dorothy:	DIEGO DIDN'T LIKE EVERYTHING HE SAW. THAT'S WHY HE HELPED THE POOR PEOPLE FIGHT THEIR WAR FOR EQUAL- ITY. THEY WERE FIGHTING FOR FAIR WAGES AND A BETTER LIFE. DIEGO LOVED HIS PEOPLE MORE THAN ANYTHING, AL- MOST ... Do we know somebody else that we were just talking about?....
2	Cm:	Benito Juarez!
3	Dorothy:	Benito Juarez. How was he the same as Diego?
4	Cm1:	Because he was in Mexico....
5	Cm2:	And he believed in freedom.
6	Dorothy:	Freedom for who?
7	Cs:	The people!
8	Dorothy:	Freedom for the poor people.
9	Richardo:	Remember we read this story before when he saw something and he like draw something——draw it in real life.
....		[Several children's faces seem to show they don't understand or recognize what book he's talking about.]
10	Dorothy:	You know what you might do? I have some of the books out and some that we've read in bags back here. Would you like to do that? Sometime when you have free time, perhaps tomorrow, you can come and try and find the book you were talking about and share it with us. Just like Leon found a book that was by the same author and brought it. That's a very——that's a *nice* con- nection. Could you remember to do that for us?
11	Ricardo:	(... ...).
12	Dorothy:	Okay. Because I'm not sure I remember the name of the book you're talking about. Maybe——perhaps you can find it.
13	C:	(... ...).
14	SCs:	Oh yeah.
15	C:	I remember that.
16	Dorothy:	Okay. Well we each kind of remember the book.
17	C:	He colored whatever he saw ... like flowers.
18	C:	He mashed the colors up.

19	Dorothy:	So what's going to happen is Ricardo is going to do the research for us. He's going to get——find that book.
20	C:	(...) look (... ...).
21	Dorothy:	But you might not remember it. But that's what we're looking for. But I'm sure that when you see it, you'll remember it. [directing her attention to Ricardo] That's a big help. [returning to the book, reading the last pages of the book]. ... DIEGO RIVERA BECAME A FAMOUS ARTIST. HIS PAINTINGS MADE PEOPLE PROUD TO BE MEXICAN. THEY STILL DO.
22	Miguel:	I am!

{Fieldnotes, Videotape, 03/22/95}

My intertextual link was an extension to the idea in the book that Diego loved his people. When I asked about someone else like that, students immediately knew that it was Benito Juarez I was talking about. Then Richardo brought up some other book we had read in which a character drew something "in real life," which was connected to the fact that Diego was an artist. I really loved the last line of the example where Miguel asserted that he is proud to be a Mexican because students being proud of their heritages was one of the goals I had in choosing the books I read.

Once I began to give them opportunities to share my responsibilities about learning with students, they brought up more and more of these intertextual links. I think my praising students when they offered links, as I did with Richardo, also caused them to occur more often.

As I mentioned, there are different kinds of intertextuality, as you saw in Example 3. Students' tying their personal stories or home experiences to books is also a kind of intertextuality—as when children talked about what their grandparents taught them, in Example 1. Two very salient cases of intertextuality occurred for me when I read *Darkness and the Butterfly* by Grifalconi (1987). First of all, just as I read the title of the book to begin the session, a boy gave the author's name. When I asked him if he was familiar with the author and illustrator, he and several other students began talk about another book, *The Village of Round and Square Houses,* written by the same author (Grifalconi, 1986), that we read earlier in the year. This was then followed by a student-led discussion comparing and contrasting the two books.

Later on during the reading of the book, another example of intertextuality occurred when a student wondered whether the book was a poem or a story. This reading happened early in March and what I learned from it went far beyond the intertextual link itself. Example 4 covers our class discussion on the poem link.

Example 4

1	Dorothy:	… "BUT LOOK AT THAT LITTLE BUTTERFLY, OSA; *SHE* MUST THINK SHE IS THE SMALLEST OF THE SMALL. DARKNESS PURSUES HER TOO——YET *SHE* FLIES ON!" SLEEPILY, OSA THOUGHT ABOUT THAT. "MAYBE SHE HAS A SECRET?" {AND} THEN SHE SHOOK HER HEAD. "BUT I HAVE NO WINGS TO FLY." OSA HEARD THE WISE {WOMAN CALL FORTH} "YOU WILL FIND YOUR OWN WAY. YOU WILL SEE." OSA NODDED, AND BEFORE SHE KNEW IT, SHE FELL INTO A DEEP SLEEP.…
2	Cm1:	That's a poem?
3	Dorothy:	Pardon me?
4	Cm1:	That's a poem. Or is that a poem or is it a story?
5	Dorothy:	Is this a poem or is it a story? What do you think?
6	Cm1:	# A story. #
7	Cs:	# Story. #
8	Dorothy:	Why do you think it's a——excuse me, why do you think it's a story? Who else thinks it's a story?
9	Ses:	[About 9 students raise their hands.]
10	Dorothy:	Cm2, why do you think it's a story?
11	Cm2:	It doesn't have <things> that rhyme.
12	Dorothy:	It doesn't have very many rhyming words.
13	Cm2:	It doesn't have stanzas.
14	Dorothy:	It doesn't——it's not written in stanzas, good.
15	Cm3:	It doesn't have four lines.…
16	Dorothy:	Okay, do some stanzas have four lines? Do all stanzas have four lines in a poem?
17	Cs:	No.
18	Dorothy:	No, do all stanzas have rhyming words?
19	Cs:	No.
20	Dorothy:	Is it too long?
21	Ses:	# Yes. #
22	Ses:	# No. #
23	Dorothy:	Well, we haven't read very long poems, I agree. But poems can be very, very long. They can be longer than a story. (…) Do you think this story could be made into a poem?
24	Cs:	Yes.
25	Dorothy:	Probably so, probably so.
		{Fieldnotes, videotape, 03/01/95}

We studied poetry and some of the characteristics of poems a few months before, so much of this discussion was a kind of intertextual link. Actually, as I looked more at that book, I realized that I didn't appreciate enough what that boy was trying to suggest by his question. Although this book is a story, the author also incorporated poem-like features in it. The format of the print is like stanzas and it has lyrical phrasing. Maybe all of us would have realized that, then, if I asked him a question like, "What makes you think that it might be a poem?" I missed a big chance here, I think.

I shared this example on videotape a few weeks later at our regular weekly meetings where my colleagues and I reviewed some aspect of our inquiries for examination together. It was at that meeting—when I heard my students giving these group "yes" and "no" responses in Example 4—that I began to see something new about these kinds of interaction. I used to think that a group response of "no" and "yes" from students indicated that they were engaged in the discussion, but now I wasn't so sure. Maybe some of them were just "following the leader" and had no idea what was going on. After that, I became wary of these group responses and of my role in eliciting them. Anyhow, I think that experience in my inquiry was probably one of the most important I gained. It made me even more committed to continue to provide opportunities for my students to initiate on their own in the read-alouds, and for me to be cognizant of how best to respond to my students' initiations. I needed to support this collaborative talk that was beginning to take place.

CONCLUSIONS

My inquiry on read-alouds helped me to realize that a lifetime pledge of continuing to grow empowered me to make changes in my teaching, and that these changes affected my students. I could see that some of my teacher responsibilities could be shared with my students, that they could have a say in the read-alouds and in whatever else I taught. I could still cover the grade-level curriculum because I was not taking as much time with skill drill, but was giving them more opportunities for group activities and peer coaching. Gradually, I acted more as a facilitator than as the sole provider of knowledge. Never before had I felt as relaxed in my teaching, and yet confident that my students were learning. All of these changes impacted their language development because, in order for their thoughts and ideas to be understood, they had to learn to express them well.

During this time of change in this 1994–1995 year-long inquiry, I made one of the biggest changes of my life. After more than 20 years, I decided to make this my last year of full-time teaching. Our nine children were reared, and my husband's business involved a lot of traveling. I felt that it was time for me to accompany him whenever possible. I had not reached the point of being burned out, nor did I really feel that I had nothing more to offer my students. To the contrary, I wanted to continue to implement new practices based on new beliefs, but it was that time in my life to make yet another change.

In both my mind and my heart "retire" does not mean what the thesaurus suggests: to abandon or quit. So instead I decided I would say I was taking my *RTD*—Reallocation of Time Distribution. My RTD is as challenging as full-time teaching and offers as many opportunities to grow and change as I could have ever imagined. I continue to share my responsibilities with students in the substituting I frequently do—mostly at Jungman—which I must admit is still difficult for me. I try to listen more attentively and more flexibly because of the changes that my third-grade students helped me to learn. I continue to do inquiry around how I read books. I try to allow students to interrupt my reading with their ideas, questions, comments, and to have them extend the book in whatever way they choose. I believe that some type of language development takes place each time. Thus, although I closed the door to my own classroom, I am still opened to growth because it is never too late to change!

ABOUT THE AUTHOR

For as long as I can remember I wanted to be a teacher. I received my bachelor's degree in elementary education from the College of St. Teresa in 1956. I taught third grade the following year, but then left on maternity leave at the end of the year.

Sixteen years and nine children later, I began to teach at Jungman. In 1985 I received a master's degree from the University of Illinois at Chicago. After 20 years of teaching, and after the year of my inquiry described in this chapter, I retired.

My husband and family are the joy of my life and taking trips with them is a favorite time. I am a people person; I enjoy reading, the theater, playing golf, and playing bridge. I have always been involved in community, church, and educational organizations.

I miss teaching, but take with me all the wonderful lessons and experiences I learned from my students during the years, but most especially the third graders who participated in this teacher research.

DEDICATION

To my family.

REFERENCES

Busca, M. C. (1991). *On the Pampas.* New York: Henry Holt.
Grifalconi, A. (1986). *The village of round and square houses.* Boston: Little, Brown.
Grifalconi, A. (1987). *Darkness and the butterfly.* New York: Scholastic.
Sage, J. (1991). *The little band.* New York: Scholastic.
Winter, J. (1991). *Diego.* New York: Knopf.

Chapter 10

Promoting English Through English Read-Alouds in a Third-Grade Bilingual Classroom

Sonia Torres Pasewark
Formerly at Jungman Elementary School

EDITORS' COMMENTS

Sonia's story tells about her journey of inquiry during her first year of teaching—at the very school she attended as a child! Her third graders, many of whom were recent arrivals, had very limited English skills. They were also scared to learn English. Sonia decided on read-alouds as the primary classroom context in which she could foster her students' understanding and appreciation of English.

In her chapter, Sonia covers many facets of her inquiry, in which she read books in English to these non-English speaking students. She tells about how she dealt with issues of translation and code-switching, how she reconsidered the kinds of questions she asked, and how she attempted to address various social issues in the books she read to them. Throughout her chapter, she raises many of the difficulties that can arise in teaching in bilingual classrooms, and offers strategies of how teachers might meet and overcome some of these challenges.

The introduction chapter of this book provides the theoretical and methodological background for the larger collaborative school–university action-research project and this chapter about Sonia's inquiry on read-alouds.

University researchers, Liliana Barro Zecker and Caitlyn Nichols, collaborated with Sonia in her inquiry.

The smell of those freshly baked peanut butter cookies was still the same. It was the same from when I attended this school 14 years ago. Not much at the school appeared to have changed. The floors were the same dark black that I remembered. The cafeteria, auditorium, and the principal's office were the same. Everything was pretty much unchanged. The biggest change was the obvious peeling paint that had aged. The school also looked somewhat older, worn with the traffic of thousands of children. The whole neighborhood also seemed used, but I love this neighborhood in Pilsen in Chicago, home to many Mexican immigrants over the years. It has a certain smell and feel to it. I was thrilled to be starting off my professional teaching career where I had grown up.

A few days before school was supposed to start, the principal gave all the teachers class lists and other accompanying paperwork. I looked at my new students' profiles with apprehension and excitement. I couldn't wait to start leading these kids on the road to love school—to make getting an education their first priority the same way my teachers had inspired me. This is what I wanted to do: help educate these kids who reminded me so much of myself. They were first-generation Mexican like myself, learning both Spanish and English, learning two cultures and intertwining them into one.

Because these children were growing up in the same neighborhood I had, with parents very much like mine, I really identified with them. I saw myself in them. I had been given the opportunity to educate them, to inspire them to read.

I thought myself very lucky to be teaching third grade. I figured these kids would be readers and I would be able to start on one of the exciting units I had so eagerly prepared at the university. I was ready to take on anything. Besides, there were two other bilingual teachers and one monolingual third-grade teacher, with years of experience, I could use as resources if need be. I had taken all the necessary theoretical bilingual courses at school, but I knew I needed more practical tips. I couldn't really depend on the way I learned Spanish to teach my students. Spanish was always spoken at home. Spanish soap operas were always on television. Every business in my Pilsen neighborhood was Spanish. I had learned English in elementary and high school. I was always taught by monolingual teachers in English. My only experience with bilingual classrooms was the theories I had learned at school and the observations I had done as part of my master's degree program. However, these observations had never yielded a "true" bilingual classroom because all I had ever seen was teachers teaching only in Spanish. This to me was not the definition of a bilingual classroom, at least not in the ways my professors taught me. As I quickly found out, Spanish-speaking-only bilingual classrooms were the case here at Jungman, too.

I try to provide a background of my first experiences as a teacher and the rationale for my inquiry to use read-alouds to promote my students' English literacy understandings. Then, I cover some of the major issues that emerged during the year, as I read books in English to third graders who not only had little knowledge of English, but were also scared to death to learn it.

DIFFICULTIES OF THE FIRST MONTH AND DECIDING ON MY INQUIRY

When I first got together with the other third-grade teachers, I found out that a team approach action plan was already devised for the upcoming year. The first thing I learned was that I was hired to teach all of the children who were categorized as *A* students, which meant that they knew little or no English. The other students were divided among the three other classrooms. The monolingual English students went with the monolingual teacher, and the students categorized as *B* and *C* (students having more and more English, respectively) were evenly placed with the two other bilingual teachers. No matter, I thought, I can still teach these kids English and support their Spanish.

The next thing I was informed of by my colleagues was that all the third-grade classrooms were to be departmentalized in the teaching of language arts. Each of us was to teach reading, grammar, writing, or drama, with me teaching reading. This language arts block would occur each morning, with each of the four periods consisting of 30 minutes, with 3 minutes of traveling time for students—approximately 30 students in the monolingual class, 20 each in the other two bilingual classes, and 17 (13 of whom were boys, with only 4 girls) in my class. I was not quite sure what teaching reading might mean in this arrangement, but I was ready to give it a go.

Finding Out More About My Students and the Chaos of the Departmentalized Language Arts Experience

I spent the first week getting to know my students and assessing their abilities. I had their records and test scores but I did not give them much credence because the majority of their scores were at or below first grade reading level in their native language. Most were recent immigrants who spoke no English and had limited prior schooling experiences. I discovered that my students were not only A category students, but also that this class had the most students having learning disabilities and emotional problems of the third graders.

The next couple of weeks I simply tried to make some sense out of the chaos we had created by departmentalizing the third grade. To make a long story short, it was awful. Students were unsure whether they were in the right classroom; they had difficulty remembering if they had homework in any particular class or what supplies were needed. I felt that each period was insufficient time to cover the day's lesson. It seemed that when

I was right in the middle of the lesson, the next group would be at my door; nothing seemed to be accomplished because by the time one set of students was settled, it was time to meet with another.

I finally went to the principal for help. I just couldn't do this departmentalized merry-go-around any more. My students, especially, couldn't learn in such an arrangement. There was no community in my classroom for these vulnerable students. The 1-month experiment of switching to different language arts subjects came to an end. However, I still had a major challenge as to how to teach my students language arts (and the other curricular areas as well).

Choosing Read-Alouds as a Context to Promote English

Because my students had such low-level literacy abilities in Spanish, I wasn't sure what to do. Should I try to strengthen their reading and writing in their native language? Should I start teaching them English? I decided to do both. I strongly feel that learning English is the way for students to succeed in the United States, an English-dominant society. Language is power and the more language a person learns, the better. English is the language of technology, medicine, and commerce throughout the world. If I did not start teaching them English, then *when* would they start? They didn't hear it in their homes or neighborhood. The only English that they ever had heard was from television. Even that was limited to when their families were not watching the immensely popular *telenovelas* or Spanish, evening, soap operas. I decided I would teach all the content areas in Spanish, but try to speak English as much as I could in between, even though they would frequently ask, "Teacher, habla en Espanol. No entiendo" (Teacher, speak Spanish. I don't understand). I also wanted another time where I could transition them from being primarily Spanish speakers to truly becoming bilingual speakers having knowledge of, and ability, in English. I decided that the least painful method to teach them would be to read aloud good children's literature in English. Through hearing English as it is used in books, I would be fostering their comprehension and other important literacy understandings.

Of course, this was no easy matter. I had problems finding books that were interesting to my students as third graders, but were of a level of English they could understand. In this chapter, I focus on the following two themes:

1. Issues of translation or code-switching in my read-aloud sessions, which also included the troubles I had in the kinds of questions I asked as I discussed the books with them.
2. The kinds of social issues we examined as I began to use books that stressed different views about race and gender roles and other kinds of power relationships in society.

CHANGES IN TRANSLATION, CODE SWITCHING, AND QUESTIONS

It was difficult to begin to read to books in English when most of the children knew little of it and were scared to learn it. At the beginning of the year, I did literal translations of the English texts. Most of this was done word by word, because they had no English vocabulary to rely on. I gradually progressed to line-by-line translation, then to page by page. Later, if a book included both the English and Spanish text, I read the total Spanish text and then the English version. Towards the end of the year, I read in English only and asked most of my questions and comments in English.

At first, however, because I wanted them to comprehend what I read to them, I ended up asking literal questions (for which I knew the answers), rather than ones that asked children to *think* about what was happening in a story or to tell their own ideas. Also, most of the questions I asked were posed in Spanish.

A good example of how this went was early in my inquiry when I read *The Biggest Pumpkin Ever* (Kroll, 1984), which is in English only. For each page, I read in English and then translated it in Spanish. This book is about two mice, Clayton and Desmond, who take care of a pumpkin and try different things to make it grow—feed it sugar water and fertilizer, cover it with blankets on cold nights, and so forth. Here are some of the questions I asked in Spanish, right after I had finished providing them with the Spanish translation:

- ¿Quién es éste?/Who is this one? (asking the children to identify one of the mouse characters)
- ¿Qué le pasó a al calabaza?/What happened to the pumpkin?
- ¿Quién le echó el agua?/Who watered it?
- ¿Qué mas le echaron?/What else did they put in it? (asking about the sugar water mentioned in the book)
- ¿Quién está cuidando a la planta de día?/Who is taking care of the plant during the day?

  {Fieldnotes, 10/26/94}

You can see how low level my questions were. However, I got some help from the other teachers in our project group in this area. I heard about different kinds of questions but never saw them put into practice. I student taught the previous year with a teacher who used very traditional methods, and that's the way it was when I was a student at the school, too. I did not think about what I was asking or why I was asking. I just tried to get some answer, just feeling my way through it. In our weekly project meetings, the other teachers talked about their dilemmas when they asked more open-ended questions and tried to have their interactions with their students be more collaborative. They also talked about the class-management difficulties that occurred when they tried to have students participate more. But, they felt that, although their sessions were noisier, students were more enthusiastic.

I had many management problems, too, mostly because I was a new teacher and also because many of my students had learning or emotional difficulties or were brand new arrivals. Through our project discussions I learned different ways I might interact with my students and how I might also deal with management problems. This didn't change overnight, but I think my questions and comments during the read-alouds got better.

More Collaborative Read-Alouds

One thing that happened was that students began to collaborate with me in providing translations. This first occurred when I was reading *The Desert Mermaid/La Sirena del Desierto* (Blanco, 1992). This book included text in both English and Spanish, and Luis, one of the most proficient English speakers in the class, offered to translate my English version into Spanish. (Note that italics in the example mark code switching in English.)

Example 1

1	Sonia:	¿En inglés o en español?
2	Cs:	¡En español!
3	Sonia:	¿Qué tal los dos?
4	Cm:	¡Los dos (...)!
5	Luis:	¡Yo lo traduzco!
6	Sonia:	*You wanna translate? Okay*!
7	Luis:	Yeah.

....

8	Sonia:	Okay, este va a ser el plan: Yo lo voy a leer en inglés y luego Luis o quien quiera me lo puede traducir, okay?
9	Luis:	¡Yo lo traduzco!
10	Sonia:	Hugo, me pones ese lapiz ahí? *Thank you. Okay, this book is called* THE DESERT MERMAID, LA SIRENA DEL DESIERTO. *The story is written by Alberto Blanco. That's the author. That's the author. The author is Al....*
11	Luis:	Alberto Blanco!
12	Cf1:	Blanco?

13	Sonia:	*Yeah! Very good, Luis! And the pictures——it is illustrated by Patricia Reva. Patricia Reva is the illustrator. What's the illustrator, Luis?*
14	Luis:	El que dibuja las cosas.
15	Cm1:	El lus——el ilustrador.
16	Sonia:	*Very good.* El que dibuja las cosas.

Translation

1	Sonia:	In English or in Spanish?
2	Cs:	In Spanish!
3	Sonia:	How about both?
4	Cm1:	Both (...)!
5	Luis:	I translate!
6	Sonia:	*You wanna translate?* Okay!
7	Luis:	Yeah.

....

8	Sonia:	Okay, this is going to be the plan: I am going to read it in English and then Luis, whoever wants to, can translate it, okay?
9	Luis:	I translate!
10	Sonia:	Hugo, can you put the pencil there? *Thank you. Okay, this book is called* THE DESERT MERMAID, LA SIRENA DEL DESIERTO. *The story is written by Alberto Blanco. That's the author. That's the author. The author is Al....*
11	Luis:	Alberto Blanco!
12	Cf1:	Blanco?
13	Sonia:	*Yeah! Very good, Luis! And the pictures——it is illustrated by Patricia Reva. Patricia Reva is the illustrator. What's the illustrator, Luis?*
14	Luis:	The one who draws the things.
15	Cm1:	The lus——the illustrator
16	Sonia:	*Very good.* The one who draws the things.
		{Fieldnotes, videotape, 12/05/94}

Luis was quite capable as a translator and he was frequently asked by me and by other students how to say things in the other language. As the year progressed, other children began to offer to be translators as they became more proficient in English. This especially occurred when I read books that had both the English and Spanish texts because they could rely on the Spanish version to offer possible English wordings.

My read-alouds became more collaborative, also, because I asked different questions from the very literal ones I used so much early on. For example, I changed by asking students for their predictions, and getting them to relate ideas in the books to their own experiences, or to reflect on a character's motivations or feelings. The next two examples come from *The Rainbow Fish* (Pfister, 1992), which tells how a beautiful fish discovers the real value of beauty and friendship. In the beginning of the book, Rainbow Fish does not want to share his wonderful, shiny scales, when other fish ask for one. Although he is very beautiful, he is very lonely. After talking to the octopus, he decides to give one to each of the other fish, who are now eager to have him as a friend. He is no longer so beautiful, but he is now happy. In Example 2, I attempted to get students to examine the Rainbow Fish's personality and why he didn't play with the other fish in the ocean.

Example 2

1	Sonia:	¿Cómo era el pez? ¿Cómo era el pez? Javier, ¿Cómo era el pez? ¿Cómo era el pez?
2	Javier:	De arcoiris, de colores.
3	Hugo:	Chico … aburrido … enano … feo.
4	Javier:	Tenía las escamas de todos los colores….
5	Sonia:	Pero, ¿qué tipo de personalidad?
6	Cm1:	Bilingüe.
7	Sonia:	Eh, Luis ¿Qué tipo de personalidad traía el pescado? ¿Silvia?
8	Cs:	(… …).
9	Silvia:	Bueno.
10	Cm2:	Mira, teacher, como brillan las escamas (…) desde acá brillan.
11	Sonia:	Juan, ¿Cúal personalidad tenía?
12	Cs:	(… …).
13	Silvia:	Era bueno.
14	Cf1:	Mala, teacher.
15	Silvia:	Bueno.
….		
16	Vilma:	Es bueno y malo.
17	Sonia:	¿Él jugaba con los otros peces?
18	Cs:	¡No!
19	Sonia:	*He didn't play with them right? Why do you think he didn't want to play with them?*
20	Cm1:	*Because,* se le ensucian las escamas.

21	Sonia:	*Why do you think he did not want to play with them?*
22	Cm2:	Porque luego se le caen (...) en el mar las escamas.
23	Sonia:	*Maybe.*

Translation

1	Sonia:	What was the fish like? What was the fish like? Javier, what was the fish like? What was the fish like?
2	Javier:	Like a rainbow, of all colors.
3	Hugo:	Small ... bored ... dwarf ... ugly.
4	Javier:	It had scales of all the colors....
5	Sonia:	But, what type of personality?
6	Cm1:	Bilingual.
7	Sonia:	Eh, Luis, what kind of personality did the fish have? Silvia?
8	Cs:	(... ...).
9	Silvia:	Good.
10	Cm2:	Look teacher how the scales shine (...) from here they shine.
11	Sonia:	Juan, what personality did it have?
12	Cs:	(... ...).
13	Silvia:	It was good.
14	Cf1:	Mean, teacher.
15	Silvia:	Good
....		
16	Vilma:	It was good and mean.
17	Sonia:	Did he play with other fish?
18	Cs:	No!
19	Sonia:	*He didn't play with them, right? Why do you think he didn't want to play with them?*
20	Cm1:	*Because,* its scales get dirty.
21	Sonia:	*Why do you think he did not want to play with them?*
22	Cm2:	Because then its scales fall (...) into the sea.
23	Sonia:	*Maybe.*
		{Fieldnotes, videotape, 4/03/95}

At first when I asked what the fish was like, children gave me responses about his appearance (and Hugo might have been referring to the other fish of the ocean). Then I tried to get them to consider Rainbow Fish's personality. Toward the end of the example, I asked why they thought Rainbow Fish did not want to play with the other fish, and I accepted students' ideas about it.

Later, in Example 3, Pedro offers that he thought Rainbow Fish was proud and was going to be happy to share his scales with other fish. I followed up this remark by asking other children if they thought if he was going to be happier.

Example 3

1	Sonia:	*Pedro said something very important. He said the fish thought he was* muy fregón *and he is going to be happy once he gives his scales away. Why do you think he is going to be happier when he gives his scales away?*
2	Cs:	(... ...).
3	Sonia:	*Why?* [pointing at Silvia to answer]
4	Silvia:	Porque van a ser sus amigos y....
5	Sonia:	*Who's going to be his friends?*
6	Cs:	#Todos los pescados.#
7	Cs:	#Todos los peces.#
8	Sonia:	*I'm just asking Silvia!*
9	Silvia:	Los pecesitos van a jugar con él porque son felices con una sola escama.
10	Sonia:	*Okay, good.*
	....	[I continue to probe later during the discussion.]
11	Sonia:	*What would you do if you had something beautiful but lots and lots of it, would you share it?*
12	Cs:	#Yes!#
13	Cs:	#No!#
14	Sonia:	*No? Just a little bit? How about you, Sara? How would you share it?*
15	Sara:	Sí, sí ... porque me miran así y después me dicen, "Me puedes dar uno?" y yo digo, "No." Y se sienten mal.
16	Sonia:	A ver Pedro. ¿Qué dijo el pulpo?
17	Pedro:	Que dé eso brilloso, que le dé a cada uno de los pescados y luego se va a hacer bueno....
18	Cm1:	(...).
19	Pedro:	¡Feliz! ¡Se va a ser feliz!
20	Sonia:	*That's right! You got it, Pedro!*

Translation

1	Sonia:	*Pedro said something very important. He said the fish thought he was very proud and he is going to be happy once he gives his scales away. Why do you think he is going to be happier when he gives his scales away?*
2	Cs:	(... ...).
3	Sonia:	*Why?* [pointing at Silvia to answer]
4	Silvia:	Because they are going to be his friends and....
5	Sonia:	*Who's going to be his friends?*
6	Cs:	#All the fish.#
7	Cs:	#All the fish.#
8	Sonia:	*I'm just asking Silvia!*
9	Silvia:	The little fish are going to play with him because they are happy with just one scale.
10	Sonia:	*Okay, good.*
....		[I continue to probe later during the discussion.]
11	Sonia:	*What would you do if you had something beautiful but lots and lots of it, would you share it?*
12	Cs:	#Yes!#
13	Cs:	#No!#
14	Sonia:	*No? Just a little bit? How about you, Sara? How would you share it?*
15	Sara:	Yes, yes ... because they look at me like this and then they tell me "Can you give me one?" and I say, "No." And they feel bad.
16	Sonia:	Let see, Pedro. What did the octopus say?
17	Pedro:	To give away that shiny stuff, to give it to each of the fish and then that would make him good....
18	Cm1:	(...).
19	Pedro:	Happy! That would make him happy!
20	Sonia:	*That's right! You got it, Pedro!*
		{Fieldnotes, videotape, 04/03/95}

I tried to get students to understand about how Rainbow Fish would become happy when he gave up his scales, which was the major theme of the book. Alongside this goal, I got them to relate this idea of sharing to their own lives, as my interaction with Sara showed. At the end of the example, I tried to support Pedro's responses regarding the octopus. Pedro was a learning disabled student who had great difficulties reading in both Spanish and English. However, he was eager to interact in the read alouds, as this example indicates, and I tried to confirm his comprehension of the text as much as I could, hoping that this area would be strong and help his other problems in reading.

Thus, as the previous two examples point out, although I was still concerned with students' understanding the meanings of the books, I got better in letting students give their own ideas and ask higher level questions that got them to think about feelings, character motivation, and so forth. I also encouraged all students to participate.

ADDRESSING SOCIAL ISSUES IN THE READ-ALOUDS

During the second half of the year, I also began to choose books that dealt with social issues. I wanted students to question stereotypes and to be open minded and more accepting of others. I especially addressed gender roles. It was interesting to see how 9 year olds believe some things about boy and girls, and about men and women. The boys see themselves in these roles and the girls also see themselves in these roles. I felt they had a really hard time accepting I was the boss, because to them, bosses can only be men. I was really adamant about questioning some of their ideas on certain things. Then, when we read *The Paper Bag Princess* (Munsch, 1980), it was interesting that they couldn't accept that this woman in the story told this guy to get lost. Why would a woman do that? Isn't that what she lives for? They go home and they see their Power Rangers and then 2 or 3 hours of Spanish soap operas, and in these soap operas the male–female relationships are very marked. They also are such typical stereotypes of race; the servants are Black. All the women have the same role. It is only a happy ending if the young, innocent, beautiful girl married her knight in shining armor, and the girls believe it and that's what they shoot for.

When I was their age and lived in this community, I thought this was the world. I can see myself in these girls and boys. There are other worlds, however, other ways of thinking that are different that these children need to know.

The Paper Bag Princess is a story that emphasizes women being strong and independent in their decision making. In the book, Prince Ronald rejects his bride to be, Princess Elizabeth, simply because she looks dirty and ugly after she fought the dragon, who had burned down Ronald's kingdom and taken him prisoner. Examples 4A and 4B cover parts of our discussion about this book, which was one of our longest read-aloud sessions. I repeatedly tried to get students to think about Elizabeth's decision to leave Ronald after he indicated that he valued her appearance more than her character. All of the students were interested and participated. You will note that my reading and my comments in these examples were in English, even though students' contributions were predominantly in Spanish. Because most of the discussion takes place in English, a separate translation is not included for these next two examples, but instead line-by-line translations are provided next to Spanish statements. Example 4A occurs toward the end of the story.

Example 4A

1	Sonia:	Let's see. ELIZABETH WALKED RIGHT OVER THE DRAGON AND OPENED THE DOOR TO THE CAVE. THERE WAS PRINCE RONALD. HE LOOKED AT HER AND SAID, "ELIZABETH, YOU ARE A MESS! YOU SMELL LIKE ASHES, YOUR HAIR IS ALL TANGLED AND YOU ARE WEARING A DIRTY OLD PAPER BAG. COME BACK WHEN YOU ARE DRESSED LIKE A REAL PRINCESS. [I show the illustrations to the whole group] See that?
2	Cs:	Ooooh! (... ...).
3	Sonia:	Why?
4	Cm1:	(...) cansando al dragón. {(...) tiring the dragon.}
5	Sonia:	He's, I don't know, I don't like him. Let's see what happens. [I read but interrupt myself to pose a question] "RONALD," SAID ELIZABETH.... What do you think Elizabeth is going to do? Do you think Elizabeth is going to come back and get all pretty and beautiful? [gesturing as if fixing my hair]
6	Cm1:	#Yeah, yeah, yeah!#
7	Cs:	#(... ...).#
8	Sonia:	Maybe? Yes? No? Maybe not, maybe yes.
9	Cs:	(... ...).
10	Silvia:	Sí, sí. {Yes, yes.}
11	Sonia:	Why do you think so?
12	Cm1:	I don't think so.
13	Cm2:	Why should she get married?
14	Cm3:	Va a venir (...). {She or he is coming (...).}
15	Sonia:	That's true. Okay, listen to what Silvia has to say. This is very important. Jairo? She said that Elizabeth was going to go back home, and put, you know, get beautiful, put——fix her hair, wash her face....
16	Cm1:	Put make up.
17	Sonia:	Put some make up on, put on a nice dress.
18	Silvia:	(...) bien arreglada. {(...) made up nicely.}
19	Sonia:	Right, so Prince Ronald will love her.
20	Cm1:	#But (...) what's going to happen?#

21	Cm2:	#Pero (...) casa (...) está, está bien fea.# {But (...) house (...) is——is very ugly.}
22	Sonia:	I don't know. Well, why is she dirty?
		{Fieldnotes, videotape, 04/10/95}

I initially told what I thought about Ronald—"I don't like him"—because of how he treated Elizabeth, who got so messy in saving him from the dragon. I began to read more, but then stopped to ask students if they think Elizabeth would come back like a princess, "all pretty and beautiful." There were divided opinions on this, but Silvia's answer reflected many of their views that the best thing for Elizabeth to do was to improve her appearance.

At the end of Example 4A, there was a heated discussion where many students were talking and giving their ideas at the same time. I asked them to predict if the story would end in marriage between Ronald and Elizabeth, and most students felt that would be the conclusion.

Then I read the very last page of the book: "RONALD," SAID ELIZABETH, "YOUR CLOTHES ARE VERY PRETTY AND YOUR HAIR IS VERY NEAT. YOU LOOK LIKE A REAL PRINCE, BUT YOU ARE A BUM!" A nobody. THEY DIDN'T GET MARRIED AFTER ALL. In the beginning students had trouble understanding the meaning of *bum*, which they thought meant ugly. I tried to give them another meaning by stating that a *bum* was someone who "is worried about how he looks more than getting a job or being responsible ... not nice." I then asked them about what they thought about Elizabeth's reasons to leave him. One boy said that "maybe she did not understand English." Another offered that "maybe she was crazy." I tried to have this student explain more, but he did not. I then reread the last page again, adding, "See? She was happy!"

In Example 4B, I tried to briefly summarize the book to see if I could find another way to get students to think again about Elizabeth's feelings and decision not to marry Ronald.

Example 4B

1	Sonia:	Look! Look! Listen! Listen! [showing illustrations] Right here in the beginning she's all in love with the prince, "Ooh, you are so beautiful, oh la la!" Right here. And then the dragon goes and you know, burns everything and takes the prince away. I mean, the dragon was going to eat the prince, right?
2	Cm1:	(... ...).
3	Sonia:	But in the end, the prince tells her, "Oh, you're so ugly." Why do you think Elizabeth got mad?

4	Luis:	Cause it was not she——it was not her fault.
5	Cs:	It was the dragon's fault.
6	Sonia:	Okay, it was the dragon's fault but what did Elizabeth do?
7	Cs:	#(... ...).#
8	Pedro:	#Well, le salvó la vida.# [#Well, she saved his life.#]
9	Sonia:	*That's it!* [pointing excitedly to Pedro] Pedro, you got it!
10	Cm1:	¿Quién? [Who?]
11	Sonia:	*You got it!* Say what you just said.
12	Pedro:	Le salvó la vida. [She saved his life.]
13	Sonia:	Who ... who saved whose life?
14	Pedro:	La señora. [The lady.]
15	Sonia:	Saved whose life?
16	Pedro:	Del señor. [The man's.]
17	Sonia:	That's right! The princess, Elizabeth. Elizabeth saved the prince's life! See? How does she do that?
18	Luis:	Cachando a ese dragón. [Catching that dragon.]
19	Sonia:	Right, she use her....
20	Luis:	Imagination.
21	Sonia:	She used her....
22	Cm1:	Her brain!
23	Sonia:	She used her brain.
24	Cm1:	Estaba pensando. {She was thinking.} [banging on his head with his hands]
25	Cm2:	Que——cómo cansarlo. {That——how to tire it out.}
26	Sonia:	Right, she used her brain.
27	Cm1:	Estaba pensando cómo (... ...). {She was thinking how to (... ...).}
28	Sonia:	To think of ways to tire the dragon so she could save the prince. Pedro was right. So she could save the prince. And then, when she saves the prince, what does the prince say, Pedro?
29	Pedro:	She——the prince says, oh, que esta fea. {... oh, that she was ugly.}
30	Sonia:	Yeah! The prince said, "You are ugly."
31	Pedro:	Y ... al principio, y al principio como (... ...) todo eso. {And ... at the beginning, and at the beginning how (... ...) all that.}
32	Sonia:	That's right. So wouldn't you be mad?
33	Cs:	(... ...).
34	Cm1:	(...) le dijo (...). {(...) told him/her (...).}

35	Sonia:	Yeah, real smart. Now let me ask you, Vilma, Silvia, Mimi....
36	Cm2:	Las tras comadres. {The three girlfriends.}
37	Sonia:	Yeah, let me ask you, if you had a boyfriend ... do you think this would be? A girl could tell a man, "Get out of here!" Right?
38	Javier:	Yo le diría apártate de mi camino. {I would tell him get out of my way.}
39	Sonia:	That's right. What would you do, Vilma? Very good Javier! What would you do if you saved your boyfriend's life?
40	Javier:	Ella no entiende, teacher. {She does not understand, teacher.}
41	Sonia:	We'll help her. Vilma ... she understands.
42	Cm1:	Sí? {Yes?}
43	Sonia:	[speaking loudly and slowly] Vilma, if you had a boyfriend——if you had a boyfriend and you saved his life but you got all dirty [gesturing as if she got something smeared on her face] and he said, "Oh, I don't want you anymore," wouldn't you be mad?
44	Vilma:	#[Shakes her head slightly indicating "no."]#
45	Cs:	#[Other children are talking at once.]#
46	Sonia:	No? You wouldn't be mad?
47	Vilma:	[Shakes her head again.]
48	Sonia:	Javier, help me, help me [pointing to Vilma] so that Vilma understands what I'm telling her. Vilma, if you had a boyfriend and you saved him....
49	Javier:	Y si tu tuvieras novio (...).... {And if you had a boyfriend (...)....}
50	Cm1:	Y lo has salvado.... {And you have saved him....}
....		[Two of the students sitting next to Vilma are translating for her too.]
51	Sonia:	And, if you saved his life but you got dirty, you know, but you got all dirty and he told you, "Ooooh, you are dirty!" Would you stay with him?
....		[Children continue to translate for Vilma as Sonia talks but what they say is inaudible.]
52	Sonia:	Tell her, Javier, tell her what I just said.
53	Javier:	(...) le salvó la vida (...) muy fea (...) y maestra, que salió allí. {(...) saved his life (...) very ugly (...) and teacher, that got out of there.}
54	Cm1:	[translating for Vilma also] Y estuvo bien fea y con toda la ropa arrugada aquí en la frente. {And she was very ugly and all her clothes were wrinkled here in the forehead.} [touching Vilma's forehead, and saying something about being dirty on her face as the illustrations in the book and Sonia had shown]
55	Vilma:	No.

56	Sonia:	No? You wouldn't stay with him?
57	Vilma:	[Shakes her head "no."]
....		[Students are talking amongst themselves. It is time for the class to go to lunch.]
		{Fieldnotes, videotape, 04/10/95}

I thought that students' responses to my questions showed initially that they didn't agree with Elizabeth's reasons to leave Ronald. I supported Pedro's idea that Elizabeth saved the Prince's life, and then Luis' that she did this by using her brain in "catching the dragon." I had them consider how Elizabeth might feel about the way that Ronald treated her and why she would decide not to marry him. Vilma initially didn't think she would be mad at Ronald, but as we all helped her understand more, switching to Spanish to provide translations, she finally considered that she might not stay with the prince because he was unfair.

FINAL REFLECTIONS ON MY INQUIRY ON READ-ALOUDS

I am not sure that students left my third grade knowing all they should, or achieving at the level that they should. However, they made big strides in their ability to understand English, and to follow a discussion. Many started to use English more fluently, with less fear. My greatest accomplishment in my inquiry, I think, was showing them that it was possible for them to learn both languages, to speak and understand both. I think they felt much better about themselves at the end of the year, and that is important. I heard their voices and also helped them to lose their fear to try their English voices.

I think that read-alouds can really help bilingual students. I have been teaching bilingual first-grade classes recently, and found that this routine is critical to support English. I have even gotten better on my questioning in these read-alouds—I stress more what they *think,* not the literal facts of books, even in the beginning of the year. Thus, children at this early level end up doing well in English; they feel good about using both Spanish *and* English.

I was not surprised at my students' reactions during *The Paper Bag Princess* discussion. It is unfortunate, but most of them see these stereotyped gender attitudes taking place on an everyday basis. Sometimes, I think that all my efforts did not accomplish my goals; I did not help them change their minds. The boys and the girls still thought that this is the way the world is and is supposed to be. At other times, however, especially now that I look back, I think that maybe our discussions made some difference. Maybe they planted some seeds that would grow with them.

ABOUT THE AUTHOR

I received my master's degree in education at the University of Illinois at Chicago, with an emphasis on bilingual education. As I indicated previously, my first teaching job was at Jungman. That experience was very challenging and introduced me to the many difficulties that bilingual education presents. Since that year, I taught at another Chicago public school in bilingual settings. Recently, I am happy to be an at-home mom raising my two daughters.

DEDICATION

I dedicate my chapter to my daughters, Sophia and Michaela, and to my husband, Richard.

REFERENCES

Blanco, A. (1992). *La sirena del desierto/The desert mermaid.* San Francisco: Children's Book Press.

Kroll, S. (1984). *The biggest pumpkin ever.* New York: Scholastic.

Munsch, R. (1980). *The paper bag princess.* Toronto: Annick Press.

Pfister, M. (1992). *The rainbow fish.* New York: North-South Books.

Chapter 11

For the Love of Reading: Inquiries in Reading Aloud and Creating Literature Discussion Groups in Fourth Grade

Susan C. Jacobson
Jungman Elementary School

EDITORS' COMMENTS

In this chapter, Sue covers two interrelated inquiries, one on read-alouds and one on *literature discussion groups* (what many also call *response groups* or *literature circles*). The reading-aloud inquiry was a continuation of a previous year's focus—the first year that she used only literature to teach reading. She shares two discussions around two books—a familiar one that she had used before, and one that was quite new to her.

The rest of the chapter centers around Sue's study on a new venture for her, creating literature discussion groups. After giving an overview of the many struggles and changes that she implemented in establishing these groups, she examines the nature of the discussions that occurred during of the last two "stages" of this process. She illustrates how students, who had been very reluctant to talk about books at all in the beginning of the year, could, at the end, engage in rich, meaningful discussions with their peers.

The introduction chapter of this book provides the theoretical and methodological background for the larger collaborative school–university action-research project and this chapter about Sue's inquiry on read-alouds and literature discussion groups.

University researchers, Shannon Hart and Diane Escobar, collaborated with Sue in her inquiry.

ABOUT OUR FOURTH-GRADE CLASSROOM

During the 1994–1995 year of my inquiry, my fourth grade "classroom" was a mobile unit that was adjacent to the main building of Jungman school, in the Pilsen area of Chicago. These mobiles were built in the early 1960s and were supposed to have a life history of no more than 5 years, so you can imagine the shape they were in. They had many layered patches of drab, gray paint to cover the various writing and other graffiti that appeared constantly. (These mobiles have been finally removed.)

The mobile unit was up off of the ground, with wooden steps built to reach the door. Because the door was always locked for safety, one had to knock on this door, which had no window, to get our attention. Many people almost broke their knuckles during the winter because the blower of the heater was so loud that we had trouble hearing anyone. Those who wanted to come in had to tell us who they were and we had to decide whether it was okay to open the door. The children and I discussed safety issues in the beginning of the year and went over who should be allowed in and what to do if they did not recognize the name of the person at our door. We all had important responsibilities as the inhabitants of our mobile classroom.

I can remember one particular incident when I taught a lesson and heard this humming sound. I thought to myself, "I am going to catch the kid who keeps on doing this." I asked the class who it was, and they all looked at me in bewilderment. So, the humming went on and I stopped again and demanded the unknown singer to fess up. As I was saying this, one brave child said, "Teacher, it's not us—it's coming from outside." So I went to the door, without opening it, and listened along with my class. To my astonishment it turned out to be a man sitting on the wooden steps singing. I immediately called the office and the man was removed from the school boundaries. Another good story about our mobile concerns the time, during a very hot spring, that the garbage in the dumpsters near our mobile was so smelly, we had to do all of our talking with shirts up over our noses. There was the day, again when it was very hot and we had to have our door open to survive, the fluff from the nearby cotton tree got into all of our noses and eyes, and even went right into someone's mouth when he was talking!

I had between 18 and 22 students (the number often fluctuated due to children transferring in and out during the school year). All were Mexican American except three children—one Puerto Rican and two African Americans. In some ways, the isolation of the mobile and all of these experiences created special and powerful connections among us.

INTRODUCTION TO MY INQUIRIES

I had two interrelated inquiries during the 1994–1995 school year. The first one involved studying the responses of my students when I read aloud. I also studied my read-alouds the year before (all of us in the project made this routine a focus of investigation) to try to make them more collaborative. That previous year was the first year that I relied on literature for most of my reading instruction, so I felt I still had more to learn in researching how I read aloud. Many of my students entered fourth grade as reluctant readers, and much instruction before mine had been basal oriented and skill based. They had not had many opportunities to hear really good literature novels, nor had they much experience in discussing them so that their interpretations were encouraged and valued. So, in my read-alouds I wanted to try out both old and newly acquired literature to see what they thought about these books.

The other inquiry was a completely new venture. I wanted to see if I could figure out how to provide even more literature discussion by creating small groups where students could have their own time to talk about good books. In the first section of the chapter, I go over and illustrate the nature of my read-alouds by providing excerpts of classroom talk about two books, and then in the second section, I spend more time on the student-led literature discussion groups because they were really new for me (and my students). Although they ended up being very successful, they also caused me many more difficulties to establish.

Both of these inquiries were rooted in my desire to foster my students' love of reading. I was, and still am, an avid reader. How could I get them hooked in the same way? Because I used basals for the first 2 years of teaching, I was not aware of the kinds of high quality literature available for fourth graders. Thus, part of both inquiries was selection of the books (and finding many multiple copies for the literature groups) for us to read.

READ-ALOUDS THAT FOSTER AUTHENTIC STUDENT RESPONSE

In the previous year, when I began my inquiry on reading aloud to my students, I had trouble deciding what to read. I wanted to read books that I had remembered as being exciting, so I began to seek suggestions from my colleagues and friends for titles. One of the first books I used was *James and the Giant Peach* by Roald Dahl (1961), which was one that a friend bought me as a gift. He said that it was a favorite book when he was a child. Students loved that book, so I also used it in the beginning of the 1994–1995 inquiry. This book is a story about a boy named James, who was mistreated by his cruel two aunts, and met overgrown garden creatures—the Centipede, the Old-Green-Grasshopper, Miss Spider, the Earthworm, the Ladybug, the Silkworm, and the Glow-worm—who join him in a fantastic adventure.

Learning New Strategies

This book was one that I loved, too. It is a wonderful thing to be reading and see students with their mouths wide open with amazement and delight. You realize that you have captured them in a way that is truly emotional, a way that made us especially connected. However, I still wanted more from our read-alouds. I realized that, while I was reading, I stopped and asked students questions about the story, and that they, in turn, answered them. This is not what I wanted, however, the old read-and-drill routine that I remembered from when I was a child in school. Instead, I wanted students to initiate their own questions and to give authentic responses that reflected what they thought was interesting about the ideas in books. This is what I worked on in the past year, and this is what I was still working on in this year's inquiry.

I was trying to ask open-ended questions so that students could offer more thoughtful comments about the meanings in books. In Example 1, I was at the part in the book where all of the insects on the peach were scared because sharks were surrounding them, and were about to eat their peach, and they asked James what to do. When I posed the same question to my students that the students addressed to James, they provided some interesting ideas.

Example 1

1	Sue:	What would you do?
2	Cf1:	The spider could, with her web, weave a string that would reach to shore.
3	Sue:	You mean like a tightrope that they could walk on?
4	Cf1:	[nods in assent]
5	Sue:	I like that idea, I think that's a great idea!
6	Alejandro:	(... ...).
7	Sue:	[moving closer, unsure what he has said] Could you repeat that?
8	Alejandro:	They could all go inside the peach and the peach could roll away.
9	Sue:	[addressing the whole class] Do you know what he's saying? He means they could to inside the peach and make it roll from inside. That's a good idea!

{Fieldnotes, 09/20/94}

Here I used the insects' question to help my students to predict what could be done in the story to solve these characters' dilemma. One of the girls thought that the spider could spin a web that would reach the shore, which I tried to clarify by asking if she had a tightrope in mind. Alejandro, who was very soft spoken initially, also came up with another possibility. Students were quiet in the beginning of the year when they spoke up. Many were still not sure of me and my really wanting to know what they thought. That's why I was enthusiastic in telling them that they had good ideas. Later on in the year I didn't have to be so overt in my message that I valued what they had to say. I also found that I repeated what they were saying too much—sometimes I was worried that my rephrasing was not really expressing the meanings they were trying say—so I tried to watch that and to have them address their ideas to their classmates without my mediation.

Besides modeling the kinds of questions they could ask themselves, and telling they had good ideas, I was hoping that students would contribute more in the future. I used questions like: "What are you thinking?" and "Anything you want to say about this chapter?" As time went on, I noticed that children began to model my questions. For example, I usually asked them to make a prediction about the next chapter, "What do you think will happen next?" Later, I heard them saying the exact thing. I knew that this would take time and many read-alouds to get to this point, but I was sure it would happen, and it did. It is very hard as a teacher, however, to keep your mouth shut and let children do more of the talking; for me that was a big change considering how much I love to talk.

Actually, students had even more ideas than Example 1 provides. Subsequently during that day, they made their own illustrations to depict what they thought this particular segment of the book was like. As students shared their drawings, with characters on the top of the peach, some on the side, some under the peach, they talked about these responses in more depth, and also noted how the pictures showed different points of view. This idea of people having different interpretations and being respectful of them was a major message I was tried to stress. It was also a big goal I had in setting up literature discussion groups.

Including Informational Books in the Read-Alouds

A new book I shared this year was *The Day that Martin Luther King, Jr., Was Shot: A Photo History of the Civil Rights Movement* (Haskins, 1992), which was the first informational book I ever used as a read-aloud. This book gave the history of the oppression of African Americans, dating back to slave trade. The day that Example 2 came from, we reviewed what we had read the previous day. When I asked, "What have we learned so far about Martin Luther King?", students eagerly offered many things they had remembered: who shot Martin Luther King, the fact he had always had to avoid following the same schedule so people wouldn't kill him, that he died at 39, that he told others to defend themselves instead of sitting in the back of the bus, and so forth.

The chapter we were about to read was titled, "Fights for Freedom," which has pictures of slave ships and talks about slaves jumping overboard while chained together. Many students were sure why the slaves jumped even though they were likely to drown. I posed a question to hear students' points of view about this dilemma. Many were eager to respond, and Felita, one of the two African-American students in the class, was the first to tell what she thought.

Example 2

1	Sue:	This is the situation. This is your choice. You either were gonna be a slave or you could jump overboard but you would risk losing your life. What do you think you would choose? Felita?
2	Felita:	(... ...).
3	Sue:	Felita, you would jump overboard, you would take the chance. Why?
4	Felita:	Because. I'd rather——I'd rather die than have people whippin' on my back forever.
5	Sue:	Okay, good point.
6	Cs:	[many talking at once] (... ...).
7	Kim:	Kill myself——it's better to jump over than to have no freedom.
8	Melvin:	I'd jump. I wouldn't have a life anyway if I was a slave.
....		
9	Sue:	How many would jump over?
10	Cs:	[all but one boy raise their hands]
11	Cm:	(... ...).
12	Sue:	Well, that's okay. He has that right to not to want to. He would choose the other way. Let's ask him why.
13	Alejandro:	Because I would stay there and fight the white people for——for——for the black people for them to have rights to do anything they want.
14	Sue:	What if they—they're keeping you though. You have no power. There's so many more of them that....
15	Cf:	I feel that——that (... ...) the other slaves might (... ...) start smashing the (...)——like you could like um....
16	Sue:	You would escape, try. ...

{Fieldnotes, videotape, 01/19/95}

This discussion continued and ended up as a very long one. At first Felita argued that she would jump and rather die than have "people whippin' on my back forever." Others seemed to agree with her. When I asked how many would jump over, everyone but Alejandro raised his or her hand in agreement. He thought that he would stay and try to fight white people. When I said I thought that would be hard to do, a girl offered a possible way, which was a very inaudible response, but must have had to do with escape (because I mentioned it in the last line of the example).

Summary

Thus, by January I was better in posing questions that elicited students' ideas. In addition, they were much more comfortable in offering their ideas, even when their classmates were of one opinion, as seen in the previous example. Actually, as I reviewed this transcript, I think I might have pushed this one view, too. Only Alejandro had an alternative idea, yet he felt he could fight against the tide, and then others began to take his interpretation more seriously. Finding ways for students to have more opportunities to share different interpretations, and to be respectful in expressing them, was the major reason I attempted my other inquiry on literature discussion groups. This would become a far more difficult task than I could ever imagine. However, in the end it was one of my greatest accomplishments as a teacher.

TRYING OUT LITERATURE GROUPS

One of the reasons I wanted to attempt literature groups was that I thought they would be a great way for students to have more chances to initiate their own responses and to allow for more interactions between them. I also viewed literature discussion groups as opportunities to help my students acquire socialization skills and to use cooperative learning. I hoped that group work would foster the interpersonal abilities that are necessary for good discussions of literature, but which are useful also in all of areas of school and life.

Telling about my inquiry on literature groups would be a long story because their operation changed, and the kinds of discussions that students had in them also changed during the year. Thus, I can only cover parts of the story here. First, I give an overview of these different phases of literature circles. Then, I go over a couple of group discussions of two books that students read to illustrate how they talked about the content of books over time.

Typically, literature groups occurred midmorning, twice a week (usually Tuesdays and Thursdays). All students read the same novel, but they discussed them in small groups of three to five students of different reading abilities. I didn't start these groups until November because I wanted to make sure that students were used to initiating their own ideas and meanings of books. Students engaged in other kinds of literacy and language arts activities before and around literature groups—for example, the reading-aloud time and art or other kinds of extension activities (the drawing a segment of the *James and the Giant Peach* book, for instance). They also wrote in Reader Response journals daily.

Students read in class a chapter or two of the book right before they met in their discussion groups. They did that in different ways: silent reading, small-group read-alouds, and frequently buddy reading. Once they met in their groups, I moved from one group to another just to listen in, or sometimes or just to be another participant. Afterwards, we had a whole-class review or debriefing session where individual groups reported what they talked about in their groups.

Throughout the year we addressed the management part of group discussion time in different ways. For example, we made a list of rules of how to behave towards each other; later we tried out having group members taking on different roles. Because students had little experience working in groups, these were important features in making literature groups work. However, I focus here more on content issues.

Changes in Addressing the Content in Literature Discussion Groups

A good way to describe the various changes regarding content is to go over how questions were constructed for discussion groups. The first phase began with the reading of *Charlotte's Web* (White, 1952) where I gave students the questions that were written on large sentence strips. I tried to make these open-ended: "What word would you use to describe Wilbur?" "How would you feel if you were Charlotte and never received any attention for your work?" Students usually answered these in very straightforward and simplistic ways, "I think Wilbur was nice"; or "Wilbur was curious"; or "I would feel bad if no one paid attention to my work." Students seemed to just take turns with their answers, without even paying attention to what others were saying. There was no follow-up from each other's ideas; there was no real, genuine discussion.

Because I was unhappy about how these discussions went, I tried to give students more responsibility for what they talked about in groups. I thought that maybe the content of their talk would be better if they chose what to discuss. When they began to read *Sarah, Plain and Tall* (MacLachlan, 1985), I encouraged them to come up with their own topics or questions to consider. Unfortunately, this didn't make the discussions much better. They usually responded by saying "I like this book because …", or "My favorite character was …" Actually, I think I was mostly responsible for this way of responding because of how I modeled. I tried to make sure that students understood that people could have different opinions about the same thing. However, when I gave them a hypothetical group interaction, I only used, "I like this or that" examples. Moreover, I never stressed that if they gave this kind of comment, they would have to provide a good rationale. Anyhow, because I felt their conversations were not very rich and because their talk seemed stilted and not like real conversations, I changed format again.

In this third phase, I returned to creating the questions on sentence strips myself. And, despite the fact I took back more of the control of what was to be talked about in groups, students began to be better in their discussions. They started paying more attention to what each said, and were able to build on individual student responses—they began to have *real* discussions. Maybe this was because they had more experience in participating in group discussions by then; maybe it was because I had become better in crafting more interesting questions for them to consider. Anyhow, because they seemed to be getting adept in developing good conversations in their groups, I changed how questions should function once more.

Finally, during the last or fourth stage, students again had control of the questions, by writing their own, on the sentence strips I provided. This was the most successful period of discussion groups. Students really talked to each other and their discussions became quite rich. Moreover, they also frequently examined important issues of sexism and racism. Next, I give examples from the last two stages: group discussions from *Bridge to Terabithia* (Paterson, 1977) and from *Blubber* (Blume, 1974).

"Was It Fair ... ?"

As I have already said, in this third stage I returned to giving students the questions for literature groups. I wrote one for each group. Groups then discussed the sentence until I gave them the signal that they should pass their questions to another group. Thus, by the end of the period, all groups had discussed all of the four questions.

This procedure in which students used my discussion questions began in February when we read *Bridge of Terabithia*. However, this time, although I was giving students the questions, the level of group discussions was much better. There were no short answers where students seemed to just say something to get through their turns to talk. Now they really seemed to be engaged in genuine discussions. *Brige to Terabithia* is about the friendship of a boy and girl that turns tragic by the death of one of the children. This book touches many topics that young boys and girls face as they grow up, and my students became quite engrossed in the characters and their views about gender roles. Example 3 shows some of the discussion of a five-member group of three girls and two boys where an issue is examined. It begins as Lisa reads the question.

Example 3

1	Lisa:	WAS IT FAIR FOR THE BOYS TO DECIDE NOT TO LET THE GIRLS TAKE PART IN THEIR RACE?
2	C:	Uh, no.
3	Armando:	It wasn't fair because girls can play. They can race too.

4	Melanie:	It was fair because they are the same thing. They should be treated equally and with respect.
5	C:	I know.
6	Armando:	Yeah. The only thing that is different is that they're a girl and he's a boy.
7	Lisa:	There's nothing——there's nothing wrong....
8	Melanie:	There's nothing different.
9	Armando:	I know.
10	Melanie:	Maybe they think that girls can't play because boys are better.
11	Lisa:	[very excited, at first she begins to raise her hand and then brings it down, now touching words on the sentence strip as if to make a point] Oh, probably, oh probably....
12	Armando:	Probably they think that girls....
13	Lisa:	SHHH! [putting her finger to her mouth]
14	Armando:	Probably they.... [he stops, smiles as if to say "whoops" and puts his hand over his mouth as Lena continues]
15	Lisa:	Probably the boys think that girls don't race....
16	Armando:	Probably the boys think that she can't race, that probably that she runs too long [meaning slow?] and that (... ...). [his voice trailing off, sometimes talking into his hands]
17	Melanie:	Probably they think, #um#
18	Armando:	#[leans over her to address the camera] Hi!#
19	Melanie:	[pushing Armando away with her elbow continues] She can't play——that girls can't play because, um——they probably think that they're only supposed to be playing like hopscotch or jump rope.
20	Cf:	Yeah, jump rope.
21	Lisa:	And patty cake.
		{Fieldnotes, videotape, 02/07/95}

In the beginning most everyone in the group thought it wasn't fair that the girls couldn't race like the boys. Then, at line 10, Melanie brought up a different topic, saying, "Maybe they think that girls can't play because boys are better." As they continued to examine this issue, they became very excited, so much so that they sometimes forgot about the rule about people having their turns (e.g., lines 11–15). Melanie persisted to make her point even when Armando fooled around in front of the video camera. Thus, students had more genuine conversations—they seemed to consider what others said, and responded to them by adding their ideas and remarks. I think that their familiarity with the concept of discussion was finally emerging in the groups. Students loved this book, too, which might have contributed to these better conversations. Throughout the year, students referred back to it. It was mentioned when certain situations occurred in the class, it was connected somehow to their own life experiences, or it was linked to some aspect of the new books they were reading. *Everything* was bridged to *Bridge to Terabithia.*

"What If Your Friend Started Picking on a Race?"

In the last phase, which began in March, students began to write their own sentences on sentence strips. Their questions got better and better, causing their discussions to be better, too. In April we read *Blubber*, which I chose because I had observed many students teasing a particular girl in the class who was overweight, and this book addressed this theme. In reading and discussing this book, I was hoping that my students might become more sensitive about this issue. Example 4 shows part of a group discussion as it examines one of the questions written for that day. The "race" in the question referred to people of a particular racial group. I had just dropped in during this group's examination of it and I also participated in the conversation. I had not known the content of the question until then.

Example 4

1	Kim:	[reading the question to group] WHAT IF YOUR FRIEND STARTED PICKING ON ANOTHER RACE? WHAT WOULD YOU DO?
2	Sue:	Ooooh.
3	Cf:	Well I'll tell them to stop it. And then if they start picking on me more I'll tell my mother and my mother will probably call the police or something.
4	Lisa:	If they keep on picking on me, I will tell my mom 'cause if I (...) they wouldn't stop. I'd tell my mom so she can go and tell the principal.
5	Melvin:	I'll go and tell the principal and then they'll probably talk to their moms.
6	Felita:	Me, I would talk to the kid personally. And then if she——if she can't do nothing about it, I'll go to my parents.
7	Sue:	Did you hear what she said? Say what you said again. Who would you talk to first?
8	Felita:	I'd talk to the kid.
9	Sue:	[to the group] She'd talk to the kid first.

10	Lisa:	What if the kid doesn't want to talk to you?
11	Felita:	I wasn't making fun of the kid so why wouldn't they want to talk to me?
12	Lisa:	Well, like I was saying, if they (... ...).
13	Sue:	We can't hear you with your face in your arms.
14	Kim:	[rereading question for Lena] IF YOU WERE——IF YOUR FRIEND STARTED PICKING ON ANOTHER RACE....
15	Lisa:	Oh yeah.
16	Cm:	If he's picking on your race and you wanted to talk with them to tell them to quit and that, he might not want to listen to you.
17	Sue:	Why wouldn't he want to listen to you?
18	Lisa:	Because he's another race?
19	Kim:	Yeah, because of the color of his skin. And they mostly don't like black kids and pick on them coming. They like——they'll say "oohh...."
20	Sue:	Who doesn't like black kids?
21	Kim:	Some people.
22	Sue:	I don't necessarily think that's true. I think it's all races because you know what I mean? I don't think it's just about black people.
23	Kim:	And the whites, they sometimes pick on white people, they tell them "Pollocks" and things.
24	Felita:	When you said——you ask me why wouldn't the kid talk to me? Maybe they think that I'm like him, that I'm probably be mean to him. But I would try to tell them I'm not like them (...).

{Fieldnotes, videotape, 04/13/95}

Students had different ideas about what they would do if their friend was picking on a person of a different race. Because the who being picked on changed throughout the discussion, different perspectives were offered by group members. The fact that there were two African-American students in this predominantly Mexican-American class seemed to encourage investigation of racism and other kinds of difference here and at other times during the year.

Did *Blubber* help students raise their consciences about how they were behaving towards Tabitha, the girl about whom I was concerned? It did seem to have a positive effect. Even more important, it seemed to affect Tabitha, which she tried to explain in Example 5. This is part of whole-class debriefing on one of the other questions students wrote and discussed that day—"Do you think Jill and Linda will become friends? Why?"

Example 6

1   Tabitha: I think (... ...). I think it's no accident that (...) we get along
            better (...) the happiness that me and Ernesto. Maybe
            they——me and Ernesto——he hasn't been picking on me that
            much because....

2   Sue: He's not. I've noticed that too. And you've really been trying,
            right Ernesto?

3   Tabitha: (... ...) happiness.

4   Sue: Well, that's true too. The good things, right? See, Ernesto. You
            can do it. [begins to read another question to hear other sum-
            maries from groups]. ...

            {Fieldnotes, videotape, 04/13/95

Although it was hard to hear everything she said in this whole-class setting, we were all moved by what Tabitha said. She thought that it was no accident that Ernesto and she were getting along much better. That is, reading and discussing the issues in the book seemed to be helping her as well as her classmates to see how hurtful the teasing might have been, and they were changing regarding it.

Thus, in the last phase or stage of my inquiry on literature groups, discussions had become very real. That is because, I think, they were based on more sophisticated questions that students themselves were able to create and examine. They, and I, had gone on a bumpy road but we had arrived!

FINAL THOUGHTS

I learned a lot in both of my inquiries—the read-alouds and especially the literature-discussion groups. Students entered my classroom not used to giving their own responses to literature or discussing with each other in groups. At the end they had traveled a long, long way. I think my attempts to make the read-alouds more interactive helped students try the in-depth discussion in small groups. Students had never talked together without the teacher present, and I never set it up so students could experience this opportunity before, either. Thus, my second inquiry had many trials and errors.

However, by the third and forth phases of literature groups, children had an interest in what the discussions were about. They listened to what other people said in their group. They definitely expressed their feelings and showed many emotions pertaining to the issues being discussed.

In June, I had them try to remember all the books we had read that year in read-alouds and in literature groups. I wrote the titles on the chalkboard as they yelled them out. I remember how excited they were, the pride they had on their faces when they realized how many wonderful books we had read.

Sure, there are still many facets of literature groups I still need to work on, but as long as the children leave, feeling this great about themselves as readers, it was worth all the anguish I went through as I struggled to try to figure literature groups out. I did it step by step because it was hard to do. I did it ... *for the love of reading.*

ABOUT THE AUTHOR

I graduated from Western Illinois University in 1990. My first teaching job was as a substitute teacher in the Chicago public schools. Subsequently, I joined the faculty at Jungman. For the first year, I taught sixth grade and then during the second year I taught an ESL pull-out program. From then on, I have taught fourth grade.

I have returned to school to pursue a master's degree in reading at the University of Illinois at Chicago. In my free time I enjoy reading, aerobics, and spending time with my family.

DEDICATION

I dedicate this chapter to the best teachers I ever had, my family: my parents John and Sonia Jacobson, and my sister Kim. Without them I would not have learned a great many things.

REFERENCES

Blume, J. (1974). *Blubber.* New York: Bradbury Press.

Dahl, R. (1961). *James and the giant peach.* New York: Knopf.

Haskins, J. (1992). *The day that Martin Luther King, Jr., was shot: A photo history of the civil rights movement.* New York: Scholastic.

MacLachlan, P. (1985). *Sarah, plain and tall.* New York: Harper & Row.

Paterson, K. (1977). *Bridge to Terabithia.* New York: Thomas Y. Crowell.

White, E. B. (1952). *Charlotte's web.* New York: HarperCollins.

Chapter 12

Reflections on Drama
in a Sixth-Grade Classroom:
A Year of Discovery

Paul Fowler
Formerly at Andersen Elementary School

EDITORS' COMMENTS

Paul was the school's literature enrichment specialist—also known as the "books on wheels" guy—who went into Kindergarten to fouth-grade classrooms to share stories with children. A month and a half into the year of his inquiry, he became a teacher of a contained sixth-grade classroom when a faculty downsizing occurred at the school. He had successfully used drama with Kindergarten to fourth-grade children and with children in an afterschool program, so he was eager to try out more long-term drama projects in this new teaching context.

However, his first efforts to implement a drama structure, described by O'Neill and Lambert (1982), into his classroom were not at all successful. Paul analyzes and explains why this particular drama venture did not do well. He then provides an account of how drama improvisation experiences of novels offered more favorable results in terms of his sixth-grade students' understanding of literature and of themselves. Paul's story of his inquiry illustrates how reflection and persistence in teacher inquiry sometimes helps teachers to overcome difficult circumstances and great discouragement.

The introduction chapter of this book provides the theoretical and methodological background for the larger collaborative school–university action-research project and this chapter about Paul's inquiry on drama.

University researcher, Hank Tabak, collaborated with Paul in his inquiry.

BACKGROUND AND IMPETUS OF MY INQUIRY

When I got my first teaching job at Andersen, I was hired as a literature enrichment specialist. Actually, I was known as the "books on wheels guy," or
just, "the man who reads us stories." As the books on wheels guy, I had a
very successful year working with kindergarten through fourth graders on
various drama-related projects. In addition, I took on an afterschool program, in which a group of first- through seventh-grade students improvised scenes from the "Ugly Duckling" and "The Princess and the Pea,"
and created very successful renditions. Yes, I decided, from the level of enthusiasm that my students showed in response to the productions, students are able to dig deeper into literature when they are allowed to be
active participants.

My experience as the books on wheels guy helped set the stage for my
next adventure in education as the teacher of a sixth-grade class. The prospect of long-term drama projects was exciting, and I began to think about
how I could fit drama into the curriculum. I also began to ask questions
about drama that I had never considered before. I came up with three questions to begin my inquiry.

First of all, I was taught in teacher's school that students would not be
interested in literature unless they were involved in some way. Prediction
is one way to do this. However, I looked for other ways to get the kids more
involved. That led to my first question, which was: Would drama provide a
doorway for my students to get truly involved in the books that I read to
them? Another thing that I learned in school was that if a teacher can
make a connection between a book and a child's personal experiences,
then that connection between the child and the book will be that much
stronger. That led to my second question, which was: Will drama help students to draw on their personal experiences? Finally, I was curious about
students *in role*. I had a few experiences in my teaching classes in which I
was asked to role-play situations. It made for an active learning experience
(as opposed to a passive learning experience) and I got more out it. I
wanted to integrate role play into my curriculum to see whether or not it
would help students grasp difficult-to-visualize concepts. With these three
questions in mind, I decided to introduce dramatic exercises to the students in my classroom.

OVERVIEW AND THE RATIONALE FOR USING
"THE LOST VALLEY" DRAMA STRUCTURE

In the sixth grade in my school, we are required to teach about the beginning of civilization. My mind raced to think of how I could use drama and
role play to make real the students' understanding of what it might be like
to create a new civilization. Fortunately, a few months before, I had taken a
class with noted and respected drama specialist Cecily O'Neill. After tak-

ing the class and reading her book, *Drama Structures* (O'Neill & Lambert, 1982), I found a role-play structure called "The Lost Valley," in which students have an experience to create their own civilization. In "The Lost Valley," students are invited to "reconstruct the life and work of a primitive society and participate in tasks related to shelter building, hunting or gathering, preparing defenses and organizing tribal celebrations" (p. 83). They are to take on various roles in building this civilization. For example, they may be shelter builders, or map makers, or experts in finding and then growing food, which can then be eaten by the population. As the students take on these roles they learn how important it is for the cooking specialist to cooperate with the farmers, who would need to cooperate with the builders (to construct levees and roads), and thereby build students' understanding of how all aspects of a society are interrelated.

I also hoped that the drama exercises would force them to draw on the knowledge of the group to solve problems related to the creation of the society. For example, the map maker might make a map of the town that is not to scale. As the road builder begins to build roads according to the map, he or she may notice that the map is wrong, and give the map maker advice on how to correct the mistake. In addition to these skills, the drama activities would hopefully build on their cooperative learning skills and improve their ability to get along in what was a very combative and angry classroom. I became their teacher a month and a half into the school year, replacing another teacher who the students liked. There had been a downsizing of the faculty at the school and because that teacher was "last to come" to the school, she was "first to go." Students didn't really understand this policy, and they were upset about the situation.

O'Neill and Lambert pointed out early in their book that drama should not simply be a series of isolated activities in which drama skills are taught. Rather, drama should be used to help students gain a deeper understanding of difficult curricular concepts, "understand complex issues, solve problems and work creatively and co-operatively" (p. 9). However, using drama in a social studies context is by no means meant to replace curricular material. It is meant to enhance the understanding of that material. For instance, as my students learned about the construction of the beginning of Western civilization from the various books and lessons that I presented, at the same time they learned, through drama, another standpoint of what it might have felt like to build this civilization and to have encountered some of the problems that people faced. They would do all of this by drawing on their own life experiences. None of my students knew exactly how it felt to be in charge of making sure that a community has enough provisions to survive a winter. Yet, all of my students knew what they do to prepare for the winter in Chicago and what it feels like to be cold. This drama structure gives students the opportunity to draw upon this knowledge and extend it to the situations faced by people creating a brand-new civilization. Using this rationale, I jumped into "The Lost Valley" with both feet.

My 28-member class consisted of mostly Latino or Latina students, mainly Mexican and Puerto Rican, a few African Americans, and a couple of children of Polish heritage. Their reading abilities ranged from second to ninth grade. As already noted, the demeanor of the class was angry—they were unhappy to have me as their teacher. For the next 4 weeks, I struggled to balance my ideas, O'Neill's and Lambert's ideas, and the needs and wishes of the class. For my troubles, I got a failed project, a confused class, and a lot of acid in my stomach. You might say, I went in with high hopes and ended up with a lemon. The object of the following analysis is somehow to make lemonade.

FIRST STEPS IN LAUNCHING THE DRAMA STRUCTURE

One of the most important hurdles that I faced was convincing this class to follow me on a journey of the imagination. There was a group of very skeptical students in the class who questioned everything I did. And indeed, as a first-year teacher in a self-contained classroom, from hindsight I made daily decisions that were questionable. I knew I had to be convincing. My task was this: I had to convince the class that we were going on a journey back in time and that they had to take on the roles of a persons who were going back in time to create a new civilization. Therefore, because I was asking my students to take on roles, I needed to do the same. I created a new persona, Mr. Johnson. Mr. Johnson had a southern accent and was very excited about the group of "volunteers" that had been assembled for the mission. I started by saying,

> "Welcome to the Scientific Institute. (Not so sure of myself, I quoted almost directly from *Drama Structures*.) I am very pleased that you are the people who have finally been chosen for this experiment. Just think of it … for the next year we shall be living as the members of a primitive tribe, without many of the benefits of the 20th century. We will be doing research on what it is like to create a new civilization. The government has funded this project so that they can learn about things that will help us today."

The students had befuddled looks on their faces. Soon they began to ask questions. (My recollections from my journal for that day in December follow.)

Example 1

1 George: [characteristically skeptical] Um, excuse me, *where* are we going?

2 Mr. Johnson: Well, certainly there must be an expert in mapping here that can tell us where we are going.

3	George:	Huh?
4	Mr. Johnson:	Well, of course we're going back in time, thousands of years, to a place where we can investigate the creation of a new civilization.
5	George:	[never one to back down from a simple explanation] And what place is that?
6	Mr. Johnson:	To tell you the truth, sir, I really don't know. I'm just leading this expedition. You all were picked because you are experts in your field. From the information that I was given, some of you are experts in transportation, some of you are experts in the environment, some of you are experts in food, some of you are experts in fire building, and there are even experts in geography. May I ask who is the expert in geography that can tell us where we are going?
7	Kendall:	[never one to be hesitant, takes the first step] We're going to a desert.
8	Paul:	Is that all, a sandy desert, nothing more?
9	Kendall:	Yes. [taking his responsibility seriously] There is also a small lake and some trees.
10	Paul:	So we will have some resources. What can we use the trees for?
11	Kendall:	Building houses and wood for fires.
12	Paul:	Well, certainly we must have a building expert here. Who is the building expert?
13	Ethan:	Yea, yea. Wood is good, but I think brick would be better for houses.
....		[A conversation ensues among the group when Ethan asks how to make bricks.]

I was excited about the beginning of the project. Some of the students seemed to take my lead quickly by plunging into their roles as experts on an important mission. I was keeping my fingers crossed that the quiet or skeptical ones would follow the lead of those who participated in the conversation.

At the beginning, it seemed possible that both the students and I had the capability to get into role. As the project played itself out in the coming weeks, I found that I had difficulty maintaining control of the class while in role. I was not able to handle all the situations without the full weight of authority that I had as Mr. Fowler. Therefore, as time went on, I found myself taking on the role of Mr. Johnson less and less. Students also seemed to have a more difficult time taking on a role. In this project, the role of the expert was exceptionally important. If students did not accept their roles as experts, then the project was doomed to failure. In retrospect, it was the undefined role of the expert that was one of the main obstacles that led to the downfall of the project. There are three reasons why it is important for students to take on the role of the expert:

1. It forces them to draw on their own experiences and knowledge in order to build meaning.
2. As experts about a variety of topics, students are encouraged to cooperate with each other in order to find out the information that they need. This helps them to understand how various disciplines are intertwined.
3. As experts, they are equipped to face new situations and to problem solve solutions.

Therefore, if students do not feel comfortable in the role of the expert, then the potential richness of learning will not take place. I did not think too much at the beginning about this, I simply took it for granted. When, during class, a student was confused over his role, I simply repeated, "You're the expert. You're the only one who knows what to do in your situation." Of course, the student did not always know what to do in his or her particular situation, nor oftentimes did classmates. My simple explanation only seemed to confuse the students more. However I, as a first-year teacher, instead of tackling this issue head on with the students, I slid around it, simply saying that they were the experts and hoping that eventually they would catch on.

DIFFICULTIES IN TAKING ON THE ROLE OF THE EXPERT

Throughout the project, the students were able to take on the roles of experts sometimes, while at other times they were not able to. A fairly successful discussion occurred about whether mushrooms were or were not poisonous. At that time Samuel had no trouble in taking on the doctor's role when the cooking group wanted information about whether they could use the mushrooms they found.

Most of the time, students were either confused or were unwilling to become experts. For example, we had one session in which a female student, Karli, agreed to take the role of a reporter. She was working for a local news program and was trying to find out why this group of people were going on this very expensive journey back in time. The network knew that people would be interested to learn about it because their tax dollars were paying for this research mission. Karli interviewed Ethan.

Example 2

1	Karli:	And what are you going to build?
2	Ethan:	Houses, boats....
3	Karli:	What kind of materials are you going to use to build?
4	Ethan:	Wood, rope....
5	Karli:	How do you know there are trees to use for materials?
6	Ethan:	(... ...). [appears to be frustrated by the question and blurts out a statement that I wasn't able to hear]
7	Paul:	Remember Ethan, you are the expert. Only you know about the materials that you are using.
8	Karli:	He isn't an expert about trees.
9	Ethan:	But the expert from the planters group told me.
10	Karli:	He did not.
		{Fieldnotes, videotape, 01/30/95}

Both Karli and Ethan seemed uncomfortable with the role of the expert. Yet, for this to work, students needed to have confidence playing in the world of make-believe. These students did not always have confidence in that world.

There were some occasions—such as during the mushrooms exchange—that the cooperative building of knowledge that allowed for the groups' survival did occur. However, a question I was asked repeatedly by the university researchers throughout this project was: "What is the educational value of this knowledge that that students are building?" In other words, where is the tie in to the subject matter or to the beginning of civilization? Is this a jumping off point from which you can learn about mushrooms and students can do research about food of that historical time? What do the students think that we are doing here? Do the students understand what they are doing and why they are doing it? How much do I leave to the imagination of my students? Where do I begin to build from that imagination and get into teaching the variety of subjects that they hit upon while doing this project? These are the types of questions that haunted me.

MY VISION VERSUS STUDENT UNDERSTANDING—REASONS FOR THE DOWNFALL

My hope was, that when the children were in role, they could create an imaginary community that would put them in the positions of some of the first creators of towns and civilizations. They would be faced with some of the same problems and be forced to problem solve solutions to these problems. They would get a feeling of what some of the inherent difficulties were in creating an interdependent community. However, it was too abstract. It seemed like they were having trouble getting into role, and specifically, taking on the role of the expert. I began to wonder whether or not sixth graders were even capable of taking on imaginary roles. I would soon find out, but at the time, it was clearly time to stop and move on.

There are many reasons why this project failed. First, I lacked the experience to manage the kinds of group activities that were required for the drama structure. When students left their desks to create different groups in various places in the classroom, I was unsure how to set up the expectations for how this participation for learning was to be accomplished. Second, in *Drama Structures*, O'Neill and Lampert expect that students have some background in the subject that is dramatized. They also assume that students will be explicitly made aware of this link. The fact that I did not make it clear enough to my students that the drama would link our class work with ancient civilizations made it lacking an objective for the children to latch onto. O'Neill and Lampert call to our attention the importance of a two-way process between the curricular subject matter and the drama. They include resources in the book that I never used in the classroom. This oversight could have been crucial to the success of the project. Finally, after the first three lessons, I fell out of character because I didn't feel comfortable managing the class while taking on the role of another character. Because I was not modeling the role-taking behavior, it is no wonder that students did not want to take the risk of entering into role either. Also, when I would say, "You're the expert," I never really had good minilessons elucidating what I really meant. I was about to learn, however, that students can and will take on roles if they feel comfortable enough to do so.

STARTING AGAIN

The project left me still wondering about my initial questions about drama in the classroom because those questions were never really answered. The experience was so negative that I found myself rethinking my excitement towards drama altogether. It was tedious and I was bored with it. It was at that point that I turned inward and began thinking about why I chose drama in the first place. It was then that I recalled my earlier personal theatre experience. The drama of the "The Lost Valley" was very different from the literature-related experience that I had in the Mr. Scrooge play when I was in my teacher education program. It was the excitement about diving deep into a piece of literature that excited me about drama in the first place. With this realization, I took a step back (and a deep breath), pulled out a dusty copy of a book that a few of my students had read, called

Bingo Brown and the Language of Love, by Betsy Byars (1989) and began to read to them out loud.

I returned to my three questions. Can drama provide a doorway to greater involvement and understanding of literature? Can drama help connect literature to students' lives? Finally, how do I get the very peer-oriented and self-conscious sixth graders to step outside of themselves and take on roles of characters?

TAKING ON A ROLE IN IMPROVISATION

I take the last question first because it really is the first step in creating a dramatic scene. As O'Neill and Lambert pointed out, "Drama is unlikely to develop successfully unless the participants are prepared to make-believe …" (p. 12). In "The Lost Valley" drama structure, my students were unwilling to make-believe in the situation that I set up. I decided that I would read the first few pages of *Bingo Brown and the Language of Love* and then give my students the opportunity to improvise the scene. The scene dealt with teenage issues to which my students could certainly relate. A brief synopsis of the story goes like this: Bingo Brown is lovesick over a girl named Melissa who just moved to another state. His mother comes to the kitchen table as his father is cooking dinner and is very upset over a "mistake" that the phone company made. It seems that there were $54.29 worth of long distance calls made by someone from her household. As she is venting her anger to her hungry and mostly uninterested husband, Bingo summons up the courage to tell his mother that it was he who made those phone calls to Bixby, Oklahoma.

As I thought about this scene, I decided that my role would be that of coach, cheerleader, and advisor. I would definitely not force my ideas about how to play the characters on students unless I felt they took something too far. However, I would guide them if I thought they seriously misinterpreted a character's motivations. I entered into the scene skeptically because I had been so unsuccessful at getting these children to open up to the world of pretend. I was pleasantly surprised at the results.

REPETITION HELPS STUDENTS TAKE ON A ROLE

On the first day that we improvised the scene, we did it four times. The first time that students acted out the part, they were hesitant. By the fourth rendition of the scene, after watching, thinking, and talking about the scene, it jelled to the point at which the students lost the self-consciousness of the first try. It was clear, however, even during the first improvisation, that students could take on roles. I was surprised only to the extent that they immersed themselves in it. After I read the scene, I asked if anyone would be willing to take the chance and take the role of either Bingo, the mother, or the father. Three kids reluctantly took the parts. A Puerto

Rican girl named Louise took the part of the mother, a Polish boy named Willie became the father, and another Polish boy named Jack became Bingo. We set a simple stage with a dinner table and some chairs. All three were tentative with their roles. They had only heard the story one time and they had to think out carefully the sequential order of the scene, while at the same time estimating the reactions of the characters to the situations that they were in.

It is unreasonable to expect that students jump into a role the first time that they act out a scene. They need to see the scene develop, see how the parts are interpreted by others, and simply see it enough times to be able to take on the attitude of the characters. During our first 45-minute period, Jack played the role of Bingo in the first and the third times that we did the improvisation. I watched Jack develop from a person who was just trying to remember what his character was supposed to be thinking and saying, to a person who clearly *became* his character. Here is a little of his first attempt.

Example 3A

1	Jack:	[sitting on a desk and speaking in a monotone to his mom] Remember the postcard I showed you and it had a picture on it and I asked you if I could——if I could call her and you just said——and your exact words were "yes you could call her, but you don't want to be a pest." Well I called her all those times but I made it short so....
2	Louise:	I told you you could only call one time.
3	Willie:	[getting antsy] Can we eat yet?
		{Fieldnotes, videotape, 05/17/95}

Notice how Jack was hesitant and stumbling around for the right words to say. He spoke quietly, but his quiet manner belied the fact that he was not really being the nervous schoolboy that Bingo was at that moment.

The next time Jack played the role of Bingo was two improvisations later. He practiced one time and saw someone else do the same role one time. This time, notice how he was able to take on more of the character of Bingo Brown.

Example 3B

1	Karli:	Bingo, did you make those calls?

2	Jack:	No.
3	Kendall:	Don't lie about it, Son.
....		[At this point the audience laughs because they know, as do the characters, that he is lying. However, Jack is making Karli and Kendall work a bit to find the truth.]
4	Jack:	[speaking slowly] Well, you remember Melissa. She moved to Oklahoma and....
5	Karli:	[motioning with her arms trying to draw more information from him]
6	Jack:	[is clearly having fun here playing with Karli and holding off on the inevitable truth for as long as possible] What, what? She moved there to Oklahoma. I *might* have made the phone calls.
7	Karli:	You what!
....		[At this point, Karli goes into a tirade and there is no way Jack can carry out the charade any longer.]
		{Fieldnotes, videotape, 05/17/95}

In this scene, Jack took his time drawing out the scene. He lied at first, he added some stutters, and he left just a shadow of a doubt at the end. It took the strong personalities of Karli and Kendall to remove any doubt from the fact that Jack as Bingo did indeed make the phone calls.

From the very first improvisation, we were having so much fun with this scene that the students (including the audience members who had not as yet participated as characters) wanted to keep trying it. This repetition allowed them to take on more clearly defined character roles and allowed them more space to experiment with their characters' personalities. My fear of drama was beginning to wane. Awkward sixth graders can get into role and enjoy it immensely!

SOLVING PROBLEMS IN ROLE

In the 1990s, educational reformers made problem solving a priority to be included in the curriculum. I would like to make the case that improvisational drama, in the context of *literary reproduction* (acting out literature), is problem solving. If students dive into the turbulent waters of improvisation, they are constantly forced to come up with instantaneous solutions to many problems that come flying their way. Next, I give examples of how two groups of students (from different improvisations), when faced with the same problem, find two very different solutions. During the first improvisation, Jack, as Bingo, seeks the solution of compromise to help get him out of the sticky situation that he is in. He knows his mother is angry about the phone bill, so he tries to placate her.

Example 4A

1	Bingo/Jack:	I'm sorry.
2	Mom/Louise:	You're sorry! Who's going to pay for this?
3	Bingo/Jack:	I'll settle ... ... for it out of my allowance.

{Fieldnotes, videotape, 05/17/95}

In the actual Byars' story that I had read so far, there was no mention of the fact that Bingo solved the problem by having his mother take the money out of his allowance. The students knew intuitively that they needed a solution to the problem. Jack came up with a very reasonable solution, one that made sense to him based on his life experience. It is interesting to note that if I had read just one more sentence in the book, we would have seen Bingo suggesting to his mom that she should take the money from his allowance.

Next, let's go to the fourth and final role play, where Kendall plays the part of the father, Karli plays the mother, and George plays Bingo. In this passage, notice how they developed the solution to the problem of the phone bill. As the scene opened, Kendall constantly moved food around the table, cut it, and ate it. Karli is very concerned about the phone bill and tends to follow up her pronouncements with a good hearty whack, with the back of her hand, to Kendall's shoulder. They clearly enjoyed themselves in this rendition.

Example 4B

1	Kendall:	[to George] Sit down, Boy. Let's eat.
2	Karli:	[gives a whack on Kendall's back] How you all gonna eat when we owe all this money to the telephone company?
3	Kendall:	I got a good job.
4	Karli:	[pointing to George] He's gotta pay for it. You shut up. [another whack on the back]
5	Kendall:	[taking on the "fatherly" role after he's gone on with this eating thing long enough, and then pointing at George] You're gonna get a paper route. Early in the morning, you gonna get up at 5:30 in the morning and get out of here at 6:30.
6	George:	[begins to say something] (...).....
7	Kendall:	Shut up!
8	Karli:	[in a very loud voice and another whack] Don't tell him to shut up! [addressing George] Shut up!
9	Kendall:	[loudly] You gonna get a paper route.

10	George:	[stuttering] I have the money already.
11	Kendall:	Where?
12	George:	In my piggy bank.
13	Kendall:	How much?
14	George:	Fifty-four dollars and twenty-nine cents.
15	Kendall:	Go get it.
		{Fieldnotes, videotape, 05/17/95}

When George came back with the money (actually a science book), Kendall counted it and decided that it was short. George dug deep into his pockets to come up with the rest of the money. Karli, not satisfied that he has been punished enough (and unwilling to give Kendall the last word), denies him use of the phone for the next 2 months.

Each character had to decide how to solve the problem, and each character came up with his or her own suggestions. Kendall thought he (Bingo/George) should get a paper route, George thought it would be easier just get the money out of the piggy bank; Karli, at the end, decided that 2 months without the use of the phone would be reasonable punishment. Both the first and last scenes show how students can, when immersed in an improvisational dramatic situation, delve deeply into a situation, find a sticking point, and then find a solution to that sticking point.

Ever since that first day, I always tried to read just to the point in a story before the solution to a problem is given. Then, when we improvise the stories, the students often come up with surprising solutions. We then take great pleasure in finding out how the author chose to solve the problems. Needless to say, sometimes we disagree sharply with the solution that the author has chosen. However, this is *active* comprehension at its best. It is moments like these that make teaching a pleasure.

CAN DRAMA HELP TO CONNECT LITERATURE TO LIFE?

This question is an important one, because if students do not find the material relevant to their lives, then it will be difficult to keep their interest. Clearly, in *Bingo Brown,* they were interested. Therefore, my question was, where can I note specific connections between Bingo Brown and their lives? First of all, the first allowance scene clearly showed a connection. Jack must have had some experience with getting his allowance withheld, because if he didn't or knew someone who had, he would not have considered it a realistic solution to the problem. Another repeated theme throughout these improvisations was the father taking on the role of disciplinarian. Even though the book portrayed Bingo's father as being more concerned with eating, and less concerned with what he considered to be a more minor issue such as the phone bill, my students couldn't seem to help themselves in seeing the father as the disciplinarian in the family. In the first session, after Jack announced his allowance solution, Willie (as father) took it one step further. They sat down at the dinner table.

Example 5A

1	Willie/father:	How much was that bill again?
2	Louise/mother:	Fifty-four dollars and twenty-nine cents.
3	Willie:	[looking over at Jack/Bingo] Let's go to the washroom, Son. (... ...). [then takes the chair (with Jack on it), drags it over to the doorway of the classroom, then begins to fake hit him]
4	Jack:	[falls to the ground]
5	Willie:	[begins to fake kick Jack]
		{Fieldnotes, videotape, 05/17/95}

I had to cut them off. I began to wonder, because the book made no mention of physical reprimands, and this was so out of the character of the father in the book, why did they do it? Clearly, it is often hard to keep kids away from bringing in a violence theme when they are allowed to develop their own scenes. However, there was no violence even implied in *Bingo Brown*. I was wondering whether, as other students took on the role of the father, they would seek the same kind of solution.

In the second role play, Jack and Willie switched roles, with Jack taking on the role of the father and Willie that of Bingo. This time it was payback time, and when Jack got to play the role of the father, he portrayed him in a violent way—he acted in a way that Willie had. Thus, in our wrap-up discussion after this second session, I tried to get the kids to reconsider their interpretation of the father. Jack as father continued in this violence vein, but Karli argued for another interpretation.

Example 5B

1	Paul:	Was there anything they (the actors) could improve upon ... as far as the characters go?
2	Jack:	I should have ... ... chopped his head off.
....		
3	Karli:	He don't care about what happens that much. He's just like, "let's eat," and she says "how can you eat when we owe all this money?", and he says, "I can eat any time."

4	Paul:	So what's the attitude of the father?
5	Karli:	He don't really care about it that much, he just wants to eat.
6	Paul:	[addressing mainly to Willie and Jack] So he might not be quite as a disciplinarian as you are portraying.
7	Willie:	Yes, he is! He's the father!
8	Paul:	Do all fathers act the same?
9	Willie:	[backing down somewhat] Possibly.
....		[Willie is drowned out in a chorus of NO's! from the group and he does not pursue it any farther.]
		{Fieldnotes, videotape, 05/17/95}

After this debriefing, I was interested to see what would happen when the role of the father was taken by another student. This time, it happened to be Kendall, and this time he took Jack (Bingo) into his room and play slapped him across the face. The audience clearly loved this. Obviously, this wasn't what I was looking for. So, when Kendall once more played the role of the father in the final improvisation, I appealed directly to him to try to be more true to the character of the father. It was during this scene that they had to find a different solution to the problem, and had to end the scene in a more thoughtful manner, which they did.

I think the violence they used at the end of their improvisation scenes brings up a number of issues. First of all, it is the sort of ending that they are exposed to the most. It brings closure in a way that students see it on television or in movies. Next, it is an easy way to end a scene. It is a simple solution to the problem of, "How do we end this?". Finally, it depicts a way of thought where the male of the household is the final arbitrator of justice, and whose solutions to problems are often physical and violent. I couldn't ask the kids whether or not they were beaten at home for similar offenses. However, it was clear that they had a hard time accepting the fact that, in the book, it was the mother, not the father, who administered the punishment.

I ended up using this information during our studies of ancient cultures, making it clear that it was not until the development of Western civilization that men became the heads of the household. I also made a point to read and talk about newspaper articles or stories that portrayed women as the heads or coheads of households in modern times. So, can drama connect literature to life? The answer I found was positive. In fact, often, they are connected so tightly that it is difficult to see where the drama ends and real life begins. Dramatic scenes can give teachers a lot of information about what their students see in the literature that they are reading. In this way, the teacher can counter students' viewpoints with other viewpoints, and can thereby influence the way he or she sees the world.

CAN DRAMA PROVIDE A DOORWAY TO GREATER
INVOLVEMENT AND UNDERSTANDING OF LITERATURE?

I remember thinking when I was acting out my role in a Mr. Scrooge play earlier in my life, that each time I played the part I learned something more about that character's personality. If I had simply read the story one time or had it read to me, I might have been able to pull out a few facts about the story, and maybe even to remember the names of most of the characters, but by being personally involved in the story, I began to ask questions about it, and was forced to find meaning in it. In this way, I enhanced my understanding of the story. I found that my students, when improvising Bingo Brown, also worked to find meaning in the story. When I saw how personally invested the students were in the follow-up discussions to the scene (and how fiery the debates were), I knew that students were involved with this piece of literature.

I wrapped up the first improvisational scene with a quick request. It turned into a very enlightening discussion.

Example 6

1 Paul: Let's talk about their performance. I want to hear some good
              things that they did in their performance.

2 Eva: Like, Bingo told the truth. He didn't say, "Ohh, I didn't do any-
              thing."

3 Willie: He didn't really say the truth. He's like, "Oh, fifty-four dollars
              and twenty-eight cents, who could have done that?"

4 Jack: He forgot about it. He forgot. He just said, "Who would have
              made fifty-four dollars and twenty-eight cents worth of phone
              calls to that Oklahoma." But then he remembered so he didn't
              lie.

5 Willie: Well, he was gonna lie.

6 George: Yea he was. He was trying to pull it off by saying who would
              make fifty-four dollars and twenty-eight cents?

7 Jack: But that was like his forgetful side. Like who would make
              fifty-four dollars and twenty-eight cents? [rolling his eyes up-
              ward toward the ceiling perhaps to make it seem like Bingo is
              kind of spacey]

           {Fieldnotes, videotape, 05/17/95}

There are a few things that are very interesting to note about this exchange. First of all, the drama fostered a situation in which students were asking their own questions and responding to them without my involvement. This type of interaction is an exciting moment in any classroom. Also, it showed that students tried to define the character of Bingo. Was Bingo a liar or was he honest? This was the real question that hung over the conversation. It was important that they discussed this question because the way they thought about the character ultimately guided the way that they portrayed him in the improvisation. It was interesting to note that both George and Willie played Bingo in the improvisations that were to follow, and both of them played Bingo as if he were basically honest, while Jack toyed with his character a bit. It was clear from this activity that students clearly were engaged in the literature enough to ask their own questions and to try to find out the answers. They realized that the way you make a statement sometimes holds more meaning than the statement itself. Finally, they were able to apply their beliefs by acting them out on the stage for all to see and respond to. It was clear that during the entire Bingo Brown exchange, students gained a greater appreciation for the problems, characters, and mood of the book than they would ever have attained by simply reading it themselves or having me read it to them.

FINAL THOUGHTS AND COMMENTS

I had many failures and a few successes in my first year of teaching sixth grade. Trial by fire certainly described my situation well. There was so much going on that I had to deal with as a first-year teacher, from how to keep a grade book or attendance book, to how to work with parents, to how to be effective in working out conflict between students. I had to figure out solutions to problems such as George's daily bathroom emergencies, how to keep track of the books the students read, when it's appropriate to admonish a student who doesn't have a pencil, to how much and what kind of homework I should give. My teacher training left me utterly unprepared to deal with situations such as these, which were blindsiding me with daily regularity. I truly don't know if any teacher training could prepare a teacher with solutions to the problems faced by a first-year teacher. With all this going on, in hindsight, I simply added to the confusion by attempting drama so soon with my class. Yet, by taking this chance I propped open a doorway of discovery that I can keep pushing open farther in teaching years to come. I learned that drama can greatly enhance the discussion of literature in a classroom. I learned that I could learn a lot about students' lives and beliefs through drama. I learned that, contrary to my earlier beliefs, students can learn to problem solve in role if given multiple opportunities of involvement to rethink and recreate. I also learned that drama does not always work, and that it is often a scary prospect for both teacher and student. Just like my initial rejection of theatre at 10 years old, when my father tried to get me interested in drama, I failed to excite my students initially in drama. Yet, without even knowing it, there must have been something in those initial experiences that stuck with me enough to make me want to try again. Then, just like my success as an actor with the Mr. Scrooge play, I had success with *Bingo Brown*. I have continued to build on this success by using drama to help kids gain a greater appreciation of literature and of themselves.

ABOUT THE AUTHOR

I taught sixth grade for 3 years and then taught seventh and eight grade social studies for 2 years. My walking shoes are worn, my backpack is light, and I can whistle a mean "Oh, Susanna." I'm off in Thailand to explore life elsewhere.

DEDICATION

I thank my dear parents for their love. It shines through me to every child I reach.

REFERENCES

Byars, B. (1989). *Bingo Brown and the language of love*. New York: Viking.
O'Neill, C., & Lambert, A. (1982). *Drama structures: A practical handbook for teachers*. Portsmouth, NH: Heinemann.

Chapter 13

How to Loosen Tongues
With Drama: Children Try
It Their Way in a Special
Education Classroom

Bernadine Braun
Andersen Elementary School

EDITORS' COMMENTS

Bernadine begins her chapter by presenting initial work she did in making her read alouds of children's literature more interactive and collaborative for her special needs students. These efforts were to "loosen their tongues," as she called it, which required that she reexamine *her* own role in this literacy event so as to make possible more opportunities for her students' participation in book discussions.

She describes the major focus of her inquiry, namely, how to support students' drama experiences with these books, and later on in the year, their attempts to write and perform their own plays. At the end, she briefly illustrates some of the lessons that the children taught when they acted as teachers at the end of the year, which she believes were only possible because of their earlier drama experiences. Throughout, Bernadine talks about her struggles and successes in these efforts, as well as what she learned through teacher research.

The introduction chapter of this book provides the theoretical and methodological background for the larger collaborative school–university action-research project and this chapter about Bernadine's inquiry on drama.

University researchers, Dian Ruben and Jane Liao, collaborated with Bernadine in her inquiry.

JOINING THE TEACHER-RESEARCH GROUP

I originally entered the teacher-research group at Andersen hoping to learn new ideas for teaching language arts to my special education students. My particular concerns involved these children's reading skills and their lack of interest in reading. As the only special education teacher at Andersen in my discipline, "cognitive disability," I usually have no one with whom to collaborate about what works well with my type of students. I found the programs written for cognitively disabled children to be lacking in imagination. Most of them were repetition after repetition. As I met with other teachers in the research group, I encountered many new ideas and methods of helping my children in reading.

Because I teach children whose abilities are at the kindergarten through third-grade level, the problem for me is being able to attend several grade meetings at one time. When the school schedule is made up it is always the same: "Well, I just couldn't fit you in. Try to change with another teacher to be included in the grade level you want." Because I usually end up collaborating with no one, this teacher-research project was a rare opportunity to meet with teachers of many grade levels to share what worked and what did not. I consider the fact that we could view others' teaching on videotapes and offer suggestions regarding their inquiries to have been quite effective for my own research on my teaching. My problems were seriously considered by all in the group, and I found suggestions, made to me by teachers with similar problems, to be helpful.

MEET THE CAST

During the year of my inquiry, my class consisted of 14 special-needs children. My room was unique because of the age span of the students. The children's ages ranged from 8 to 14 years old. Three of these children spoke no English, and because my own Spanish is limited, my communication with them was assisted through a Spanish-speaking teacher aide, who was frequently called away to help elsewhere in the school, and also by some of the children who could translate.

Because it is a special education class, I keep my children for more than 1 year. Some of the children had been with me 3 and 4 years. Along with their academic difficulties, most of them had overlays of emotional problems. Most of the children in the group were labeled "cognitively disabled"; a few were labeled "severely learning disabled" (in my room by special request of their parents).

One thing I try to foster in my classroom is a feeling of family. As the children arrive in my room in the morning they are allowed to tell me anything that is on their minds, and are encouraged to conference with me privately, if they have trouble they feel they cannot handle by themselves. I also try to make the atmosphere in our room as non-threatening as I can. I want the children to feel that they can ask any question, no matter how stupid it may seem, and get an answer. I want them to realize that we can work together to find ways to overcome their problems. As a result, they are very caring and also look out for each other. Sometimes they tease each other, but they get very upset with anyone else who teases one of them.

The majority of children I work with have met so much failure before coming to me that it is very difficult to interest them in trying anything. I always try to consider the background of the child when I am planning a new strategy. During the year of my inquiry, I was particularly concerned about two of my students who would be graduating that year. Planning for Ana and Cecilia was very difficult because they refused to try anything that involved speaking in front of the class. These two sisters came to my class so traumatized that they would not move out of their seats, which were next to each other; they held hands so tightly that their knuckles would get white. I had never had children this traumatized in my class before. Never once in the first year I had them did they initiate a question or volunteer an answer in front of the class. At the time of the research, I had had them for 4 years. They had learned to move as individuals, but I was still having trouble getting one of them, Ana, to answer questions or to share her opinions with the class.

SELF-CRITIQUE AND BACKGROUND ON MY INQUIRY

I was told that I did too much for these children—that I did not let them answer their own questions or decide what they were supposed to do. My students are so easily frustrated when they first come to me that I usually arrange things to keep them from failing for awhile. As they begin to see that they can do things by themselves, I try to slowly withdraw my help and ask them to put forth more effort to achieve what was asked of them. In my inquiry I attempted to see if I was indeed helping too much. I found it very hard always having to decide, at that moment, whether to interact with the children. I taught so long using the lecture-and-answer-all-questions technique that it was difficult to know when to stay out and when to intervene. I found myself vacillating between not giving enough guidance and giving too much information. Children became so used to me giving them the answers all the time, that I had a terrible time getting them to answer. It takes time to find the right mix, but I was determined to be the guide, not the total provider.

In my inquiry I studied how the use of drama might help my students be better readers, but also be more active participants in their learning in general. However, before I talk about these drama efforts, I need to cover my inquiry on my read-alouds that I had done during the preceding year, an area in which I was still having ongoing struggles. In my mind, students having opportunities to initiate their own responses and questions to the books being read was a prerequisite to their being able to dramatize stories and books. Underlying both of these concepts in the drama part of my teacher-research, however, was this issue of mine regarding how and when I should intervene.

STAGE I: READ-ALOUDS

During the 1993–1994 school year, my colleagues and I did inquiries about reading aloud to children. My inquiry was to find out if reading stories to them would foster a desire for reading and increase their vocabularies. Initially, when I read a story to my students, they sat and listened with little enthusiasm. At the end of the story, there would be a sigh of relief. If I asked questions, children sat silently waiting for me to give answers. If I called on someone else, that child would sit quietly until I got impatient and either asked someone else or gave the answer.

When I started the study on read-alouds, I chose fairy tales. The children seemed to enjoy the stories, but at first it was difficult to get them to discuss or respond to questions raised about the stories. Many of the children continued to be afraid to state their opinions or to discuss a subject due to embarrassment, shyness, or lack of English-language ability. When I saw that they were losing interest in the books I chose, I asked the children to choose the books for the read aloud, but this was not much better. The only book they really listened to with any interest was *Matilda* by Roald Dahl (1988). I tried to get them to tell me what they were interested in, but as usual they shrugged their shoulders and became mute.

As I indicated, in the beginning, I received only one-word answers or a shrug of the shoulders as responses to my questions. I felt, however, that many of these reactions might be attributed to the fact that I was not asking enough open-ended questions, and or, not waiting long enough for an answer. I began to see that I needed to change if I wanted them to respond more and to initiate discussion. Using different types of questions, patiently waiting for answers, and providing more spaces for their initiations were the ways that finally worked. This was a very frustrating experience for me, but I was determined. Gradually they began to answer more quickly and then they began to respond by asking questions and stating opinions as the stories progressed.

In the 1994–1995 year of the drama inquiry, I used many of the same books, thinking that children would be somewhat familiar with the stories, therefore enabling them to ad-lib or make up dialogue more easily. When I reread these fairy tales that they would use for dramatic play, most children were finally uninhibited enough to comment as we went along. They even related some of the events to things that happened in their lives. Example 1 illustrates this active participation in our reading of *Jack and the Beanstalk Retold in Verse* by Beatrice Schenk de Regniers (1990). Our discussion began with my introductory question.

Example 1

1	Berna.:	Was Jack's sale of the cow for five beans a good deal?
2	Cs:	No!
3	Arnie:	It's a bad idea.
4	Berna.:	Then why do you think it's a bad deal?
5	Arnie:	Because if you would sell the cow for three beans——if the mother threw them out and in the morning the thing growed.
6	Berna.:	So was it a good bargain or not? Would you sell your cow for five seeds? How much would you want for your cow?
....		[Students responded with varying amounts of money. Then just as I began to read the book, I mentioned that it was in rhyme and Stan offered an explanation of what that term meant.]
7	Berna.:	HERE'S A STORY ABOUT A BOY NAMED JACK, BOLD AS BRASS, SHARP AS A TACK. IT'S ALSO ABOUT A GIANT ——NOT VERY BRIGHT, BUT MEAN AND *BIG*. IN JUST ONE BITE HE CAN SWALLOW A PIG BUT WHAT THIS WICKED GIANT LIKES MOST ARE BOYS——AND GIRLS——BROILED, ON TOAST....
8	Cs:	[in disgust] Eeeeeuuw!
9	Julissa:	I'd rather have cooked pig. Cooked pig is good!
....		
10	Berna.:	BUT HE HAD A COW NAMED MILKY WHITE. SHE GAVE MILK EVERY MORNING. SHE GAVE MILK EVERY NIGHT. BY SELLING THE MILK THE COW WAS GIVING, THEY WERE BARELY ABLE TO MAKE A LIVING.
11	Arnie:	Ms. Braun, how do they sell the milk?
12	Berna.:	They put it in a pan or a jar and they sell it to you.
13	Julissa:	[pointing to the udder of the cow in the illustration] What is this?
14	Berna.:	That's the cow's udder.
15	C:	That's where the milk comes from?
16	Berna.:	That's where the milk comes from.
....		[There is a long discussion about other aspects of a cow's anatomy, its gender, and where cow babies come from. Then more of the book was read with discussion.]
17	Berna.:	[I am now finishing reading the part where the beanstalk has appeared and am showing the illustrations on that page. The left-hand page depicts the night before——Jack had had a hard time sleeping and has left his bed in shambles. The right-hand page has Jack——with his spiky hair standing out high from his

head——putting his clothes on as he sees the beanstalk outside his window.] ... JACK JUMPS UP, PUTS ON HIS CLOTHES, THEN GOES TO THE WINDOW. WHAT DOES HE SEE? SOMETHING LEAFY AND GREEN ... IS IT A TREE? NO. IT'S——....

18	C:	It is a tree.
19	Berna.:	Is it a tree?
20	Cs:	No. It's a beanstalk.
21	Julissa:	#Look at this hair! Look at his hair!#
22	Berna.:	#It's a beanstalk.#
23	Arnie:	[loudly] Look at his bed!
24	Berna.:	Yeah, look at his bed.
25	Julissa:	Look at his hair!
26	Arnie:	[pulling his hair up] His hair looks like this.
27	Berna.:	Yes, his hair looks like that.

....

28	Berna.:	[I finish reading the next page, which shows a two-page illustration of the beanstalk.] ... "THE MAGIC BEANS MY MOTHER THREW INTO THE YARD TOOK ROOT AND GREW AND GREW AND GREW UP TO THE SKY."
29	Arnie:	Ms. Braun, he has to climb all the way to the top?
30	Cs:	No.
31	Arnie:	He'll fall. Does he have to fly all the way to the top?
32	Berna.:	He could.
33	Arnie:	Is it a magic cloud?
34	Berna.:	Is it a magic cloud?
35	Cs:	No.
36	Arnie:	It could be....
37	Berna.:	It could be because the giant's house is on it*...
38	Stan:	But that's a fake....
39	Berna.:	Could a giant's house sit on a cloud?
40	Cs:	#Yes.#
41	Cs:	#No.#

....

42	Melissa:	Excuse me ... my friend went to Puerto Rico. She was in Mex——<Gloria>, she went to Puerto Rico. This giant fell from the sky. I'm not joking.
43	C:	<You> never seen no giant.
44	Melissa:	Excuse me! Uh my——<Gloria> went to Puerto Rico ... and she saw a giant fall from the sky. ...

45	C:	(...)
46	Melissa:	Down to the ground.
....		[The conversation goes into another direction.]
		{Fieldnotes, videotape, 01/10/95}

This example shows many kinds of student responses I had been looking for all along. For example, in line 8 they reacted in disgust to the idea of the giant's eating of boys and girls. Julissa also indicated that she preferred cooked pig. They asked questions of their own—about how they sell milk, about the udder of the cow, about how Jack might fall if he climbed to the top of the beanstalk, about the possibility that the cloud might be a magic one, and so forth. Julissa and Arnie exclaimed about Jack's hair after a night's sleep, with Arnie illustrating how it would look on his head. Finally, in response to students' consideration of the fantastic idea of a giant living in a house on a cloud, Melissa brought in her own personal story of what she had heard from her friend about a giant falling from the sky in Puerto Rico. After the discussion about where milk comes from, they even reaffirmed concepts they learned in an earlier study of anatomy and family life (which I didn't include in Example 1 due to space constraints).

As I mentioned previously, I struggled with the balance between giving the children all the answers and guiding them so that they could find their own way. I think I did pretty well in accepting and valuing many of their initiations and providing answers that helped them extend their ideas more fully. However, some of my responses reflected that I still had work to do. I thought I had an okay open-ended question in the beginning to get them to recall what they thought about the book we had read before, and I followed up well with Arnie's comment that he thought it was a bad idea that Jack sold the cow for five beans by getting him to provide an explanation for it. However, my response in line 6 to his answer was troublesome—I asked three questions in a row with little pause in between! Also, a couple of times, instead of my answering their questions immediately, I might have turned them over to the class for consideration—for example, when Arnie asked how they sell milk (line 11) or when Julissa asked about the udder in the illustration (line 13).

Nevertheless, in general the read-alouds became a comfortable atmosphere wherein children actively responded, and I became better at guiding the read-alouds. I felt that in this new environment I would be ready for the next stage, namely, to launch my inquiry on trying out drama with my students.

STAGE II: ENACTMENT OF DRAMA

During the 1994–1995 school year, my inquiry was to find out if drama could increase the children's vocabulary and reading skills. I was also thinking that drama might provide a means for helping some of my students—especially the two sisters, Ana and Cecilia—become more active in their participation in class. I hoped the experiences of the previous year's read-alouds, which were continuing this school year, would lead into the drama activities I planned as the focus of the second year's inquiry.

When we began, I felt that drama consisted of my reading a story and then having the students remember the sequence of that story by stating an approximation of the words they heard in the story. As a result, in the beginning I was very controlling in my interactions with them, just like I was in the beginning of my read-aloud inquiry in the previous year. By the end of the research, however, I changed my ideas of about I expected of the children—and myself. Children could change the story to suit themselves and could make up new dialogue as they went along. This was a big difference from the beginning, when I was telling them each line as they needed it and when no one seemed to want to act.

So, my dominance was present a few days later as we enacted the *Jack and the Beanstalk* book. When it seemed to me that the children were unable to speak the words of the story or to follow exactly the story line by making up things that did not happen in the story, I directed them back to the story line. Neither the children nor I were happy with the outcome. In retrospect, of course, it would have been better to have let them just have fun enacting the drama. They might have gained more from the experience, and I might have learned more about their understanding and interpretations of the book. Again, as I was with the read-alouds, I decided to be the director instead of letting the children have some of the control.

There were many more occasions like this in other dramatizations of other books. It felt like it was back to the old ways of the read-alouds. Most of the children did not seem to recall the stories; they did not want to do it, telling me that they were embarrassed to get up in front of their peers. I was running everything—telling them every word they were to say. It was not the right way to go, so I began to wait for the children to respond. It took a month or two before they began to feel free enough to enact the stories, and that occurred because I found a way to give them both my support and their freedom.

Using Storyboards in Dramatizing *Horton Hatches the Egg*

The following incident was the first time that the children were given sufficient power to make their own decisions. This enactment turned out to be one of the best. The story was *Horton Hatches the Egg* by Doctor Seuss

(1940), which is the story of an elephant, Horton, who is asked by Mayzie Bird, who never intends to return, to sit on her egg so she can rest for a while. Horton agrees to sit on the egg, is laughed at, and then is deserted by his friends. Hunters point guns at him, intending to kill him, but change their minds and sell him to a circus. When Mayzie sees Horton again, the egg is hatching and she wants it back. When Horton gets off the egg, it hatches into an elephant bird who ended up flying to Horton.

I read the book to them 2 days before the enactment. The next day, each child folded a drawing paper so that it had eight boxes. This is called a *storyboard,* a technique I became aware of when I shared edited versions of my classroom interactions in our weekly discussions with other teachers in the research program. Together, the class and I decided what parts of the story to put in each of the boxes. These represented the scenes they would then act out. Each child drew his or her pictures in the boxes to refer to during the drama.

Thus, I supported students' drama efforts ahead of time, also in coming up with the props they thought they needed, and in setting the various locations in the classroom for the drama. During the enactment I deliberately sat back and enjoyed myself. The children really did take charge of this enactment, which was the major goal of my inquiry. Example 2 shows students' dramatization of the beginning of the story when Mayzie Bird, played by Stan, asked Horton, who is Polly, to sit on her egg.

Example 2

1	Berna.:	[to Darla] Do you have your storyboard so you know where we're going? Okay, it's all up to you. Go ahead Mayzie.
2	Polly:	[Walks over to where Mayzie Bird (Stan) is sitting on the egg.]
3	Stan:	"Will you sit on my egg?"
4	Polly:	"No, I have some work to do." [stands in front of Stan for several seconds awaiting his reply]
5	Stan:	[Looks at me and seems to want me to help.]
6	Berna.:	[I do nothing.]
7	Polly:	[Is becoming impatient as she pats her foot and drums on her thigh with her fingers. Finally she turns partially around and addresses me.] Ms. Braun ... [in an exaggerated manner suggesting increasing impatience]
8	Stan:	I don't know what to say next.
9	Cf1:	You talk to her. You convince her.
10	Cf2:	Say please......
11	John:	You beg her!
12	Stan:	"Please, can you sit on my egg?"

13	Polly:	"No, I have some work to do."
14	Steven:	[Looks at me with a nervous smile.]
15	Berna.:	[I do not respond.]
16	Polly:	[whispers to Stan] (... ...).
17	Stan:	"I'm tired of sitting on this egg. I'll come back in a little while."
18	Polly:	[whispering] "Go, bye."
19	Stan:	[Leaves and goes to another part of the room.]
20	C:	[off camera] You're at the beach.
21	Berna.:	Excuse me. He knows where he's going.
22	Darla:	[Enters the scene and hesitates.]
23	Berna.:	What happens next? If you forget, look at your storyboard.
24	Darla:	[Walks over and looks at storyboards they had made that are laying on a desk nearby. She and Konrad, John, and Stan are hunters in the story. As the boys enter with guns drawn, she joins them.]

{Fieldnotes, videotape, 03/02/95}

It is easily seen in this example how much the children took active parts in the play. They helped each other—for example, when several of them (lines 9–11) helped Stan out when he said that he didn't know what to say next, and then later when he seemed lost, Polly whispered to him to prompt him (lines 16 & 18). That was because I tried not to be the source of help (lines 6 & 15). Instead, when I did intervene, it was to suggest that they refer to their storyboards (lines 1 & 23) or to encourage their ability to do what they thought best—as when I supported Stan's actions (line 21). Because I took a new role, children really worked together as a team for this enactment.

Things weren't perfect. Sometimes children acted silly, and when acting in front of another class, some of them became so shy they just stood and did nothing. Trying to remember their parts was always a challenge. However, because as a rule I let the children enact the story a second time, these more reluctant students began to participate in these repeated dramatizations. They now saw how it could be done and they were more at ease knowing what was expected. In addition, children began more spontaneous acting, for example, during their free time. Sometimes they made up things and sometimes they enacted things they had seen or heard at home. It was eye opening when they acted things from their lives. It gave me an insight into the children and a knowledge of what their home lives were like. Sometimes this made a difference in the way I handled the different children. Acting out stories of their own creation also helped the group to become more supportive and understanding of one another. They sometimes reenacted incidents when they had gotten themselves in trouble, and then the class and I tried to show how the situation could have been changed if they had handled it another way. Thus, once I began to change my way of interacting with students in drama, children began to use drama to express themselves in many ways.

STAGE III: BECOMING STUDENT PLAYWRIGHTS

I finally let the children write and then perform their own plays. Unfortunately, and I don't know why, I felt that I should not give them any help at all. I found a nice balance of support finally in their dramatizations as the *Horton* enactment showed. From one extreme to another: first I helped them with everything, then I helped them with nothing.

We started by talking about what they should do in order to produce their own play:

1. Decide (what you want your play to be about)
2. What do you need (props etc.)
3. Write (the parts of your play)

They could do anything they wanted. Their drama could be an original play, a story from a book, or a life experience. Students divided themselves into three groups, with some children playing in more than one drama.

The first group consisted of mostly the two sisters who were the two shyest girls in the room (though sometimes Donia, who spoke only a few words of English, joined them). They decided to write their play about "The Little Mermaid" tale, which in their version had an evil queen who had a crystal ball and held the mermaid hostage. The mermaid's father saved the mermaid and they ran away with a goldfish and lived happily ever after. Ana and Cecilia worked very hard and produced a reasonable script, with the help of one of the university researchers who was helping me in my inquiry. In rehearsing or performing their play, they read from that script. Frequently, they stood sideways with their backs almost facing the audience, reading with their scripts held partly covering their faces. Nevertheless, they spoke in front of an audience for the first time, and they got better as they did it over and over.

The second group decided their play would be about "The Lion King" movie. Arnie and Konrad did most of the work, thinking through the scenes of their play. Most of their play focused on incidents that happened at Pride Rock, which is where the lion could view his entire kingdom. Most of their drama, which had little dialogue, was play fighting, with the help of three other boys (Paul, Stan, and John), who where the hyenas in the production. Arnie, playing the father lion, Mufasa, and Konrad as the young lion, Simba, frequently discussed and decided on their lines throughout their performances. Because they did not ever write a script (even though I kept asking them to do so), they usually provided very confused dramas that mixed up different parts of the movie.

The third group worked on the play, "The Dead Cheerleaders," which seemed to come from some horror movie. In this play, three cheerleaders—Melissa, Polly, and Darla—have some kind of power to bring back from death an entire football team (played by John, Arnie, Konrad, and Stan). All of the action in the drama occurred at a graveyard and the girls spent a lot of time making headstones as props and painting their faces to look gory. They did not produce a script either, and most ad libbed their lines during each performance, which did not improve much.

We did have some after-drama discussions about what children liked and disliked about performances, where I gave them some opportunities for self-evaluation. However, having a meaningful discussion of their performances was very difficult. This is illustrated in Example 3, when we were evaluating one of "The Lion King" performances. I tried to let them know that their own evaluations were legitimate, but I also worked on having them be specific and helpful. Example 3 begins after John and Stan said of the play, "It stinks!", "It sucks!"

Example 3

1	Berna.:	No! Don't tell me it stunk and it sucked! I want to know what can you do to make it better!
2	Arnie:	You know … you could——don't be scared … prepare more….
3	Paul:	Don't try to play the two parts … uhm … together.
4	Berna.:	Okay, let's not——who's got paper? Get a paper, write this down so you don't forget. Somebody in your play. Write it down!
5	Cs:	[John, Arnie, and Konrad all get paper to write on.]
6	Berna.:	[Quietly repeats Paul's suggestion.]
7	Arnie:	[repeating softly each of the words as he writes them down) (··· ···) to … gether … together!
8	Berna.:	Right! All right, what else was a suggestion?
9	C:	(··· ···).
10	Berna.:	Someone suggested that you speak louder. All right, put that down.
11	Konrad:	[Writes "spec" ("speak")….]
		{Videotape, 04/25/95}

Thus, these discussions helped my students realize that their evaluations were worthwhile. However, although their remarks were genuine and fairly accurate, they centered mostly on the process aspects of performances (except for Paul's idea that the content of two parts not be played together). Also, I never had them follow-up on these assessments in their subsequent dramatizations, although I had the class participate in performing negative comments with alternative ways of critiquing. Through this method, children finally learned to comment on the play itself, rather than the about person performing.

Except for the "Little Mermaid" group, children did not write out a script. Most of the performances weren't very successful for that reason. They did not know how to organize in their minds what they wanted to present, and I was at a loss at times what to do to guide them. I went from group to group asking questions, but offered little help. I should have given them more guidance. I never thought of their using storyboards for their plays, which had been so helpful to them in dramatizing stories (see Example 2). That would have scaffolded their ideas about their plays, but instead, I left them on their own.

SOME OTHER OUTCOMES

Although there were difficulties in developing effective drama experiences for my students, they did get better and better in their enactments. I also think that other positive outcomes came from them. Next I briefly describe two—their discussions about death, and about their roles as teachers.

Talking About Death

Although "The Dead Cheerleaders" play was not so wonderful as a play, it did spark useful discussions about the topic of death, which helped some of the children who had recently lost someone close, to deal with their losses. In the play, children had to make headstones to hide behind and had to come up with dates of birth and death. Learning their own years of birth (which most did not know), and determining the date of their deaths according to the headstones they made, caused them to consider how long people live. They also figured out how old their loved ones were when they died, and some were even prompted by the discussion to ask their parents when they (parents) were born and how old they were.

This continued into a discussion of how long people live, which lead to a heated discussion of life after death. Some of the children never thought about what happens after death. They all said they would be with God in heaven, but some were very disturbed to find out that their body was only what someone called a "piece of meat" and so rotted in the ground. They seemed relieved when one of them asked about spirits and ghosts. They also brought up other death-related topics—spirits, angels, God, devil, and hell.

These discussions occurred over a period of 3½ weeks. Questions relating to death and what happens after death even surfaced for some of them a year later. Thus, although this play was a lot of nonsense, it certainly centered and focused the thoughts of the children on death, spirits, and an afterlife. This was a valuable outcome.

Students as Teachers

After the performances, we had only a couple of weeks of school left. When asked what they would like to do, the children asked if they could teach the class just like a real teacher. They wanted to act out being teacher for a day. I asked if they thought they could plan enough to keep us busy for a full day, but most of them agreed it was not possible. I then suggested that they each teach for 5 minutes. They liked this idea, so we scheduled a time when they would do their teaching.

I explained that they did not have to teach school subjects, that they could teach us about anything they wished. All of them had something to teach. They worked for one week in the classroom refining their lessons. They used their friends and their families as sounding boards. Many of them worked on their projects at home, and the work they put into perfecting their lessons showed in their final presentations. Here are some of them:

- Arnie taught us about the workings of a carburetor. He went into much detail about how the gas made it run. He even made a picture to show us. I was astonished because I knew he liked cars, but I did not know he understood exactly how they functioned.
- Cecilia taught us how to listen to a short story. This amazed me because she was one of the two children who never spoke and rarely showed any overt interest in our read-alouds. She read a story she wrote and then had the class discuss it.
- John, who was a 12 year old emergent reader, taught us the alphabet; Donia, who knew only a few words of English, taught us about addition. She made the whole class work on problems she made up as board work.
- Ana told us about her game "Girl Talk." This was the child who rarely initiated anything in 4 years and would not speak in class.
- Jose, who came to the class later in the year, spoke no English, taught us the "Spanglish" alphabet where some of the letters he said in English, and some he said in Spanish.

This project of teaching was one of the valuable things that came out of this inquiry on drama. Students who normally refused to present in front of the class presented. Students who never looked into a book went to the library and brought back a book, asked for help in reading it and presented very good lessons. They practiced them without being reminded.

CONCLUSIONS: GAINS FOR MYSELF AND MY STUDENTS

My students gained much due to my inquiry. My continuing inquiry on read-alouds has made me more aware of the type of questions I ask, which has led to using more open-ended and higher level questions when discussing things. I also now refer questions to the children more often, and wait longer for them to initiate and offer their own ideas.

Children became quite adept, and not as inhibited, in dramatizing stories. They still dramatized things during their free time, using the clothes provided in the play area. They learned new vocabulary and sequencing, but learned much more in these dramatic experiences. They began to initiate discussions about things they wanted to learn. They also interrupted when they did not understand something. They became more eager to do their own projects. Overall, they became more self-reliant.

I learned quite a lot as a teacher researcher. I found the research journal, a new tool for me, to be a helpful guide to what I was doing. I had never used a journal to record my lessons and my reflections. When I looked at my notes, I discovered that certain children had skills of which I was unaware. Reviewing these entries later was a big help in showing me who participated, who had a real grasp of what I was trying to teach, and in the general growth of children.

The tape recorder was another new tool that was a great help. I recorded a lesson on an audiotape cassette and listened to it later. Sometimes I was so involved in a lesson as it was taking place that I did not hear all that was going on. This review helped me rethink how I handled discipline, how I was tracking students' participation, how I could find ways for students to demonstrate what they knew, and so forth. It helped me to evaluate more objectively my own teaching style. I found several things in my teaching style that I did not like: giving answers instead of referring children's questions back to them to consider, too much lecturing instead of tapping either the knowledge of the children or sending them to find the answers in books, and reprimanding students in front of the whole class. These are things that are hard to notice during the moments of teaching, but the cassette recording made them very clear.

The most difficult part of my inquiry was learning how I had to give the children some control of their learning. I also learned that turning total control over to children is not a good idea, as when I gave them the opportunity to write and perform their own plays and didn't support them enough. It is much harder to guide them than it is to tell them what to do. It is necessary to try to invent ways to bridge the gap between exercising all of the control and delegating some of the control to the children. My task has to be how to lead children through their tasks so they can tackle them on their own. I have thought of retiring, but I would miss the children. I enjoy greeting them in the morning and finding out what my challenge will be this day. Although the job is often frustrating, it is always challenging, is never dull, and is very rewarding at times.

ABOUT THE AUTHOR

I received my bachelor's and master's degrees from institutions in the city of Chicago. I have taught, or shall I say that my pupils have taught me, at the same school, Andersen, for more than 36 years. I taught special-needs children for about 30 of those years.

I like to learn new things and how to do old-time things. I enjoy creating things, crafts, cooking, knitting, poems, decorating cakes, refinishing, decorating, woodworking, weaving, or a new way to teach a subject to my students.

DEDICATION

I dedicate this writing to all the students whom I have loved and who have rewarded me by progressing farther than anyone expected.

REFERENCES

Dahl, R. (1988). *Matilda.* New York: Viking Penguin.
de Regniers, B. S. (1990). *Jack and the beanstalk: Retold in verse for boys and girls to read themselves.* New York: Macmillan.
Seuss, Dr. (1940). *Horton hatches the egg.* New York: Random House.

Chapter 14

Teaching Research Writing: Our Search for Voice in the Eighth Grade

Michael Rassel
Formerly at Andersen Elementary School

EDITORS' COMMENTS

Michael's inquiry focuses on his attempts to help eighth graders learn to write informational research reports *with voice*. His interest in the topic of voice in this genre has long, personal roots.

With a wonderful humor, he describes his struggles and successes in his journey to foster voice in research writing. He talks about his minilessons on getting students to brainstorm questions about their topics and about helping them on paraphrasing. He invites you to some of his conferences with students. He also provides examples of student writing. He offers some especially useful advice for teachers working with second-language learners.

At the end of the year and the study, students even developed a metaawareness of voice as they learned the research process of writing informational texts.

The introduction chapter of this book provides the theoretical and methodological background for the larger collaborative school–university action-research project and this chapter about Michael's inquiry on research writing.

University researchers, Dian Ruben and Jane Liao, collaborated with Michael in his inquiry.

One evening in the fall of 1994, I noticed my 16-year-old daughter working on a research paper. Despite her protest, I managed to get a glimpse of her writing. It seemed fragmented. It lacked fluency and, above all, it certainly didn't sound like my daughter. The piece, an assignment given by her history teacher, was about World War II. After reading just the first page, I realized that all she really did was to take an article out of the *Grolier Encyclopedia* and rearrange the text. When I began to raise some questions about her process, she immediately became insulted and insisted (as most teenagers do) that I just stay out of her writing. As a concerned parent, I wondered if I should demand that she rewrite the piece. As a teacher, I came to the conclusion that she (and many of my own students) sincerely believed that informational writing meant "just taking somebody else's stuff and re-organizing the writing." I finally decided that I would drop the issue and let her turn it in so she could learn, the hard way, that what she had done was totally unacceptable. Two weeks later, I was horrified when I learned that not only was her paper accepted, but she received a B for the project!

As a result of the World War II incident, I began to inquire about the writing that was going on in the eighth grade at Andersen, my school. The principal, along with many colleagues, felt that our graduating students should write a research paper before moving on to high school. Somehow this idea turned into a project with rather high stakes. This meant that any student who did not turn in a research paper would not be allowed to participate in the graduation activities at the end of the school year. Although I did not necessarily agree with this approach, I thought the idea of teaching eighth-grade students how to write a research paper provided me with a wonderful opportunity to investigate and find some of the answers to my questions about writing-to-learn projects. Therefore, I agreed to start a writing workshop (1 hour per day) in Rebecca Gipson's eighth-grade class. This turned out to be the perfect place to pursue my inquiry, which began in January. Rebecca Gipson is an enthusiastic, talented, and compassionate teacher (she'll say, "Oh ... stop!" when she reads this!) who is extremely collaborative, not only with colleagues, but more important, with her students. She is a reflective teacher who is always willing to take risks. As a result, her students exhibit the same kind of commitment to their work. I cannot thank her enough for allowing me to work in her classroom community.

IN THE BEGINNING ...

During the years in which I taught fourth and fifth grades in a self-contained setting, I attempted to address many questions about the teaching of writing. The school community in which I work decided to adopt a whole-language approach to teaching several years ago. So naturally we were all exposed to the ideas of wonderful teaching-writing-as-a-process gurus like Lucy Calkins (1986), Donald Graves (1983), and Nancie Atwell

(1987), a motivational writer and speaker who has this remarkable ability to bring tears to my eyes when she shares not only her own experiences as a writer, but also the experiences of her students. As I became familiar with their work, I entered a constant period of transition as a teacher, a phase that I am currently in and, hopefully, one in which I will always remain. I came to realize that when I cannot reflect and question my own teaching, I cannot enjoy my work.

Having adopted a process approach to the teaching of writing causes me to constantly reflect on my own experiences as an adolescent writer. Few of my high school teachers taught from a process-oriented perspective. Therefore, the decision to teach research writing in the eighth grade in this way brought forth some rather embarrassing memories. As I recalled, I also turned in one or two "rearranged" pieces as a teenager. This kind of research writing is so prevalent that it became the focus of a recent Doonesbury comic strip (Trudeau, 1996), during which a junior high school student is seen reading a paragraph from the encyclopedia, and then writing a paragraph of his research paper. Only subtle changes are seen (e.g., "initiated by Thomas Jefferson" is modified to "at the invitation of Thomas Jefferson"; "the purchased area" is altered to "the area that was purchased"). In the final frame, his mother is seen with his research paper in her hands as she exclaims, "My ... what a dramatic improvement in our writing." He responds with a humble ... , "Thanks." Every colleague who has seen the comic strip finds it particularly amusing. You know what they say about writing good comedy: If the material is about the kinds of experiences that most people have, you'll have them rolling in the aisles.

Reflecting on my daughter's and my own adolescent attempts at research writing brought forth many questions about teaching eighth graders how to write informational pieces. The biggest question in my mind had to do with writer voice. Why did so many older students lack voice as they composed informational texts? One colleague in my graduate program, Carol Gaul (personal communication, 1996), a seasoned writing teacher and recent recipient of the prestigious Illinois Golden Apple Award, attributes the problem to students not realizing the purpose of research writing. She says that many of her intermediate level students will initially "define a report as something that comes from a source other than themselves, like an encyclopedia or magazine. So, to them, copying it word for word is the same as giving a scientific explanation of what they're studying. They know they've copied, but they really think it's okay to do that because of the nature of their work." Another expert, Ralph Fletcher (1992), argued that it's because many upper grade classrooms are less child-centered. The nurturing writing workshop of the primary grades gives way to the content-driven curriculum of the upper grades. As a result, research writing often becomes what Fletcher calls "dump-truck" writing. "Dump-truck" writers are "students who pick up a clump of words (usually from an encyclopedia), drop those words onto the paper, and are genuinely surprised when teachers accuse them of plagiarism" (p. 76). What confused me was why so many teachers did not scream "Plagiarism!" and were willing to accept very "rearranged" research pieces.

FINDINGS OF MY INQUIRY OF THE WORKSHOP IN ROOM 321

Most of the writing workshop periods were structured so that we would have a 20-minute, whole-class meeting. At first, a critical part of my inquiry was to investigate how well students attempted some of the strategies that were modeled during these meetings. Therefore, these were followed by a writing time, during which I roved around the room to conference and help writers on an individual basis. Writing time was also a period during which students could help each other. I wanted to see what would happen if I wrote in front of them and did some of my own thinking aloud. Would they understand how I approach research writing? Would they be able to take on the same approach?

I was able to draw the following three major conclusions in my inquiry about how young writers and their teachers ought to go about the business of writing research reports:

1. If students are not really interested in their topics, if they aren't driven intrinsically to find out something, then forget it! Wholesale copying and rearranging is all that you get.
2. Young writers should not be expected to apply one specific process as they attempt to write informational pieces. Individual writers have their own individual processes. The teacher's goal is to help each writer discover that process.
3. Some "rearranging" of a professional writer's text (i.e., a resource book that students might have used in their research) may represent a necessary scaffold, especially for second-language learners. Otherwise, how can they develop what students themselves subsequently called "the sophisticated voice" of a research writer?

An elaboration of the events that led me to these conclusions follows.

WHAT DO YOU REALLY WANT TO FIND OUT?

At the very beginning of the process, I had whole-group meetings on brainstorming questions about a particular topic. These were productive because when kids created their own questions, it gave me an opportunity to see if they were really interested in what they chose to investigate. Students having difficulty coming up with questions had topics that really didn't interest them. Because the research paper was a graduation requirement, too many students just chose anything in order to meet the topic-selection deadline imposed by teachers. To make matters worse, I insisted that they choose topics related to the areas of science or social studies because these were important curricular goals of the teachers. Thus, their initial ideas sometimes had to be altered. For example, one young author wanted to write about cars called "Low Riders." Because I knew about the popular magazine with the same name, we negotiated, and the decision to write about how cars operate was made. I just didn't want students choosing to write about famous cars, entertainers, or sports figures because they were almost too familiar with these topics. After all, the finding out part is really what research writing is all about.

After the first few meetings about brainstorming, I realized that the most important step toward getting kids to find their voices in this genre was to make sure they were choosing to write about issues that they really, really, really wanted to find out about. It became easy to determine whether or not they were involved by examining the kinds of questions they wrote while brainstorming. I began to question the questions and I refused to accept those that had obvious or irrelevant answers. As a result, some writers became rather frustrated until they started to ask more important questions such as: "What was it like for my parents growing up in Mexico or Puerto Rico?" or "How do the astronauts use the bathroom in outer space if there is no gravity?" These kinds of questions gave me the important signal that students were beginning to choose topics that they were genuinely curious about.

As the drafting of questions took on more importance, it became easier to persuade these young writers that this whole thing wasn't going to be as difficult as they anticipated. In fact, I might have even convinced some of them that research writing could be a rewarding experience if you can find the answers to some of your questions. On the other hand, I don't recall any student saying, "Wow! Mr. Rassel, this is really fun!"

Working with Thomas on Good Inquiry Questions

The following workshop conversation is illustrative of the kinds of interactions I had with students. Here, I am trying to help Thomas, a second-language learner who arrived from Poland only weeks after the class started the project. Thomas, who spoke English with limited proficiency, started the notetaking phase of his research paper. He seemed organized with a page of notes from two or three resources, but he wasn't sure what to do next. Because he wasn't present for the early meetings about deciding what it is that one wants to find out, he just began to jot down (copy) passages from his sources. My goal during our conversation was to find out if he was really interested in his topic, "Stars." The only way that I knew was to listen to the kinds of questions he had about the topic.

Example 1

1	Michael:	How's it going?
2	Thomas:	Okay.
3	Michael:	Have you narrowed it down? [I look at his note cards and resources] So you want to write about stars?
4	Thomas:	Yes.
5	Michael:	I see that you already have a page of notes. Before using them, let's get out a sheet of paper and make a list of the things that you want to find out about stars. Can you think of any?
6	Thomas:	What is the star closest to the earth?
7	Michael:	Okay! Put that one down. Another one?
8	Thomas:	Is the sun a star?
9	Michael:	Put that down, good one!
10	Thomas:	Can they be counted?
11	Michael:	Excellent! Can they be counted?
12	Thomas:	What's the biggest star?
13	Michael:	Ah! ... What is the biggest star? I've got one that might be important to you. What are they made of? What exactly are stars made of?
14	Thomas:	[jots down the question]
15	Michael:	Now, all of these questions can become the headings that you put on the top of your note pages or index cards. As you look for the answers, you might think of new questions that can become headings. For example, you might find something on temperature. Make another card or note page. If you jot some information down on the card, write the title of the book that you found it in along with the page number at the bottom. Do you need more index cards or paper? Don't forget to write a bibliography sheet for the books that you are using....

{Fieldnotes, 01/26/95}

It became clear, from the kinds of questions he asked, that Thomas was genuinely interested in his chosen topic. After my suggestion—"What are they made of?"—I got him to see the questions as tools in the research process. I explained how he might use many of the questions as headings on index cards or notebook pages so that when he found some information during reading, he could simply make notes on the appropriate card or paper. Although I probably confused him with all of the other advice at the end—making sure to put down the name of the book, keeping a working bibliography, and so on—I hoped that he was at least back on track at this stage of his inquiry.

Beginning the Process of Looking for Answers

When I felt that all of the students were really interested in their topics, we began to go about the business of finding answers to their questions. One very important issue became getting the materials needed in order to record their first findings. Those materials became different for each of them. I wanted to make sure that, during whole-group meetings, I introduced them to more than just one way of taking notes and then, later, of organizing those notes. I didn't want them to be bound by the familiar or traditional structures associated with doing a research paper. Therefore, students could either take notes on index cards or on sheets of paper. My rationale for this grew out of my own frustration, as a child, at being made to use small index cards. If I tried to use the huge index cards or notebook paper, teachers complained that I wasn't using the proper materials! There never seemed to be enough room to write, and the small cards often got lost in my desk or in some of the books I was using. Some of my best notes are probably still sitting in a book somewhere at the Hollywood Public Library in Florida! Consequently, once I became a teacher, I promised myself that students would always be given the freedom to choose whatever method works best for them.

At a future juncture during the project, it also became important to me that they not be limited by the traditional structures for organizing their notes. If they preferred to use the traditional outline, that was okay. However, I also showed them how to create a semantic web, or how to just lay their note cards on the table (excuse the pun), organize them into particular categories, and then just jump into the drafting process.

I hoped that teaching students how to come up with good questions and use various methods for organizing the answers to those questions might lead them to write down data from books in their own words. This would help to prevent wholesale copying. However, as you see later, that was big time wishful thinking on my part.

Plagiarism: Mortal Sin or a Necessary Scaffold for Novices (Especially If They Are Second-Language Learners)?

After what seemed like an inordinate amount of time negotiating topic selection and then ways of organizing notes, I encountered what I knew would become the pivotal point of this project: Finding enough good resources for these young writers to go to for their answers, and then showing them how to share those answers in their own voices. Yes ... this was the "paraphrasing, summarizing, can-you-tell-me-what-it-means-in-your-own-words-without-copying-from-the-book?" PROBLEM!

The plagiarism problem reared its ugly head because I probably put too much emphasis on how to organize findings too early in the process. I should have first devoted much more time to modeling more than just a few paraphrasing strategies in more than just a few whole-group meetings. The result of my mistake was that most kids were doing a wonderful job of organizing note cards and had notebook pages filled with great informational text that was written by somebody other than themselves … aaaaaaarrrrgh! To make matters worse, I decided that I would remedy the situation by doing what I will call kamikaze minilessons on paraphrasing. Out of my frustration, I conducted these minilessons after sitting down with an encyclopedia and paraphrasing a paragraph or two. Having analyzed the steps that I took, I broke them down into what would become "Mr. Rassel's sure-fire-lock-step method of putting things into your own words." Here's what I came up with:

- Step 1 Read a chunk.
- Step 2 Jot down a few key words or ideas. Do not write in complete sentences.
- Step 3 Put those key words or ideas into complete sentences using your own voice.

Did the students use or even understand Mr. Rassel's recipe? Of course not! It didn't take long to realize how ridiculous it was to assume that there is only one way of paraphrasing information that you learn from other resources. It was even more ridiculous to assume that a good writer uses only one strategy for putting things in her or his own voice. What actually happens to a research writer involves a complex thought process as he or she interacts with informational text. I began to realize this while doing some research writing as part of my graduate studies at Loyola University. It became clear that the process was definitely too complex to isolate into some sort of lock-step strategy that could be taught and learned all at once. Furthermore, while my initial attempt at teaching paraphrasing was embarrassing, it illustrates how frustrating teaching experiences can lead teachers to engage in extremely ludicrous methods out of desperation.

Having learned the hard way that paraphrasing is really a complex process, I gradually attacked the paraphrasing problem by working with kids on an individual basis, as much as possible. During writing time, my colleague, Rebecca, and I worked hard to try to visit each of our 28 writers for at least 15 to 20 minutes per week. Because many students were knee deep into the drafting phase, our goal was to have them select chunks from their drafts that didn't really sound like their own words. To put it bluntly, we focused on those portions that we knew for sure had been plagiarized.

Examples from Conferences on Paraphrasing

In the following conference with Leon, who decided to become an expert on George Washington, I attempted to address the issue of lifting wholesale versus paraphrasing. My goal was to help his text sound more like Leon and less like the resource that he was "borrowing" from!

===

Example 2

1	Leon:	[reading] ALTHOUGH GEORGE WASHINGTON HAD VERY LITTLE OR NO FORMAL SCHOOLING, HIS ...
2	Michael:	What does that mean?
3	Leon:	What? "Had very little or no formal schooling?"
4	Michael:	Yeah.
5	Leon:	He had like, a little bit of schooling or he never went to school....
6	Michael:	So you could put "George Washington had a little bit of schooling." So like if we were going to take this sentence——do you have a sheet of paper?
7	Leon:	[gets paper]
8	Michael:	If we were going to take this sentence and we were just going to write down key ideas, what would they be? What would be the key words or phrases? You could put "little bit of schooling," right?
9	Leon:	Yeah.
10	Michael:	Put it down. You said "little bit of schooling."
11	Leon:	[writes]
12	Michael:	What else did you say ... about the second part?
13	Leon:	AND HE READ WIDELY IN GEOGRAPHY.
14	Michael:	What could you put? You don't have to put all that, "he read widely in geography." What could you put?
15	Leon:	Read widely in geography.
16	Michael:	Do you have to put "widely"?
17	Leon:	[shakes his head "no"]
18	Michael:	Just put key words ... or key phrases. What could you put?
19	Leon:	Read geography.
20	Michael:	Yeah, read geography.
21	Leon:	[writes]
22	Michael:	What's geography about?

23	Leon:	Finding places.
24	Michael:	Put that——now, maybe between here and here [pointing to Leon's list] you could put something about the notebooks.
25	Leon:	Yeah.
26	Michael:	What could you put?
27	Leon:	[seemingly thinking out loud] Early notebooks.
28	Michael:	Think about how we know he read about finding places. How do historians know that?
29	Leon:	Cause he kept a lot of things in his notebooks.
30	Michael:	Good, that sounds great. He kept a lot of things in his notebook.
31	Leon:	[writes more notes]
32	Michael:	About what?
33	Leon:	About geography.
34	Michael:	Okay, so put "about" and then draw an arrow to "geography." There we go. Okay, now——[turning over the original sheet from which Leon was copying his key words and phrases] now, you have some notes there, right?
35	Leon:	Uhhuh.
36	Michael:	Write a couple sentences about his education. Make sure you make it complete sentences. Put it in your voice. This [referring to the key words and phrases list] is your voice, not——this sounds like you.
37	Leon:	[writes "George Washington had very little schooling, but he kept notes in his notebook about geography."]
38	Michael:	Read it.
....		[Leon reads what he's written.]
39	Michael:	Now that sounds like you. See? See how you took that information and you've internalized it and now you're going to teach somebody else in your voice. That's what research is. That's really what research papers are all about, isn't it?
40	Leon:	[nods his head in understanding and agreement]
41	Michael:	So now what you need to do is … so that you don't——don't think that you have to go through every single sentence in here. Just get the key words from each page and write them down.
42	Leon:	Just get the key words from each page and write them down.
43	Michael:	Right, just take the key words. For example, you could draft another sentence here if you wanted to about how this shows that he did know how to read because he read books about….
44	Leon:	Geography.

45   Michael: Right, because how else could he put those notes in his notebooks?

46   Leon: Right.

47   Michael: So ... I know you can do this. Don't worry about how long it is anymore. I know that that's a note on the outside of your folder, but I'm sure that Ms. Gipson and I would rather have three to five pages of this [referring to the sentence that he wrote in his own voice] where you tell us everything that you understood about what you read than have 10 pages of something that doesn't sound like you. I want you to do what you just did. I don't want you to worry about length. I want you to go through this thing and I want you to teach me some things that you felt you understood about this literature. And, you'll prove to me that you really understand it because you'll use your voice.

{Fieldnotes, videotape, 05/09/95}

As the long conversation illustrates, asking students to further explain or define what they read was a way of helping them to find voice without screaming "Plagiarism!" In many of the conferences, saying something like, "Well, why don't you just put down what you've just said to me in place of what you read aloud," or "Now that sounds more like you!", really helped the students to find voice. On other occasions, when students had difficulty explaining a passage because they didn't understand the material, I tried to ask questions that would lead them to internalize concepts so they could restate them in their own voice. For example, in a conference with Maribel, one of several students in the community who also received special instruction because of a mild learning disability, I tried to help her transform something she really did not understand about her topic of hurricanes and how they form into something she could, and then to say it in her own words. In this case, her copied notes were, "As great masses of this warm wet air rise up, towering rain clouds form." As I worked with her, Maribel gradually came to understand the plagiarized passage. It became easier for her to explain the concept in a different way, "While warm air is going up, great big clouds form." It took considerable time to work individually with those students who were struggling. It is my opinion that the time was well spent. It should also be noted that another important outcome of our lengthy conversation was that I think Maribel learned new vocabulary, including "masses" and "towering." Perhaps she will use these words in future writing projects.

More Ideas on Plagiarism

After I had several productive conversations with students such as Leon and Maribel, I tried to let students have more in-class time to write. I became more confident about this decision after having a lengthy conversation with Dr. Kenneth Kaufman (personal communication, 1996), a professor at Loyola University. While sharing stories with me about his encounters with plagiarism at the university, he made the following comment:

> You have to understand that you ought to let children write in the classroom. And, by the way, that takes care of a lot of plagiarism because ... they'll begin to realize that ... what's written in the classroom can't be that much different from their final product. There's got to be some relationship [between what they do in class and what they attempt on their own] and so I think a lot of coaching and mentoring and one-on-one conferring and actual writing [in class] is the way to get it done. (personal communication)

When I asked about confronting those who may have plagiarized, his remarks included,

> "What if I'm dead wrong and I make this accusation and this person really does write poorly ... and then writes brilliantly ... and I've got to kind of be able to prove it?"

As Kaufman suggested, determining whether or not a student lifted certain passages can become a problem during one-on-one conferences. However, because students were beginning to do most of their reading and writing for the project in class, I just asked them to show me the source from which they got information that sounded "unusual." Eventually, I discovered that students attempting to share information that had been learned from books by just changing a few words here and there was a necessary step as they struggled to find their own voices. For example, one student who read, "Mexico is roughly triangular in shape," wrote "Mexico is kind of a triangular shape." What ended up in her final draft was, "Mexico is a sort of triangular shaped country."

Initially, I was very disturbed when I discovered that more than just a few students were engaged in the "I'll-just-substitute-this-word-with-another-word" process of research writing. Just making minor changes in wording or syntax is definitely considered to be a form of plagiarism. Nevertheless, I began to think about whether or not I should accept such plagiarism on the part of some of my ESL students. Eventually, I decided that what they were doing was an approximation and that I needed to accept it for them to feel some level of success. After all, at least they weren't just lifting passages word for word anymore. They were developing new vocabulary as they enthusiastically substituted one word for another as well. My acceptance of such writing was no different than that of a primary teacher who teaches spelling from a developmental perspective. Those of us in the upper grades should also recognize that, even when students are not exactly where they should be, they have taken steps in the right direction.

IMPLEMENTING AN "I-SEARCH PAPER" APPROACH

In addition to accepting these approximations, I also tried to help my students find their voices by introducing them to *The I- Search Paper* (Macrorie, 1988) method of writing a paper. Macrorie suggested that students not only share new knowledge as they compose informational text, but also share the journey taken in order to acquire that knowledge. In other words, we should encourage them to write about how they became interested in a particular inquiry as well as the steps they took in pursuit of their findings. According to Macrorie, "A natural way to begin an I-Search paper is to tell readers What I Knew (or didn't know) and What I Wanted to Know—in story form. You don't have to write an essay or a pretentious declaration, just tell the story of how you got into the search" (p. 100).

For my young writers, this structure was a vehicle that helped them find their voices on paper. It also provided a kind of safety net for those students who had difficulty starting their first drafts. As you will see in the next two samples, however, writing a more narrative "Introduction"— which had no inklings of plagiarism—led to different results for different students as they began the rest of their papers.

Eva's Writing on Puerto Rico

Eva's text included her introduction, and then provided the first part of the next section, which she called the "Early History":

Introduction

The reasons why I'm writing about Puerto Rico are: I wanted to find out more about its history and government. Another reason is that my grandmother used to live there and I wanted to find out what was happening at the time she was living there, which was in the early 1940s. Also, the fact that I've been to Puerto Rico so many times just gave me more of an incentive to write about it.

My last trip to Puerto Rico was in 1992. It was a fun and interesting trip. Fun because of all the malls and beaches I went to and interesting because of my cousin's job. My cousin and I would go to San Juan every day, and there, I helped her work. I did stuff like make copies and fax papers.

While going to San Juan, we always passed Ponce, Lares, Vega Alta and other beautiful and fantastic cities in Puerto Rico. We also saw cows and horses. We also saw high mountains and nice forests.

When my grandmother was living there in 1940, there were no televisions. People used radios to obtain information from the outside world. Everything, especially the culture, was really different in Puerto Rico during the 1940's and, until this day, it still is.

Early History

About 2,000 years ago, the Arawak Indians traveled from Venezuela to Puerto Rico. These Indians were the first people of Puerto Rico. Boriquen was the name that the Arawaks named it when they first got there. Since a lot of people lived in Boriquen, the Arawaks just made themselves at home.

There, in Boriquen, the Indian women gathered berries and pineapples and other fruits while the men spent most of their time hunting. These Indians also farmed. They planted corn, peanuts, sweet potatoes and other crops. ...

Eva's introduction and beginning passage on the early history show how students can develop a voice for informational writing when they are given a framework that enables them to share their prior knowledge along with what they find in other sources.

Maritza's Writing on Mexico

However, some students had considerable difficulty when making the transition from writing about what they know, to writing about what they've recently learned. You can really sense a shift in the following example written by Maritza, on Mexico. It's comparable to riding in a car with a bad transmission system. It feels like whiplash! You will feel this difference when she finishes the "Introduction" and begins the "History" section—that's when you will feel like you want to fasten your seat belt:

Introduction

Mexico is where most of my family comes from. The last time I went to Mexico was in 1989. In this paper I will give you a brief description on what I saw. I will also be telling you about the history, people, culture, education, government, land, natural resources, and about the many sports played in Mexico.

The last time I went to Mexico, I went to a place called Trojes, Michoacan. Over in Trojes the land is very dry, even though at some places there are some lakes, ponds, rivers, and beaches.

I also visited a place called Colima, Colima. In Colima my grandfather Jose, and grandmother own a store. Every time I would go to their store they would give me free candy.

The streets in Trojes are very smooth, but in Colima the streets are very rocky. In Mexico there are a lot of palm trees, a lot of mountains and very nice beaches.

In Trojes during June through August it is very rainy. It is also very odd for it to snow at all; from what I know it has never snowed in Mexico. In the afternoons it is extremely hot, but as the sun starts setting it gets very cool.

When traveling from one place to another it seems as if you would swerve off the road, because the roads are very narrow, and the cliffs are very steep.

History

Mexico was the site of the earliest and most advanced civilization in the western hemisphere. The Maya lived on most of the South Eastern Mexico, and Northern Central America during the first thousand years.

The Mayan culture, according to archeological research, successfully achieved its greatest development in about the 6th century A.D. During the first 100 years of the Christian period of time, another Indian group, the Toltec, migrated from the north and, in about 800, established themselves in the valley of Mexico. ...

Fortunately, Maritza's rocky ride only represented a small percentage of students who had extreme difficulty internalizing and restating new information. As we compared the work of all those involved in this project, we discovered a wide range in terms of voice. Another positive outcome was that nobody, not a single student, turned in a paper that was completely devoid of voice. Also, there were no papers in which voice was present in the introduction and then was never to be found again. For all of the writers, voice would phase in and out of their final copies as they struggled to expand on newly acquired knowledge.

CONCLUSIONS

During final whole-class, share-time sessions, students had ample opportunities to comment on each other's work. What was interesting to me was how the issue of plagiarism was addressed as students listened to their peers. Many of them accused each other of copying passages that, in fact, were not plagiarized. However, these discussions also illustrated a new understanding on the part of the students, namely, that a writer can develop a "sophisticated voice" during the process of writing research papers. The following comments in Example 3 are made after Jasmine read a passage from her piece about Puerto Rico.

Example 3

1	Michael:	Good. Reactions? What do you think? Does it sound like Jasmine?
2	Miguel:	No, it sounds like plagiarism.
3	Michael:	What should she do to make it sound like her?
4	Jasper:	She uses big words.
5	Carmen:	It's sophisticated writing.
6	Michael:	Is it possible to slip into a sophisticated voice because you're trying to teach something or to impress the teacher? You don't use words that you use everyday.

....		[I give an example of a colloquial word and what might be used instead in written expression. Then Fernando reads his piece on cheetahs.]
7	Tania:	It doesn't sound like him.
8	Michael:	Well he didn't plagiarize. I read his piece and I could tell from the misspellings.
9	Jose:	I never heard him say "nonaggressive" or "approach."
10	Michael:	What does "aggressive" mean?
11	Fernando:	[does not have time to think and respond]
12	Maritza:	Being charged up.
13	Alberto:	[responding to "nonagressive"] Happy ... not harmful.
14	Michael:	[to Fernando, who has not come up with an acceptable response] You might want to change that.
....		[Darrell reads and I ask about the word "remarkable," which he is able to explain. All of the students believe that the writing is in Darrell's voice.]
15	Michael:	You must think he talks more sophisticated? I like his piece because you can see the thing just sitting there.
....		[I call on Maribel to read about hurricanes. I comment, "I'm going to Florida, and I need to know." Maribel reads her text. Darrell thinks that she has copied from a book, but Maritza defends Maribel's writing.]
16	Michael:	Do you think writing changes——if you keep on writing, will it change the way you talk?
17	Francisco:	Yeah, you'll start to speak the stuff you write.
18	Alberto:	But we don't talk intellectual to each other.
19	Michael:	Do you try to sound more sophisticated when you write, not plagiarize, but your own voice? Tell me this, do you think she knows something about hurricanes?
20	Candida:	Yeah, she knows what "twirling" means.
21	Michael:	And "moisture"....
22	Maritza:	I visited Mexico in 1989 (... ...).
23	Michael:	Wow, that's interesting. It's in conversational voice and at the same time it's teaching.
24	Francisco:	That's good, I know she didn't plagiarize.
25	Michael:	If you know what a word means, you can keep it. Everybody go through and find a part that doesn't sound like your sophisticated voice but somebody else's voice ... make it better.

{Fieldnotes, 05/16/95}

Hearing comments like, "it's sophisticated writing" or "she uses big words" helped to confirm my belief that challenging my students about making sure that they wrote in their own voice was worth the effort. They learned new vocabulary that was theirs. Moreover, it was a student who brought out the "sophisticated writing" idea that we all then examined and elaborated on. This new awareness was a very important understanding, despite the fact that all of their papers didn't end up written entirely in their own voice.

Finally, as our journey came to an end, I began to think about some of the grave mistakes made by those who forced me into my first writing experiences. Their insistence on my working within traditional structures instilled a fear of writing that, even today, occasionally surfaces. Working through the fear led to one of the biggest breakthroughs in my career: My inevitable realization that if I really want to teach young people how to write, I have to be a writer. I have to avoid the illusion that, just because I made it through college and became a teacher, I know how to teach writing. I have to really listen to what I've read in so many of the books written by those who teach writing. I have to write and write and write. I have to write on a regular basis so that I can feel some of the same kind of fear that my students feel when they write. I have to find strategies for conquering the demons that sometimes cause me to feel paralyzed while writing. I have to teach those strategies to my students. I have to constantly remind myself that one the most important requirements for becoming a successful writing teacher is that I continue to write.

ABOUT THE AUTHOR

I have been teaching at Andersen for more than 12 years. I completed my undergraduate work at DePaul University in the Goodman School of Drama in 1984. I recently received a master's degree in education from Loyola University in Chicago in 1997. In addition to my work as a teacher, I have performed in and directed several plays in the Chicago area. For me, the classroom and the theater have been one and the same—a place to grow, to collaborate, and above all, to learn. I am presently an assistant principal at Foreman High School.

DEDICATION

To my wife, Carmen, who makes me feel like writing during those dreadful periods when I don't feel like a writer.

REFERENCES

Atwell, N. (1987). *In the middle: Writing, reading, and learning with adolescents.* Portsmouth, NH: Boynton/Cook.

Calkins, L. M. (1986). *The art of teaching writing.* Portsmouth, NH: Heinemann.

Fletcher, R. (1993). *What a writer needs.* Portsmouth, NH: Heinemann.

Graves, D. (1983). *Writing: Teachers and children at work.* Portsmouth, NJ: Heinemann.

Macrorie, K. (1988). *The I-search paper.* Portsmouth, NH: Boynton/Cook.

Trudeau, G. (1996). "Doonesbury" cartoon.

Chapter 15

Summary and Ongoing Reflections: Struggles and Significance in Creating Collaborative Interactions and Talk in Urban Classrooms

Christine C. Pappas
University of Illinois at Chicago

Liliana Barro Zecker
DePaul University

Although all of the teachers in this book focused on their own inquiry questions and developed their own routines and activities with students, several common themes or threads can be seen throughout all of their accounts. The aim of this summary chapter is to both highlight and further examine these themes.

This chapter is organized into three major sections. The first section revisits the New Literacy ideas that are found in the chapters and discusses how they relate to a particular view of literate thinking. The second section addresses how New Literacy notions were realized in the collaborative talk in the various classrooms. It considers what is meant for teachers to share authority with students and explains why collaborative classroom discourse supports student literacy learning. The third, and last, section talks about the struggles entailed in teacher research and elaborates on some of the ideas in the previous sections by further examining the *political* implications of teachers sharing power with their urban students in collaborative literacy instruction.

REVISITING NEW LITERACY IDEAS: EXAMINING
THE CONCEPT OF EPISTEMIC ENGAGEMENT OF TEXT

In chapter 1, we indicated that a major aim of New Literacy is to make reading and writing more meaningful for students, and that this requires that the locus of control, or the power relationships between the teacher and students, be altered in the classroom work. In Willinsky's (1990) words:

> [T]o shift this meaning of literacy also necessarily alters the relationships between teacher and student. The teacher, as an authority on what needs to be known and done, begins to turn over more of this responsibility to the student and to the meaning that comes from somewhere within the student's work with literacy. In these terms, then, the New Literacy's proposal is to reshape the *work* of the classroom around a different form of reading and writing. The moral, psychological, and social worth of this literacy begins with the students as sources of experience and meaning. To alter the form of literacy in this fashion clearly entails redefining the role and relationship of teacher and student. (p. 7)

Thus, in all of the chapters, teachers gave students more responsibility and opportunity to contribute and control the meanings of the texts they were reading, writing, and interpreting.

This occurred in many different ways. It happened when Sonia Soltero encouraged her Spanish-speaking kindergartners to bring up, discuss, and debate topics such as "the stealing of Mexico," "wetbacks," and other issues of immigration that were extremely relevant to the everyday lives of these children. It occurred when Dee Collier encouraged her kindergartners' efforts to approximate texts as emergent readers. It was seen when Anne Barry, Hawa Jones, Dorothy O'Malley, and Sonia Pasewark allowed for their students' initiations in read-aloud sessions. It was present when Renuka Mehra and Sue Jacobson offered ways for their students to share their own responses to novels. It was noted when Bernadine Braun and Paul Fowler enabled their students to take on roles as actors to provide their own interpretations of texts. It was evident when Pam Wolfer, Sarah Cohen, and Michael Rassel helped their students, as authors, to share and gain feedback on the meanings they expressed in their written texts. Thus, all of the teacher researchers worked at crafting interactions in which their students' voices—their ideas, comments, questions—were encouraged and valued.

Promoting "Epistemic" Engagement of Text

A major tenet of the New Literacy perspective, then, is viewing *"literacy as a social process with language that can from the beginning extend the student's range of meaning and connection"* (Willinsky, 1990, p. 8, [emphasis in the original]). This idea of extending and connecting student meaning is consistent with Wells' (1990) conception of what it means to be literate, and the fact that it can be applied at all levels of learners, even to the very young primary-age children who use emergent approximations of adult, conventional forms of written language (Sulzby & Teale, 1991). Wells' definition is, "To be literate is to have the disposition to engage appropriately with texts of different types in order to empower, action, thinking, and feeling in the context of purposeful social activity" (p. 379).

To further explain this notion of literacy, Wells proposed and described several modes of engagement of text. He argued that one of them, what he called the *epistemic* mode of engagement, is the most powerful. An epistemic mode of engagement exists when "meaning is treated as tentative, provisional, and open to alternative interpretations and revision" (p. 369). This mode of engagement is so influential because it takes advantage of the potential of literacy by empowering the thinking of those who use it. It provides opportunities for students to reexamine and reconsider their ideas and those of others.

In this sense of engagement, Wells' meaning of *text* is extended to include oral texts such as classroom discourse. Of course, before they enter school, children have learned to interpret and contribute to oral texts in many ways in the various social contexts that supported their language development. However, in most of these settings, language accompanied action, and attention focused only partially on what was said (Halliday, 1978; Pappas, Kiefer, & Levstik, 1999; Wells, 1986). Thus, according to Wells, children engaging in oral texts from an epistemic orientation view the role of language differently. It introduces them to literate thinking because it fosters reflection on, and reformulations of, meanings. As a result, this primarily silent and covert mental ability is made explicit to children.

However, just providing opportunities for students' meanings in various literacy routines per se is only one step in fostering epistemic engagement of text, or in realizing the aims of New Literacy. What is also important is the ways in which teachers sanction students' efforts, what teachers *do* with the meanings that students offer, how teachers contingently respond to students' initiations. So, when Sonia Soltero kept asking, "Why?" or, "How do you know?", in response to her kindergartners' comments, she made possible openings for student clarifications and justifications of an alternative historical interpretation regarding United States–Mexico boundaries and the related topic of wetbacks. When Anne Barry read ABC books, her first-grade children contributed *other* possibilities for the sound–symbol relations than what these books offered, and she was able to extend them or to provide essential feedback. Students also provided extra intertextual links to other texts from the ones they were presently considering (Bloome & Egan-Robertson, 1993; Lemke, 1985; Oyler, 1996). Indeed, making intertextual connections, that is, juxtaposing other texts—other books, songs, movies, personal stories from their homes and community, and so forth—was a topic that many of the teachers discussed and illustrated in their chapters. Intertextual links occurred frequently because the teachers let students know how exciting and valuable these relationships were as reflections on the interpretations of the books they were reading.

Such an epistemic stance was also promoted in the chapters on writing because Pam Wolfer, Sarah Cohen, and Michael Rassel emphasized revision, thereby helping their students see the tentativeness of the meanings expressed in written texts and how these could be reexamined so as to state these meanings more fully or clearly. Offering provisional meanings and then reformulating these meanings was seen in other chapters as well, such as when Renuka Mehra's second-grade students created extensions—a play, a puppet show, and so on—in their study of the *Ramona Quimby, Age 8* (Cleary, 1981) book, or when Paul Fowler's sixth graders did repeated improvisations of the *Bingo Brown and the Language of Love* (Byars, 1989) book.

These epistemic engagements are very similar to what Lindfors (1999) calls *inquiry,* that is, "language acts by which children bring others into their sense-making" (p. ix). Inquiry here is not just students asking questions; it also includes their engaging others in many various expressive ways—their negotiating, agreeing, comparing, evaluating, generalizing, disagreeing, predicting, reflecting, and so forth. All of these inquiry acts, or epistemic engagements of text, to accomplish the New Literacy ideas of student-meaning extension and connection were possible because of the new and modified classroom interactions that the teacher researchers created in their classrooms. They took on collaborative styles of teaching that were realized in collaborative classroom discourse. Hence, the nature of collaborative talk warrants more examination.

CREATING COLLABORATIVE DISCOURSE TO FOSTER URBAN STUDENTS' LITERACY LEARNING

New Literacy requires a shift or a redefining of the power relationship between teacher and student. It challenges the teacher-controlled *IRE pattern*—teacher *initiating,* child *responding,* and teacher *evaluating*—that dominates traditional education with its transmission orientation (Cazden, 1988; Edwards & Mercer, 1987; Gutierrez, Rymes, & Larson, 1995; Young, 1992). In such IRE student–teacher interactions, the teacher has a fixed, strict agenda that allows for little room for deviation. There is a lack of open-mindedness where different points of view or exploratory ideas or approximations can be raised and examined (Barnes, 1992, 1993; Barnes & Todd, 1995; Freedman, 1993). Such activity structures are commonly found in urban classrooms (Bartolome, 1994).

In contrast, collaborative talk represents an alternative to this teacher-controlled IRE structure. The role of collaborative discourse is not a means to transmit knowledge, but serves as a critical mediator of knowing and knowledge building (Wells, 1998). As a result, *students,* not the teacher, frequently initiate the topics and meanings of discussion. Moreover, as already indicated, collaborative talk is not merely hearing students' voices, but requires that teachers' voices—their contributions—are also present, but in very different ways from the IRE model.

Collaborative Discourse as Dialogue for Knowing and Knowledge Building

Wells (1998) recently argued that a major mistake in education has been to emphasize knowledge rather than knowing. Too much attention has been given to memorizing facts and being able to reproduce information, rather than on developing an understanding of information that can inform and guide action. Knowledge building occurs in a particular place and time in which participants attempt to solve a problem of some kind. For this knowing to advance, learners need others with whom to dialogue. In this knowledge building, classroom talk is characterized by Wells (1998) as having *dialogic responsivity*:

> In order to make a useful contribution, speakers first have to interpret the preceding contribution(s) and compare the information presented with their own current understanding of the issue under discussion, based on their experiences and any other relevant information of which they are aware. Then they have to formulate a contribution that will, in some relevant way, add to the common understanding achieved in the discourse so far by extending, questioning, or qualifying what some else has said. Other participants contribute similarly, turn by turn. (p. 29)

In other words, and as we saw in the various chapters, in collaborative interactions, there is a *cognitive worktable* where the talk has both students and the teacher attempting to link puzzle pieces together to create coherent, joint meanings (Almasi, McKeown, & Beck, 1996).

As Lindfors (1999) argued, when teachers promote and take seriously children's inquiry, they give up *control* but not *power*. In collaborative interactions and discourse, teachers actually become powerful in new, different ways. Thus, it is important to emphasize that, although the teachers in this book engaged in what Oyler (1996) termed "the dance of shared teacher authority," it does not mean that they no longer provided their expertise or knowledge. When students are given space and voice to initiate and offer their own meanings, it does not follow that teachers have "given up" power, authority, or privilege. Authority is not a possession (Manke, 1997; Oyler, 1996). It is not a fixed-amount entity where garnering power or authority means that there is a corresponding loss for another (Lindfors, 1999). Instead, when teachers share authority, they learn to create new strategies or new dance steps to use in their interactions and relationships with their students (Oyler, 1996; Oyler & Becker, 1997).

Thus, the teacher has a new role in collaborative discourse. The teacher can revoice a hesitant student voice by reformulating that student's contribution, thereby allowing him or her to retain some ownership and credit to the reformulation (O'Connor & Michaels, 1993). The teacher can contingently respond to students' initiations so that these student contributions are sustained, so that students' claims of expertise are valued and further encouraged. Or, the teacher response to students' ideas can be extended by the teacher's introducing additional information or alternative interpretations so that students are challenged to go beyond their current understandings (Wells, 1990, 1993, 1994, 1998; Wells & Chang-Wells, 1992). Thus, when students are given opportunities to give voice to their ideas—even if, and especially when, these student ideas are conjectures or might represent partial or mistaken understandings—the teacher's contribution can serve as follow-up or as feedback or uptake (Nystrand, 1997; Wells, 1993, 1998). This is the most valuable position for teachers to have because this is the way that they can truly be responsive to students' understandings, be able to *guide* the construction of students' knowledge building (Mercer, 1995). Teachers can now *be explicit,* but to a particular purpose and at the level of students' current understandings. Moreover, in such arrangements there are many opportunities for the teacher to provide strategic and contextualized skill instruction, which was seen to be especially critical for linguistically diverse students (Delpit, 1988, 1995; Gutierrez, Baquedano-Lopez, & Turner, 1997; Reyes, 1992).

This new dynamic role of the teacher in the classroom discourse is extremely powerful. This collaborative, dialogic classroom talk serves as a significant mediator in fostering students' learning in the ways that Vykotsky (1962, 1978) proposed with his notion of the "zone of the proximal development." Collaborative discourse becomes the kind of cultural tool or resource that enables students to accomplish and understand with others in a way that they had not been able to do on their own. The teachers' efforts to promote and create classroom discourse described in the chapters, then, reflect a major achievement in supporting their urban students' literacy learning.

STRUGGLES IN TEACHER RESEARCH IN SHARING AUTHORITY, AND THE POLITICAL SIGNIFICANCE OF COLLABORATIVE TEACHER-STUDENT INTERACTIONS AND DISCOURSE

The Nature of Teacher Research—Ups, Downs, Bumps, and Ongoing

All of the teachers were successful in developing collaborative styles of teaching to accomplish New Literacy's goals. However, as they all indicated in their chapters, their efforts to forge collaborative interactions and discourse with their students were sometimes fraught with difficulties. Frequently, the writing of teacher researchers indicates a rosy picture of the cycles of action researcher, however, the path that teacher researchers take to change and rethink their practices are not always so easily traveled. The journey of teacher inquiry is sometimes quite bumpy, characterized by both ups *and* downs.

To figure out ways to give their students spaces to express their meanings meant that the teacher researchers in this book sometimes had to scrutinize long-held, underlying assumptions about their teaching and about children's learning. As Dorothy O'Malley discussed, she had to rethink her "teacher responsibilities"—namely, to impart knowledge to her students. Sometimes it was difficult to get students to share their ideas because they already learned from their prior schooling that their voices were not expected or valued. Even at kindergarten, as Sonia Soltero found out, her young children viewed her questioning—"Why?", or "How do you know?"—suspiciously. When Hawa Jones finally found ways to encourage her second graders to express their ideas in read alouds, she had to address a new challenge in her inquiry—she now needed a system to deal with all of her students' initiations. Anne Barry was used to getting her first graders to share their ideas in read alouds and to decifering invented spelling in their emergent texts, but dealing with their approximations of their current letter–sound knowledge as initiations, as she read ABC books to them, was a completely new matter.

Thus, these teachers had difficult questions to solve. How was Dee Collier to persuade all of her kindergartners, especially the boys, that they could be readers? How could she find ways to assess and scaffold the reading reenactments (Holdaway, 1979) of students who had a range of literate understandings? How were Pam Wolfer and Sarah Cohen supposed to find out how to convince first and second graders that they *could* be authors, and even to revise their texts? Or, as Michael Rassel tried to discover, how could he help eighth graders to write as experts in their own voices instead of writing down others' words in their research reports? Consider Sonia Torres Pasewark's dilemma in her first year of teaching: how could she get Spanish-speaking third graders to understand books read in English? Paul Fowler was in a similar situation because he left his days as the school's books on wheels guy to become—in October—the teacher of a contained sixth grade, dealing with all of the difficulties of a beginning teacher while he tried out his drama ideas with his students. Bernadine Braun also tackled drama, and after several tries, figured out how to support her special-education students as actors only to find that she still had trouble in being a consistent guide. Renuka Mehra and Sue Jacobson encountered problems as they attempted to scaffold peer collaboration while groups of third graders created various literature extensions, and fourth graders discussed novels in literature response groups, respectively.

To understand *students'* understandings meant that teachers also had to reexamine their roles in student learning. New strategies had to be developed to elicit students' meanings. New repertoires for scaffolding or intervening had to be created. New ways to share and contribute their own knowledge and expertise had to be discovered so they could be effective in building on students' contributions during classroom talk. In this process, there was no script or formula for teachers to follow (Zecker, Pappas, & Cohen, 1998). Thus, teachers sharing authority and power with students, so that they can be responsive to the local cultural meanings of students who come from diverse ethnolinguistic backgrounds, is a critically important educational goal, but not one that is achieved without lots of hard work. Sharing teacher authority with students frequently also means sharing vulnerabilities (Oyler & Becker, 1997). Moreover, figuring out how to create the kinds of collaborative interactions the researchers sought did not result in outcomes that were set in stone. That is, the teachers' inquiries enabled them to solve current tensions or questions for themselves, but also raised new questions and inquiries in or about their teaching. Thus, in some real sense teacher research is never settled or finished; it is always ongoing. Teachers' reflections on their present inquiry frequently serve as springboards for future avenues or areas in which to further examine their teaching.

The Political Significance of Collaborative Interactions and Discourse

Despite the difficulties that the teachers had in their efforts to create new ways of interaction in literacy instruction, the chapters show how capable the children were in these classroom events. In fact, the teachers frequently remarked that it was the children's exciting, interesting, and intelligent questions and ideas that kept these teachers resolved to overcome the problems that arose in their inquiries.

Such an account, then, reveals a different view of urban children's capabilities in literacy learning than is commonly seen. That is, there is more going on here than teachers merely finding the right "methods" to improve the literacy learning of students who have been historically oppressed (Bartolome, 1994). In forging collaborative arrangements with their students, the teachers challenged the deficit view that many urban-school personnel—and many in the society at large—still hold regarding low-socioeconomic status and ethnic-minority children (Pappas, 1999). Instead of seeing their students as "at risk," which is usual term for such children, these teachers viewed them as "at promise" (Oyler, 1996; Swadener & Lubeck, 1995). They actively worked to structure classroom activities to allow and encourage the students' rich cultural "funds of knowledge" (Moll, 1992) from their homes and communities to come into the classroom discourse. As the various chapters show, given the opportunity to present their own current understandings of a topic and to initiate their own questions or comments about the content or task at hand, these students demonstrated convincingly that they had ample linguistic, cultural, and intellectual resources, which could form the bases of their schooling.

Thus, sharing power with students in collaborative classroom interactions and discourse not only provides better literacy instruction, it also has a broader political significance. Geertz (1973) argues that "to rework the pattern of social relationships is to rearrange the coordinates of the experienced world" (p. 28). This is what happened in these teachers' inquiries. As they purposely changed the patterns of social relationships into more collaborative ways, children's experienced world were transformed. Student voice was encouraged and appreciated; students' prior knowledge was accepted, valued, and further extended. Students' literacy learning was facilitated by guided participation and talk (Mercer, 1995).

Although all of these teacher researchers here had different foci in their inquiries, they all attempted and examined how they might alter the power relationships that typically occur between teachers and students in urban classrooms. The interactions between students and teachers in the chapters reflected the "transformative potential" of relations of culture and power in the society (Cummins, 1994). That is, the collaborative interactions in the chapters are significant because they illustrate how to resist and challenge the historically entrenched deficit views of how to teach urban students. Power relations are learned and become a part of children's identities as they participate in particular social practices of particular communities. Schools can also provide the conditions for interaction that *expand* students' expressions and possibilities to learn new identities.

In their inquiries, the teachers took Maxine Greene's (1995) call for "releasing the imagination" in teaching seriously. They disrupted the broader society's views—and power structures—as to how urban children have been, and ought to be, seen as knowers and learners. Greene argues, "We who are teachers ... have in mind a quest for a better state of things for those we teach and for the world we all share. It is simply not enough for us to reproduce the way things are" (p. 1). Teachers, as illustrated in this book, can take on such a quest to construct collaborative classroom experiences and discourse in which urban and all children learn to be literate in powerful ways. In doing so, they can create discourse for social change (Fairclough, 1992).

REFERENCES

Almasi, J. F., McKeown, M. G., & Beck, I. L. (1996). The nature of engaged reading in classroom discussions of literature. *Journal of Literacy Research, 28,* 107–146.

Barnes, D. (1992). *From communication to curriculum* (2nd ed.). Portsmouth, NH: Boynton/Cook.

Barnes, D. (1993). Supporting exploratory talk for learning. In K. M. Pierce & C. J. Gilles (Eds.), *Cycles of meaning: Exploring the potential of talk in learning communities* (pp. 17–34). Portsmouth, NH: Heinemann.

Barnes, D. & Todd, F. (1995). *Communication and learning revisited: Making meaning through talk*. Portsmouth, NH: Boynton/Cook.

Bartolome, L. I. (1994). Beyond the methods fetish: Towards a humanizing pedagogy. *Harvard Educational Review, 64,* 173–194.

Bloome, D., & Egan-Robertson, A. (1993). The social construction of intertextuality in classroom reading and writing lessons. *Reading Research Quarterly, 28,* 305–333.

Byars, B. (1989). *Bingo Brown and the language of love*. New York: Viking.

Cazden, C. B. (1988). *Classroom discourse: The language of teaching and learning*. Portsmouth, NH: Heinemann.

Cleary, B. (1981). *Ramona Quimby, age 8*. New York: Avon.

Cummins, J. (1994). From coercive to collaborative relations of power in the teaching of literacy. In B. M. Ferdman, R.-M. Weber, & A. G. Ramierz (Eds.), *Literacy across languages and cultures* (pp. 295–331). Albany: State University of New York Press.

Delpit, L. (1988). The silenced dialogue: Power and pedagogy in educating other people's children. *Harvard Educational Review, 58,* 280–298.

Delpit, L. (1995). *Other people's children: Cultural conflict in the classroom*. New York: The New Press.

Edwards, D., & Mercer, N. (1987). *Common knowledge: The development of understanding in the classroom*. London: Routledge & Kegan Paul.

Fairclough, N. (1992). *Discourse and social change*. Cambridge: Polity Press.

Freedman, L. (1993). Teacher talk: The role of the teacher in literature discussion groups. In K. M. Pierce & C. J. Gilles (Eds.), *Cycles of meaning: Exploring the potential of talk in learning communities* (pp. 219–235). Portsmouth, NH: Heinemann.

Geertz, C. (1973). *The interpretations of cultures: Selected essays*. New York: Basic Books.

Greene, M. (1995). *Releasing the imagination: Essays on education, the arts, and social change*. San Francisco: Jossey-Bass.

Gutierrez, K., Baquedano-Lopez, P., & Turner, M. G. (1997). Putting language back into language arts: When the radical middle meets the third space. *Language Arts, 74,* 368–378.

Gutierrez, K, Rymes, B., & Larson, J. (1995). Script, counterscript, and underlife in the classroom: James Brown versus Brown v. Board of Education. *Harvard Educational Review, 54,* 445–471.

Halliday, M. A. K. (1978). *Language as social semiotic: The social interpretation of language and meaning*. London: Edward Arnold.

Holdaway, D. (1979). *The foundations of literacy*. Sydney, Australia: Ashton Scholastic.

Lemke, J. L. (1985). Ideology, intertextuality, and the notion of register. In J. D. Benson & W. S. Greaves (Eds.), *Systemic perspectives on discourse: Selected theoretical papers from the 9th international systemic workshop* (Vol. 1, pp. 275–294). Norwood, NJ: Ablex.

Lindfors, J. W. (1999). *Children's inquiry: Using language to make sense of the world*. New York: Teachers College Press.

Manke, M. (1997). *Classroom power relations: Understanding student-teacher interaction*. Mahwah, NJ: Lawrence Erlbaum Associates.

Mercer, N. (1995). *The guided construction of knowledge: Talk amongst teachers and learners*. Clevedon, England: Multilingual Matters.

Moll, L. C. (1992). Literacy research in community and classrooms: A sociocultural approach. In R. Beach, J. L. Green, M. L. Kamil, & T. Shanahan (Eds.), *Multidisciplinary perspectives on literacy research* (pp. 211–244). Urbana, IL: National Conference on Research in English.

Nystrand, M. (1997). *Opening dialogue: Understanding the dynamics of language and learning in the English classroom*. New York: Teachers College Press.

O'Connor, M. C., & Michaels, S. (1993). Aligning academic task and participation status through revoicing: Analysis of a classroom discourse strategy. *Anthropology and Education Quarterly, 24,* 318–335.

Oyler, C. (1996). *Making room for students in an urban first grade: Sharing teacher authority in room 104.* New York: Teachers College Press.

Oyler, C., & Becker, J. (1997). Teaching beyond the progressive–traditional dichotomy: Sharing authority and sharing vulnerability. *Curriculum Inquiry, 27,* 453–467.

Pappas, C. C. (1999). Becoming in the literate in the borderlands. In A. Goncu (Ed.), *Children's engagement in the world: Sociocultural perspectives* (pp. 228–260). Cambridge, England: Cambridge University Press.

Pappas, C. C., Kiefer, B. Z., & Levstik, L. S. (1999). *An integrated language perspective in the elementary school: An action approach.* New York: Longman.

Reyes, M. de la Luz. (1992). Changing venerable assumptions: Literacy for linguistically different students. *Harvard Educational Review, 64,* 427–446.

Sulzby E., & Teale, W. H. (1991). Emergent literacy. In R. Barr, M. L. Kamil, P. Mosenthal, & P. D. Perason (Eds.), *Handbook of reading research* (Vol. 1, pp. 727–757). White Plains, NY: Longman.

Swadener, B. B., & Lubeck, S. (Eds.). (1995). *Children and families "at promise" : Deconstructing the discourse of risk.* Albany: State University of New York Press.

Vygotsky, L. S. (1962). *Thought and language.* Cambridge, MA: MIT Press.

Vygotsky, L. S. (1978). *Mind in society: The development of higher psychological processes.* Cambridge: Cambridge University Press.

Wells, G. (1986). *The meaning makers: Children learning language and using language to learn.* Portsmouth, NH: Heinemann.

Wells, G. (1990). Talk about text: Where literacy is learner and taught. *Curriculum Inquiry, 20,* 369–405.

Wells, G. (1993). Reevaluating the IRF sequence: A proposal for the articulation of theories of activity and discourse for the analysis of teaching and learning in the classroom. *Linguistics and Education, 5,* 1–37.

Wells, G. (1994). The complimentary contributions of Halliday and Vygotsky to a "language-based theory of learning." *Linguistics and Education, 6,* 41–90.

Wells, G. (1998). Some questions about direct instruction: Why? To whom? How? And When? *Language Arts, 76,* 27–35.

Wells, G., & Chang-Wells, G. L. (1992). *Constructing knowledge together: Classrooms as centers of inquiry and literacy.* Portsmouth, NH: Heinemann.

Willinsky, J. (1990). *The New Literacy: Redefining reading and writing in the schools.* New York: Routledge & Kegan Paul.

Young, R. (1992). *Critical theory and classroom talk.* Clevedon, England: Multilingual Matters.

Zecker, L. B., Pappas, C. C., & Cohen, S. (1998). Finding the "right measure" of explanation for young Latina/o writers. *Language Arts, 76,* 49–56.

Author Index

Subject Index